Troubleshooting NetScaler

Gain essential knowledge and keep your NetScaler environment in top form

Raghu Varma Tirumalaraju

BIRMINGHAM - MUMBAI

Troubleshooting NetScaler

First published: April 2016

Production reference: 1270416

Published by Packt Publishing Ltd.
Livery Place
35 Livery Street
Birmingham B3 2PB, UK.

ISBN 978-1-78217-535-3

www.packtpub.com

Credits

Author

Raghu Varma Tirumalaraju

Reviewers

Naval Khanna

Anton van Pelt

Dennis van Remortel

Travis Scotto

Neil Spellings

Craig Tolley

Acquisition Editor

Reshma Raman

Content Development Editor

Riddhi Tuljapurkar

Technical Editor

Mohita Vyas

Copy Editor

Merilyn Pereira

Project Coordinator

Sanchita Mandal

Proofreader

Safis Editing

Indexer

Mariammal Chettiyar

Graphics

Disha Haria

Jason Monterio

Abhinash Sahu

Production Coordinator

Arvindkumar Gupta

Cover Work

Arvindkumar Gupta

Notice

The statements made and opinions expressed herein belong exclusively to the author and reviewers of this publication, and are not shared by or represent the viewpoint of Citrix Systems®, Inc. This publication does not constitute an endorsement of any product, service, or point of view. Citrix® makes no representations, warranties or assurances of any kind, express or implied, as to the completeness, accuracy, reliability, suitability, availability, or currency of the content contained in this publication or any material related to this publication. Any reliance you place on such content is strictly at your own risk. In no event shall Citrix®, its agents, officers, employees, licensees, or affiliates be liable for any damages whatsoever (including, without limitation, damages for loss of profits, business information, or loss of information) arising out of the information or statements contained in the publication, even if Citrix® has been advised of the possibility of such loss or damages.

Citrix®, XenApp®, XenDesktop®, CloudBridge™, StoreFront™, and NetScaler Gateway™ are trademarks of Citrix Systems®, Inc. and/or one or more of its subsidiaries, and may be registered in the United States Patent and Trademark Office and in other countries. Some of the images in the chapters are taken from the Citrix® website and documentation.

About the Author

Raghu Varma Tirumalaraju has been in the networking industry for around 10 years, with a good part of this time at Citrix working with NetScaler in various support roles. As someone who thoroughly enjoys packet analysis, he finds that NetScaler lends itself perfectly to troubleshooting if you just know where to look, and he would like to share some of the techniques he's picked up over the years.

Writing a book for the first time is a daunting experience regardless of the subject. I would like to thank the solid team at Packt Publishing—Riddhi Tuljapurkar for managing to keep us moving forward with endless patience as I struggled for time on several occasions and her thorough inputs on presentation, Shaon Basu for his initial guidance and encouragement, and Mohita Vyas for ensuring that the book is at the standard it should be. I would also like to thank the reviewers especially Craig Tolley, Anton Van Pelt, Dennis Van Remortel, Travis Scotto, and Neil Spellings, whose insightful inputs have helped turn this book from its original amateurish form into something (hopefully!) much more readable.

Being given the opportunity to write a book while being employed is also a matter of trust. I would like to thank my current and previous managers, Bal Garcha and Nicholas Ibourk, for their support and for resisting the worry that working on a book could impact the quality of my work.

Finally, as I learnt, a book doesn't get written in a day. I would like to thank my wife, Fanny, for understanding my ambitions and willing to forego our countless weekends and a fair share of evenings that we could have done something else with, and our families for their support during this time.

About the Reviewers

Naval Khanna is a diligent and seasoned trainer as well as an experienced Network Security professional. He has more than 10 years of experience in the industry and is mainly focused on niche skills such as data center technologies, virtualization, cloud computing, and application delivery controller environments. He has been providing training online, as well as classroom sessions to individuals and corporates and has successfully trained more than 500 IT personnel.

He has been associated with organizations such as F5, Oracle, Citrix, Cisco, and Microsoft. He has also worked on various projects of implementation and designing large data centers. Currently, he is working with some education/training organizations Networkers Zone and Bitzone technologies (`http://www.bitzonetechnologies.com/`, `http://www.bitzoneindia.com/`, and `http://networkerszone.com/`).

He has most of the industry leading certifications such as CCIE.

I would like to thank my family and my brother for supporting me in taking out time for this accomplishment and my dear friends who all cooperated with their valuable inputs.

Anton van Pelt is an enterprise mobility consultant with over 10 years of Citrix experience. Anton's focus is primarily on Enterprise Mobility solutions such as Citrix XenMobile, ShareFile, and NetScaler. He has a broad knowledge in complex IT environments.

Anton is active in presenting his technical knowledge throughout the community (Citrix IRC channel, Citrix Support Forums, NetScaler KB, and so on) and as a speaker at various international conferences. He is also the co-author of *Enterprise Mobility Management Smackdown*, PQR and *User Environment Management Smackdown*, PQR.

Anton has been awarded the Citrix CTP (Citrix Technology Professional) and RSVP (RES Software Valued Professional) titles.

You can contact Anton at ape@pqr.nl, follow his Twitter handle at @AntonvanPelt, or follow his blog at https://www.antonvanpelt.com/.

Dennis van Remortel is a senior consultant at ilionx. ilionx is an ICT service provider which aims to make your organization more successful using its services and solutions.

In this position, Dennis is responsible for designing and implementing both cloud and on-premise infrastructures. Furthermore, he has 14 years' experience with Lotus Notes/Domino. He is a Certified NetScaler Administrator and has been working with NetScaler for the past 8 years.

He previously reviewed Lotus Quickr 8.5 for Domino Administration.

Travis Scotto has been involved in the tech industry since he was 14. He began his career as a part-time web guru for a small local company and has improved ever since. He now works as a system Administrator with specialization in Citrix technologies and virtualization as a whole. Over the years, he has worked on multiple versions of Citrix XenApp, XenServer, Provisioning Services, and Netscaler. He has worked on large and small Citrix deployments with some deployments as large as 2500+ concurrent daily users. He has been involved in the architecting and maintenance of these systems as well. His Netscaler experience started with version 9.3 and continues through version 11. He has used Netscalers for access gateway, load balancing, and other various clever uses of the product. It is one of his favorite technologies to work on. Currently, he works in the healthcare technology field, but in the past has also worked on state government management systems. He also holds a small part-time position as an e-mail marketing designer. He earned his bachelors at Central Pennsylvania College in Information technology and is currently pursuing his masters in Information technology at Johns Hopkins University. This is his first book and he looks forward to writing and reviewing many more in the future.

I would like to thank all my employers and colleagues for giving me the opportunities and experience to learn these technologies, so I can better apply them to business needs and help others learn about them. I would also like to thank my family for being supportive of me as I worked on this book.

Neil Spellings is an independent virtualization and cloud infrastructure consultant who has worked with Citrix products since the early days of Winframe and Metaframe and was instrumental in the initial deployments of server-based computing technologies into a number of large financial institutions in the UK and Europe.

Neil is a Citrix Certified Expert – Virtualization and is certified across numerous other Citrix and Microsoft products to give a balanced view of the virtualization marketplace. He is a recognized SME by Citrix Education having contributed questions to numerous XenApp 6, 6.5 CCA, CCAA and CCEE exams, and has also helped write the recent XenDesktop 7 Design exam.

Neil is an active member of the Citrix community in the UK, traveling around Europe to both present and attend E2E/PubForum events, Citrix Synergy and is one of the founding members of the UK Citrix User group and remains on the steering group. Neil blogs at `http://neil.spellings.net` and frequently shares his opinions on twitter via `@neilspellings`.

Neil was awarded Citrix Technology Professional (CTP) status in 2013 for his contributions to the community.

Neil is a STEM Ambassador and runs a CodeClub in a local primary school with the ambition to inspire and encourage children to take up a career in ICT and learn to code.

Neil lives in Surrey, England, with his wife, Ina, and a 7-year old daughter, Zoë.

Craig Tolley is a senior systems engineer at the University of Cambridge with over 10 years' experience designing and managing IT in various educational environments. He is currently designing and implementing solutions using Citrix products to provide secure segregated environments for handling sensitive research data. Alongside this he is implementing configuration management and automation at the University's Clinical School. Craig remains happy to turn his hand to any IT related challenge and is proud to support local charities in providing bespoke IT solutions.

When he is not sitting behind a computer, he can be found listening to music, in his workshop perfecting his carpentry skills, or hill walking with his wife Alex and their beloved dog Bubbles.

www.PacktPub.com

eBooks, discount offers, and more

Did you know that Packt offers eBook versions of every book published, with PDF and ePub files available? You can upgrade to the eBook version at www.PacktPub.com and as a print book customer, you are entitled to a discount on the eBook copy. Get in touch with us at customercare@packtpub.com for more details.

At www.PacktPub.com, you can also read a collection of free technical articles, sign up for a range of free newsletters and receive exclusive discounts and offers on Packt books and eBooks.

https://www2.packtpub.com/books/subscription/packtlib

Do you need instant solutions to your IT questions? PacktLib is Packt's online digital book library. Here, you can search, access, and read Packt's entire library of books.

Why subscribe?

- Fully searchable across every book published by Packt
- Copy and paste, print, and bookmark content
- On demand and accessible via a web browser

This book is dedicated to the NetScaler Community and the army of NetScaler Developers, Testers, Support Engineers and Product Managers many of whom I have had the chance to work with and learn a lot of interesting things from

Table of Contents

Preface

NetScaler is a high performance Application Delivery Controller (ADC). Making the most of it requires knowledge that straddles the application and networking worlds.

As an ADC owner, you will also likely be the first person to be solicited when your business applications fail. You will need to be quick in identifying whether the problem is with the Application, the Server, the network, or NetScaler itself.

This book provides you with the vital troubleshooting knowledge needed to act fast when issues happen. It gives you a thorough understanding of the NetScaler layout, how it integrates with the network and what issues to expect when working with the Traffic Management, Authentication, NetScaler Gateway and Application Firewall features. We will also look at what information to seek out in the logs, how to use tracing and explore utilities that exist on the NetScaler to help you root cause your issues.

What this book covers

Chapter 1, NetScaler Concepts at a Glance, provides a short review of NetScaler background concepts. NetScaler runs as a User Process on top of FreeBSD and therefore its layout will unsurprisingly be familiar to Unix and Linux Administrators. However, some folders are of particular importance to NetScaler and the chapter reviews these folders. We will also look at the different types of IP addresses that NetScaler administrators need to be aware of, as well as how the various modes offered impact NetScaler behavior.

Chapter 2, Traffic Management Features, explains the concept of Traffic Management, which is the umbrella term used to describe the traffic handling features of NetScaler. These are load balancing, SSL Offloading, Content Switching, and GSLB. In this chapter, we will look at how to troubleshoot uneven distribution when using load balancing. There are also several options here that need to be considered when they are enabled. We discuss these considerations before looking at some useful counters that help understand how NetScaler is load balancing requests in greater detail and finish the section with a step-by-step approach to troubleshoot page load failures when using load balancing. We then look at SSL Offloading, which adds security on top of normal load balancing. We look at the SSL Handshake and Certificate related failures when implementing SSL offloading and also how to decrypt an SSL trace so you can see the requests in clear text, which is something you will be doing very often when troubleshooting SSL issues. We conclude this section with some SSL Best Practices. We continue on to Content Switching to discuss how to resolve some of the common errors seen with this feature. Finally, we look at troubleshooting GSLB failures using counters, nslookup, and nsmap.

Chapter 3, Integrated Caching and Compression, explains Caching and Compression which are HTTP standards-based optimization features. They help conserve bandwidth and help pages load faster in the process.

In this chapter, we discuss Caching-related terminology and how the policy evaluation process happens. This knowledge is key to troubleshooting as it helps determine whether an object should or shouldn't have been cached. We then look at caching best practices before focusing on troubleshooting. We also look at a number of wireshark examples to highlight the necessary details.

We then look at Compression starting with some guidance on which kind of content should and shouldn't be compressed before looking at how Compression works at a header level. We then conclude the chapter by looking at troubleshooting for Compression.

Chapter 4, AAA for Traffic Management, covers AAA for Traffic Management that adds AAA (Authentication Authorization and Accounting) to the otherwise un-authenticated traffic and it does so using encryption so that the exchange is also secure. In this chapter, we focus on the various protocols that NetScaler supports for Authentication and there are a few of them. Using Wireshark we will examine LDAP, RADIUS, Client Certificate, Form Based, Kerberos, and SAML authentication mechanisms in good detail. The last of these two protocols are especially gaining importance recently in the NetScaler world. Each of these protocols also has their own set of troubleshooting techniques which we look at in tandem.

Chapter 5, *High Availability and Networking Issues*, explains NetScaler High availability, which is how nearly all NetScaler deployments are currently done. We look at how heartbeats work and the conditions that cause a failover, how to identify them going back in time and how to remedy them.

In the second half of this chapter, we look at how NetScaler handles packets at the NIC level. This serves to explain why NetScaler has picked up or dropped a packet. We then differentiate between normal and error conditions based on interface outputs before focusing on the wider Networking-related issues that are often seen in NetScaler deployments and discuss how to troubleshoot them.

Chapter 6, *Application Firewall*, describes Application Firewall as a Firewall for Web Applications. Instead of regular connections that focus on TCP connection state and connection rules, Application Firewalls use input validation at layer 7. This input validation is in part set up by the Administrator based on the understanding of security risks associated with the application, for example, potentially risky SQL commands if the Application is a database a   pplication. In this chapter, we cover the essential background such as what those vulnerabilities are and how Application Firewall can protect against them. We also examine changes that Application Firewall makes to requests to offer that protection. We then look at the logging mechanisms available on NetScaler for this feature and how to use them to identify why the request is failing.

Chapter 7, *NetScaler Gateway*, explains that NetScaler Gateway is the remote access feature of NetScaler. Apart from being an SSL VPN solution, which works with and without a Client, it is also the preferred way to extend XenApp, XenDesktop, and XenMobile access across the Internet.

In this chapter, we examine using wireshark how each of the capabilities such as VPN, XenApp, XenDesktop, and XenMobile integration work. This will provide you with good baseline information that you can use as a comparison during troubleshooting. We then discuss the common issues in each of these areas and how to troubleshoot them using the logs available on NetScaler, Wireshark, and helpful error codes where available.

Chapter 8, *System Level Issues*, discusses the issues that can impact the NetScaler system as a whole. These vary from issues such as features being unavailable and software bugs such as crashes and hangs, performance issues such as CPU and Memory to hardware issues.

We conclude the chapter with a brief discussion of the various types of builds available for the NetScaler, which will hopefully help you when it comes to deciding on a build for your next upgrade or deployment.

Chapter 9, Troubleshooting Tools, introduces the tools available on NetScaler to aid with troubleshooting. While the information covered here is also laced throughout the book in examples, a quick read of this chapter upfront will prove very useful as it covers all of this information in one place. We cover tools such as tracing and nsconmsg available on NetScaler itself along with external tools. We also discuss some points to consider when troubleshooting the Command Center and Insight Center tools themselves.

What you need for this book

- NetScaler VPX Software—you can obtain a free trial on the Citrix Website
- An ssh client such as Putty for CLI and Shell Access
- A Standard Browser software for GUI Access
- Wireshark for Analysis
- A Text editor such as Textpad or Notepad++
- An HTTP header tool such as Fiddler

Who this book is for

This book is aimed at NetScaler Administrators who have a basic understanding of the product, but are looking for deeper exposure and guidance in identifying and fixing issues to keep their Application environment performing optimally.

Conventions

In this book, you will find a number of text styles that distinguish between different kinds of information. Here are some examples of these styles and an explanation of their meaning.

Code words in text, database table names, folder names, filenames, file extensions, pathnames, dummy URLs, User input, and Twitter handles are shown as follows: "Go to the page at `https://<XenMobile_Server_IP>:4443/support.html`."

A block of code is set as follows:

```
User level > Group level > VSERVER level > Global
```

Any command-line input or output is written as follows:

```
nsconmsg -K /var/nslog/newnslog -s ConLB=1 -d oldconmsg
nsconmsg -K /var/nslog/newnslog -s ConCSW=1 -d oldconmsg
```

New terms and **important words** are shown in bold. Words that you see on the screen, for example, in menus or dialog boxes, appear in the text like this: "Click on **XenMobile** and you will find a **Test Connectivity** button in the top right-hand corner."

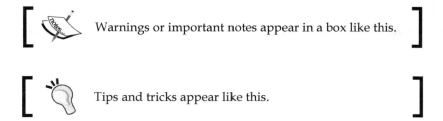

Warnings or important notes appear in a box like this.

Tips and tricks appear like this.

Reader feedback

Feedback from our readers is always welcome. Let us know what you think about this book — what you liked or disliked. Reader feedback is important for us as it helps us develop titles that you will really get the most out of.

To send us general feedback, simply e-mail feedback@packtpub.com, and mention the book's title in the subject of your message.

If there is a topic that you have expertise in and you are interested in either writing or contributing to a book, see our author guide at www.packtpub.com/authors.

Customer support

Now that you are the proud owner of a Packt book, we have a number of things to help you to get the most from your purchase.

Errata

Although we have taken every care to ensure the accuracy of our content, mistakes do happen. If you find a mistake in one of our books — maybe a mistake in the text or the code — we would be grateful if you could report this to us. By doing so, you can save other readers from frustration and help us improve subsequent versions of this book. If you find any errata, please report them by visiting http://www.packtpub.com/submit-errata, selecting your book, clicking on the **Errata Submission Form** link, and entering the details of your errata. Once your errata are verified, your submission will be accepted and the errata will be uploaded to our website or added to any list of existing errata under the Errata section of that title.

To view the previously submitted errata, go to https://www.packtpub.com/books/content/support and enter the name of the book in the search field. The required information will appear under the **Errata** section.

Piracy

Piracy of copyrighted material on the Internet is an ongoing problem across all media. At Packt, we take the protection of our copyright and licenses very seriously. If you come across any illegal copies of our works in any form on the Internet, please provide us with the location address or website name immediately so that we can pursue a remedy.

Please contact us at copyright@packtpub.com with a link to the suspected pirated material.

We appreciate your help in protecting our authors and our ability to bring you valuable content.

Questions

If you have a problem with any aspect of this book, you can contact us at questions@packtpub.com, and we will do our best to address the problem.

1
NetScaler Concepts at a Glance

The first chapter in this book naturally is a review of concepts that are key to the rest of the book. In this chapter, we will look at:

- How the NetScaler file system is laid out and what folders we are likely to often visit when troubleshooting
- The different address types and their purposes
- Request Switching and Connection Multiplexing
- The different modes of operation, their significance, and considerations

The NetScaler filesystem

The NetScaler code runs on top of FreeBSD as a userspace process, so it pays to understand the underlying file system structure.

 A question that comes up often, given the system is based on FreeBSD, is, "Is the system automatically vulnerable to any FreeBSD security issues that (as with any software systems) are reported by advisories?" The answer is, it depends; the NetScaler is a hardened appliance with several of its modules customized to reduce a potential security impact. For a definitive answer, you will need to contact Citrix Support, who would then work with a Security Response team for a validated response.

While the base layout will be familiar to anyone familiar with UNIX-based systems, the files that we would look at when troubleshooting are custom to the NetScaler.

Start by using `df`. This is also a great way to see how you are doing in terms of disk space:

```
root@ns# df -ah
Filesystem      Size    Used    Avail   Capacity   Mounted on
/dev/md0c       272M    206M     61M       77%     /
devfs           1.0K    1.0K      0B      100%     /dev
procfs          4.0K    4.0K      0B      100%     /proc
/dev/ad4s1a     3.7G    109M     3.3G       3%     /flash
/dev/ad0s1e     312G     32G     254G      11%     /var
```

The command `df` stands for diskfree, a Unix command to show disk usage statistics. By using the `-ah` option, we are asking for all the folders to be displayed in a human readable format, with percentages, for easy comprehension.

Let's take a look at the two important ones here for troubleshooting: `/flash` and `/var`.

`/flash`, as you've probably guessed, maps directly to the Flash drive/SSD installed in the NetScaler. This is the most important partition on the NetScaler as it contains the operating system along with the configuration, license, and essentially everything needed to boot the NetScaler.

The `/var`, which is the largest of partition and equals the hard disk on the NetScaler, contains: logs, crashes, traces, and other items that are to do with the maintenance and monitoring of the NetScaler.

In the case of a VPX, which is a virtual appliance with no physical drives, these folders become references to virtual partitions on the drive. Let's have a brief look at the important subfolders among these.

Folders on /flash

`/flash` contains the following folders:

- `/nsconfig/`: This contains the NetScaler configuration files (`ns.conf.*`). Each time you make a configuration change, it does get applied but doesn't get committed to the disk. To commit changes you need to click on **Save config**. Five such files, each resulting from a "save config", are saved in the `/nsconfig/` folder. So, you can get back to a last known good configuration if you are in trouble after saving configuration changes.

```
root@rvtns# ls -la | grep ns.conf
-rw-r--r--    1 root    wheel     13681 Mar   6 14:39 ns.conf
-rw-------    1 root    wheel     11685 Mar   6 14:39 ns.conf.0
-rw-------    1 root    wheel     11375 Mar   5 17:23 ns.conf.1
-rw-------    1 root    wheel     11287 Mar   5 15:32 ns.conf.2
-rw-------    1 root    wheel     11208 Mar   5 15:26 ns.conf.3
-rw-------    1 root    wheel     12077 Nov  30 13:30 ns.conf.4
```

- The best practice of course is to not leave it to chance and use well named backup files. The current versions offer a handy way to do this: navigate to **System | Backup/Restore**, choose a file name, and select either **Basic** backup (configuration, location database) or **Full** (basic backup along with certificates). You can then download the backup.

 A copy of these backups is sent to the /var/ns_sys_backup/ folder.

- The /nsconfig/ folder is also home to other configuration files, most notably that of the routing engine ZebOS:
    ○ /nsconfig/license: This contains the license files.
    ○ /nsconfig/ssl: This contains the SSL certificates, keys, and requests.
    ○ ns-root.* and ns-server.*: These files come by default; the ns-root.* files are used for signing, while the ns-server.* files are bound to the internal services, so care must be exercised with any folder cleanup here. The ns-server certificate is what you are presented with when accessing the NetScaler, and consequently, this is the key-pair that you would change as a best practice with a signed certificate you trust.
    ○ /nsconfig/monitors: This is the folder for any USER (script-based) monitors that you upload to the NetScaler.

Monitors provided as `Perl` files are used when creating a monitor of the type USER. Going by the list in the following screenshot, you can guess that these are usually monitors that provide application knowledge beyond basic port or protocol response checks. In newer versions, the home for these files is `/netscaler/monitors/`; it's when you upload any with modifications that they are stored in `/nsconfig/monitors`.

```
root@ns_80# ls /netscaler/monitors
nsall.pl          nsftp.pl          nsnntp.pl         nsrdp.pl          nssnmp.pl         nswi.pl
nsappc.pl         nsldap.pl         nsntlm-lwp.pl     nssf.pl           nstftp.pl         perl_mod
nsbmradius.pl     nsmysql.pl        nspop3.pl         nssmtp.pl         nsumon-debug.pl
```

- Notice that all this while that we've been referring to this all important folder as `/nsconfig/` and not `/flash/nsconfig/` - that's because `/nsconfig/` is a link to `/flash/nsconfig/` and they represent the same folder.

Folders on /var

`/var/log` contains text based logs. Let's look at some of the important ones:

- `ns.log`: This is of paramount importance when troubleshooting, and as you will see during the course of this book, it is a file that we often turn to get a *live view* in easily readable messages in order to understand what is happening in the background, such as why is that User denied access, or why is the request blocked?

 A very handy way to examine this file is to run a tail - f while you reproduce the issue. You might also find it useful, to demark the entries (I use a series of hyphens) before you begin reproducing the issue, to be able to spot with a bit more ease what you are looking for.

- `messages.*`: These are your standard Linux/FreeBSD system logs. This is where I would look first if I were to go back in time to understand when a reported reboot of the unit happened, or when a shell command was run.

- `license.log`: This is the log to look at if the licenses fail to apply, such as when the `hostID` used during allocation is incorrect.

- `/var/nslog`: This folder contains the binary `newnslog` files. While the `ns.log` files we just discussed are very easy to read by text and are our preferred go to when dealing in a controlled environment, we most certainly can't digest patterns in a heavily used production unit, and that's where `newnslogs` come in. This is a highly efficient form of logging that tracks the value of each counter (there's a few thousands of them) at every 7 second interval. These logs also serve as a basis for any external tool's plotting patterns, such as traffic, CPU, or errors.

This folder also contains the AppFirewall learning related logs:

- `/var/core` and `/var/crash`: This is where the crash files go.
- `/var/core`: This contains any crashes related to the NetScaler software, and you will almost always have them labeled in the format `NSPPE-0x-xxxx` where the `NSPPE` stands for the **NetScaler packet engine**, the first x for the packet engine number, and the rest for the PID; recall what we said about the Packet Engines running as User processes, therefore they will have PIDs.
- `/var/crash`: This is where any core dumps by the Kernel will go.

A brief look at NetScaler address types

In this section, we will briefly go over the various address types in NetScaler:

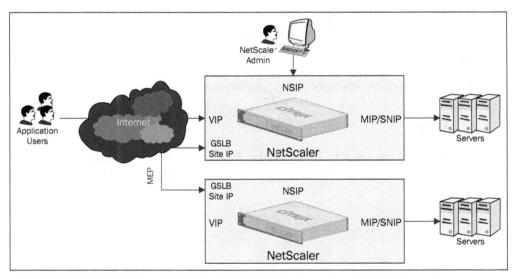

IP addresses used in a regular NetScaler deployment.

NetScaler IP

NetScaler IP (NSIP) is the Management IP address, unique to each unit. The following are some of the features:

- Needs to be configured as part of the initial setup
- Any subsequent changes will require a reboot
- Typically is a private IP address for security reasons

[Authentication requests will be sourced from this IP by default]

Virtual IP

Virtual IP (VIP) is the IP that users land on and is usually added as part of configuring a feature.

Mapped IP

Mapped IP (MIP) is an IP that the NetScaler can also use to talk to the Server. Its features are as follows:

- Essentially relaying requests and receiving responses on behalf of the client.
- You can add as many MIPs as you like but only if they are from the same subnet as the NSIP.
- MIP only exists these days for legacy reasons; everything you can do with a MIP you can do with a SNIP. So follow on to the next.

Subnet IP

Subnet IP (SNIP) is the defacto IP for NetScaler to Server communication. This IP is everything the MIP is, but without the limitation of having to be in the same subnet as the NSIP.

As a bonus, adding a SNIP will also add a direct route on the NetScaler to facilitate communication with the Servers. Check out the illustration with a routing table, as follows:

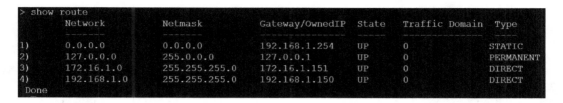

```
> show route
        Network         Netmask          Gateway/OwnedIP   State   Traffic Domain   Type
        --------        --------         ---------------   -----   --------------   ----
1)      0.0.0.0         0.0.0.0          192.168.1.254     UP      0                STATIC
2)      127.0.0.0       255.0.0.0        127.0.0.1         UP      0                PERMANENT
3)      172.16.1.0      255.255.255.0    172.16.1.151      UP      0                DIRECT
4)      192.168.1.0     255.255.255.0    192.168.1.150     UP      0                DIRECT
 Done
```

Here, `192.168.1.150` is the NSIP that evidently sits in a different subnet from `172.16.1.151`, which is the SNIP. In this case, the NetScaler will add a direct route to `172.16.1.0` with itself as the gateway.

You can, also use the SNIP to manage the NetScaler (among other IPs) by enabling management access. This especially helps in the HA environment by ensuring you always arrive at the primary when logging in to make any changes:

```
> set nsip 172.16.1.151 -mgmtAccess ENABLED
```

GSLB Site IP

A **GSLB Site IP (GSLBsiteIP)**, in general terms is a Data Center. This IP only comes into play if you use GSLB.

This exists to enable communication between different sites allowing them to exchange operational information via a customer protocol called **Metric Exchange Protocol (MEP)**.

You would also use the `-mgmtAccess` command with the GSLBsiteIP for one specific use case. Thus enabling the GSLB configuration to be synchronized between sites. Failure of the GSLB config sync functionality has very often come down to just this.

Request Switching and Connection Multiplexing

NetScaler's fundamental performance secret is a patented traffic handling technique called **Request Switching**. It allows the NetScaler to decouple Layer 7 protocol requests from TCP connections. This allows for a more granular load balancing by making decisions for each individual Layer 7 request.

NetScaler combines Request Switching with Connection Multiplexing. **Connection Multiplexing** is a technique where *warm* connections are maintained with each of the Servers using Keep-Alives. The result is that server side connections are already scaled up to maximum speed/window size. The NetScaler then multiplexes requests from several client side connections and potentially several users to a single server using a single TCP connection.

If you consider the server side processing cost of setting up a TCP connection and tearing it down, the round trips needed to do so, not forgetting that each of these connections also has a memory cost, the benefits of request switching become immediately apparent.

Along with helping the server scale better, there are also other benefits to this technique. Because NetScaler is looking at traffic at the request level instead of the connection level, it is capable of offering better protection by looking at individual requests, instead of letting all traffic on a connection through and similarly, policies and load balancing decisions can be applied more granularly on a per request basis.

 The patent number for anyone interested in delving deeper is 6,411,986. This was later licensed to other vendors.

The following screenshot shows NetScaler Request Switching and Connection Multiplexing:

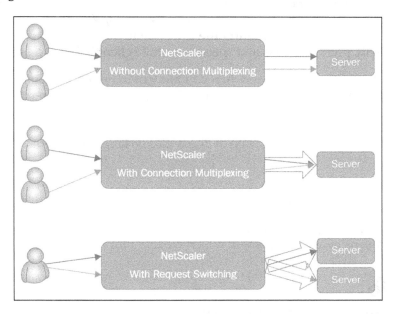

For troubleshooting, you might, on occasion, want to temporarily disable Connection Multiplexing, for example, to rule out issues of it not playing well with the Server. To do so, you can either use a HTTP profile with -conMultiplex DISABLED bound to the service, or by setting -maxreq to 1 on the service. Make this change at the service level to avoid impacting the performance of the environment as a whole.

User interface options

You have some options around what tools you can use to manage the NetScaler. This is a quick review of what's available and when best to use them.

GUI

This is the easiest of the lot to use, and comprehensive. Its benefits also include the ability to more easily spot DOWN entities such as services/VIPs. You can also navigate to **System | Diagnostics | Command Line Interface** to invoke the CLI/shell, though I would personally prefer the ease and speed of an SSH client if that access is needed.

The ability to view reports is huge when you are looking at performance issues. Apart from the standard port 80 or 443 for SSL, you also need Java ports 3008/3010.

 11.0 is now fully HTML5 and thus no longer needs Java.

CLI

Administrators coming from a Unix background might prefer CLI. This provides you an easy means to access the shell, which we use a lot for troubleshooting.

Console

It is highly recommended that you have this access when you are making network-related changes to the NetScaler; many damage control operations have been possible when all network access to the unit was lost following a change, purely because console access was available.

Console access is also handy when recovering from a corrupt kernel or changing a lost password. Another way of accessing the console on some physical NetScalers is via the **Lights Out Management (LOM)** Interface. This is a dedicated module on the NetScaler that has its own network and SSL settings that you can use the NetScaler CLI to revert any recent changes you have made, or even remotely reboot the NetScaler.

Shell

Accessed from the CLI, shell commands are the preferred way to Grep log outputs as well as to look at counters, that is, you would spend a lot of your troubleshooting time using the shell.

Another use case (though not often) is when you need to manipulate files such as the `rc.netscaler` or the `nsbefore.sh`/`nsafter.sh` files.

Of course, shell access is mighty, so you might want to restrict who you provide access to using command policies.

Nitro

Nitro is a move away from the original APIs that the older releases supported and has the inherent benefit of being lightweight and fast, and as with any API, it allows you to manage the NetScaler programmatically. It's a great way to automate configuration.

Here's an excellent text taken from the docs that describes it better. Source: `http://support.citrix.com/proddocs/topic/netscaler-main-api-10-map/ns-nitro-wrapper-con.html`:

> *NITRO exposes its functionality through Representational State Transfer (REST) interfaces. Therefore, NITRO applications can be developed in any programming language. Additionally, for applications that must be developed in Java or .NET, NITRO APIs are exposed through relevant libraries that are packaged as separate Software Development Kits (SDKs).*

And here's a quick example to get you excited about the possibilities with Nitro. When you are ready to save the configuration on a unit next time, try the following URL from your browser: `http://<your_ns_ip>/nitro/v1/config/nsconfig?action=save`.

Now imagine being able to use several commands like this to build your own page of handy actions or write PowerShell scripts for the most common tasks you need to perform. The log to look for is `/var/log/nitro.log`.

SFTP

Finally, you can use SFTP, which is based on SSH, for the purposes of browsing through the file system and copying in and out files. My favorite SFTP client is WinSCP, which is free and has a very easy-to-use interface.

NetScaler modes

Let's take a look at the various nodes that the NetScaler operates in. First, we'll look at two different ways in which the NetScaler behavior is influenced, based on how your Virtual IPs are configured.

Endpoint and Nonend point mode

Let's clarify upfront that this isn't a knob you will find on the NetScaler and, as such, it doesn't pertain to the set of options you can select under **System | Settings | Configure Modes**. Instead, it refers to how the NetScaler handles the TCP connection when features such as Compression, TCP Buffering, SSL Offload, and AppFw (which require the packet to be written) are in play.

As a consequence of this rewriting, when operating in the Endpoint mode, the NetScaler takes ownership of reliable TCP delivery, managing window sizes and MTU independently for both legs of the conversation. So, if in your troubleshooting, you see that NetScaler is ACKing a packet before the server has sent in its ACK, it is down to the NetScaler acting in the Endpoint mode.

Now, with this understanding out of the way, let's look at some of the modes that are not enabled by default and what their impact on your environment will be.

ANY, L4, or L7 modes

You need to consider what level of protocol processing is in play. NetScaler has the most to offer in performance when it's running a protocol natively (as in, you select a VIP type that matches the type of traffic), for example, HTTP. This is also where it can offer the most security as it is able to inspect pretty much everything in the flow.

When troubleshooting, however, you might occasionally see a situation where you will need to *dumb down* the processing for a moment so you can understand whether the optimizations that are being offered are causing the failure that you are troubleshooting. A technique I sometimes find myself using is to move momentarily from a VIP configured as the native protocol type (HTTP) to TCP. This will still offer TCP optimizations but will help to understand whether, for example, one of the packet rewriting features is causing the App to fail.

Very rarely have I had to consider going a level further down for troubleshooting purposes and reconfigure the same HTTP VIP as type ANY, such as when deliberately bypassing the inbuilt window-based protection mechanisms to prove raw throughput in a POC. By setting up the VIP as type ANY, we pretty much turned the NetScaler into a Layer 3 Load balancer.

 Apart from troubleshooting, there are valid cases where you need the ANY VIP, such as for protocols that use random destination ports to the server.

The mode switches on the NetScaler

Now, we're coming to the area that you can turn ON and OFF by navigating to **System | Settings** on the NetScaler.

Modes that are enabled by default

Let's start with the ones that are enabled by default. The fact that they are enabled by default also means they play along well for the most part with most deployments.

Fast Ramp

Fast Ramp is a performance friend. Traditional (read RFC-based) TCP follows a very conservative approach to increasing window sizes; while this made perfect sense in the days of unreliable pipes, it stems the TCP connection from quickly reaching its top speed. Especially in the context of the NetScaler, which will sit closer to or at least have very solid connections to the Server, Fast Ramp works great and is one of those features that rarely has to be touched.

Edge Configuration

Even though it's enabled by default, the **Edge Configuration** mode only impacts very specific use cases. Notably, Link Load Balancing and Cache Redirection. It's called edge mode because it's sitting literally at the edge of the network learning services that are not even part of your infrastructure, purely with the goal of load balancing. There are two desired behaviors for such deployments:

- To be able to increase the number of internal services that are allowed on the NetScaler
- To turn off binary performance logging for such services, thereby increasing performance and at the same time reducing the impact on log size

Remember though, this is only when cache redirection or link load balancing are in use, not system wide.

Using Subnet IP

As we discussed in the IP review section, SNIPs are the recommended way to configure IPs for the purpose of NetScaler to Server conversations. This mode, abbreviated as USNIP, simply enables your SNIPs to be used.

The Layer 3 mode

The Layer 3 mode is enabled by default. If you need the NetScaler to forward packets to an IP not owned by it, you need this mode. When enabled, NetScaler will behave like a router, looking at the routes it has learned or that has been configured with to forward packets. Disabling it will mean anything the NetScaler receives that doesn't have the destination IP as one of its IPs will be dropped. Situations where you would turn this off would be to prevent Servers in the backend from talking to each other or if you want routing to be entirely handled by a separate device (such as a router or firewall).

Path MTU Discovery

Path MTU Discovery, or PMTUD as it's known, is a pretty well-known networking technique that uses ICMP to learn what the lowest MTU along the path is. This way fragmentation is avoided and that is always a good thing. Fragmentation is inefficient, it costs performance at multiple points in the network, and then needs reassembly at end points.

Modes that are disabled by default

First, let's get the advertisements out of the way — SRADV, DRADV, IRADV, SRADV6, and DRADV6.

When you enable dynamic routing on the NetScaler, you do so to have it participate in routing and learn routes from other routers in its neighborhood. You then also have the ability to have it advertise the routes it knows. This is when you choose to enable the respective advertisement.

Next, there are a couple of RISE-related enhancements. These are RISE_APBR and RISE_RHI. First let's begin by understanding what RISE is. **Remote Integrated Services Engine** is a Cisco technology, which allows the NetScaler when used with the Cisco Nexus series of appliances, provides a tight integration between the two products and this enables some configuration automation and in turn easier management.

Here is a quote from the Cisco Whitepaper. Reference: http://www.cisco.com/c/dam/en/us/products/collateral/switches/nexus-7000-series-switches/white-paper-c11-731370.pdf:

> *"Each device can retrieve and program the hardware and software tables of the other (for example, the forwarding tables, routing tables, and access control lists [ACLs])."*

The two RISE modes represent two of the fundamental use cases of this integration:

- **RISE_APBR (RISE Auto PBR)**: USIP configurations require special routing handling in place so that the return traffic goes through the NetScaler; otherwise, the client that isn't expecting a response from the Server will drop it. APBR allows the PBRs needed for this to be set up dynamically, which helps with scale.

- **RISE_RHI (RISE Route Health Injection)**: Route Health Injection allows active-active load balancing of VIPs by using injecting routes into the routing table to point to one of the several NetScalers as the target for a given VIP. The RISE implication here is that the addition of these routes can be done dynamically.

Let's now get to the modes that we are most concerned with while troubleshooting:

- **Layer 2 Mode**: As you can tell from the name, this turns the NetScaler into a switch, forwarding any packets that are not meant for its MAC addresses. So yes, this does induce a very real risk of a loop if enabled without proper network evaluation. This is why it's turned off by default. Luckily, most deployments do not require this option (a couple of such exceptions are the AppFw transparent mode and CloudBridge Connector).

- **Bridge BPDU**: It's important to first note, that the NetScaler doesn't participate in understanding Spanning Tree Protocol. By default, it drops BPDUs, and this is perfectly okay for most deployments because the L2 mode is disabled by default. The best practice in fact is to not have STP enabled at all on any of the switch ports that the NetScaler (with L2 mode off) is plugged into, so that the instances come on instantly without cycling through the intermediate states. If you, however, are enabling the L2 mode, consider bridging BPDUs so that the switches can detect loops and turn off redundant interfaces if they need to.

- **Use Source IP (USIP)**: When enabled, NetScaler preserves the original client IP as visible to it while forwarding traffic to the Servers. As simple as that is, there are network implications to consider in order to avoid dropped packets. When USIP is enabled, the Server can see the Clients IP address, and unless it's set to route traffic back to the NetScaler, might attempt to talk directly to the client. This, of course, will be rejected by the client. To get around this, you will need to either set the NetScaler as the default gateway for the Servers, route traffic back to the NetScaler using PBR, set up a non-ARPing loopback address, or alternatively use NAT for the reverse traffic.

If it's purely for Client IP logging purposes that you are turning on USIP, consider Client IP Insertion or Web logging instead. The latter is especially designed for high performance logging. Another point to bear in mind while enabling USIP is that it reduces the reusability of a connection on the Server side. Why is that? Because when the NetScaler tries to look for a connection in its reuse pool, it looks for something that matches among other things, the source IP. Whereas, by default, you have a lot of matches given the SNIP remains somewhat a constant; with USIP, this gets chopped up into several small pools of connections.

A common question is what happens if both USNIP (which we discussed earlier) and USIP are enabled? USIP always overrides USNIP. Also, USIP can be enabled either at the Global level or at the service level. The service level setting takes precedence over the Global level setting.

- **Client Keep-Alive**: Known as CKA, in short, this is a HTTP technique to allow for connection multiplexing on the Client-side of the connection. When enabled, NetScaler drops the `Connection: close` header, which would have otherwise signified the end of the conversation and caused the client to close the connection and insert a replacement header of its own `Connection: Keep-Alive`. The result is that the client doesn't need to re-establish newer connections for other requests on the page it's trying to load. The technique, as such, is perfectly valid and most browsers support it, however you might run into cases where the browser (by behavior) doesn't load the page until it receives the `Connection: close` header. This once manifested for me as a certain browser not redirecting me on seeing a HTTP 302 for 180 seconds! Such situations would require you to leave this mode disabled.

- **TCP Buffering**: In a typical deployment, the NetScaler has a much more reliable and faster connection to the Servers than it does to the Clients who are connecting to it. This could easily mean that the Server builds up a queue of responses that it hasn't been able to send out, as the Client doesn't acknowledge as fast as the Server is generating data. This is where TCP buffering comes in. When enabled, the NetScaler queues this data for the Server thereby taking the load off it and lets it continue working on data for other clients. The reason this mode is disabled by default is that it has, along with the memory requirement (configurable), a CPU impact. So, in summary this is a very helpful feature for Internet-based clients but proper testing to evaluate the impact for a given profile and the volume of traffic is needed.

- **MAC Based Forwarding**: MBF is a cache-based forwarding technique. It notes the MAC address of the incoming Client request and automatically assumes what the destination MAC address should be for the response. For very static and symmetric environments, this could mean hugely increased forwarding performance as the whole route lookup process is bypassed. If your environment relies on specific routes for the return traffic (think PBR), those get bypassed too. So it needs careful consideration for such environments. There are certain scenarios, such as Firewall or VPN load balancing where MBF is indispensable due to the way it avoids asymmetric routing.

Summary

Let's quickly recap what we've covered in this opening chapter. We have looked at the NetScaler folder structure and the files and folders that are most interesting from a troubleshooting perspective. Key to note was the `/var/log/ns.log` file, which when used with a tail `-f`, spews out a lot of useful information while an issue is being reproduced.

The different IP addresses that you, as an Administrator, assign to the NetScaler and their purpose. We looked at Request Switching and Connection Multiplexing, which gives the NetScaler its high performance. We looked at the different ways to interact with the NetScaler and what each UI is best for.

We looked at the various modes of operation that the NetScaler functions in and those that can be configured. Among the modes that are configurable, we noted that there are very important considerations, especially for those features that are disabled by default. As we move to the next chapter, we will look at troubleshooting areas in the features that form the bulk of NetScaler deployments.

2
Traffic Management Features

This chapter is focused on the features that form the basis of most NetScaler deployments. They are available under the traffic management node in the UI. These features are as follows:

- Load balancing
- SSL offloading
- Content switching
- GSLB

Let's explore and discuss troubleshooting these features one at a time.

Load balancing

The NetScaler started off as a high performance load balancer and is still its most prominent use case. In this chapter, we will look at a range of issues/questions that you come across when setting up or managing a load balanced environment with the NetScaler.

Considerations

First, let's look at some considerations around the general settings of load balancing.

Startup RR factor

Let's consider a scenario where you've created a new **load balancing (LB)** vServer or bound a service to an existing vServer that already has a bunch of services. You will notice that even though you have the LB method as the default (also happens to be the recommended) of least connections, NetScaler starts to send requests to the backend in a round robin fashion. This is a deliberate behavior to ensure that the new service you've just added doesn't get inundated with requests; after all, being a new server, it will have the least connections. This behavior is controlled by adjusting the tunable Startup RR factor.

To USIP or not to USIP

By default, when you create a load balancing VIP (we will shorten this to LB VIP for conciseness), NetScaler uses one of its own IPs, usually a SNIP to send that packet to the servers. This is controlled by the USNIP global mode setting. USIP (use client IP as the source IP), on the other hand, is needed only for specific scenarios.

Some scenarios where USIP really is required are as follows:

*   With Direct Server Return, where the return traffic bypasses the NetScaler
*   With some applications that need to use the actual Client IP to function

Occasionally, USIP gets deployed purely with the goal of getting visibility into the Client IP. There are definitely better ways to achieve this requirement:

*   By using Weblogging for HTTP/S, which is both high performance and logs a lot of useful info
*   By using **Client IP Insertion (-cip)** on the service, which then presents the Client IP in a header that can be extracted on the server

Why should you avoid USIP?

*   The first reason is routing. When you present the Client IP address as the source IP to the Server, without any special configuration in place, it will try to reach out to the Client directly; this will trip the client and the packet will be dropped, so you will need either PBR or to set the NetScaler as the default gateway for the Servers.
*   Next is performance. When USIP is enabled, the reuse pool, which is how the NetScaler maintains optimized connections to the backend, is not used efficiently, since it now means that it is fragmented as per IP, that is, a connection optimized for one User cannot be used for another. So, this means more connections are opened on the Server.

- Because of the preceding reason, if you now enable surge protection (not surge queue, they are completely different), you will see very aggressive throttling, and that will mean users can't get to their applications.

Choosing a VIP type

To get the most performance out of the NetScaler, as much as possible you should choose one of the native VIP types, such as HTTP, SSL, DNS, or MYSQL. Apart from performance, this also gives you granular control, such as your choice of rewrite policies. For applications that don't have a native protocol, or use a mix of sub protocols, a layer 4 protocol would be the right choice, such as TCP, UDP, or SSL_TCP. Some applications might need you to forward traffic with even minimal handling; this is when `SSL_Bridge` or the `ANY` type of VIPs are in use, where the NetScaler is essentially just flinging packets it receives on the VIP to the services as fast as it can.

Special considerations for load balancing Firewalls or CloudBridge appliances

When load balancing Firewalls and CloudBridge devices, there are a couple of options that are not very evident. Let's take a look at what these are because they are the only way to achieve the necessary scenarios.

Prefer Direct Route

If you are setting up Firewall load balancing, this will require you to have a vServer of type `ANY` with IP and Port set to * (Wildcard) and MBF enabled so that you are not introducing asymmetry in routing. This all works great except when you also have the L3 mode set to `ON` (default) and have more specific static routes, or when you have one of these destination IPs available on the same NetScaler as a VIP:

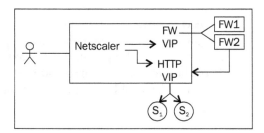

The **Prefer Direct Route** option will route traffic directly to this destination VIP directly without passing it through the Firewall first. If you are using FW LB and using routing, or have a corresponding VIP, disable this option; if you are not, leave it at its default.

vServer specific MAC – when daisy chaining FW VIPs or CloudBridge appliances

When you want traffic to pass through different sets of firewalls, the limitation you will run into is the NetScaler's default behavior of only intercepting packets for a * VIP once for VIPs that have the forwarding mode set to MAC instead of IP. This behavior exists to avoid issues resulting from packets running in a loop between two wildcard VIPs. To enable the interception more than once, enable the **–vServerSpecificMac** option:

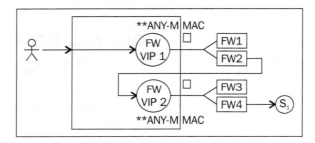

httpOnlyCookieFlag setting when enabled, inserts a flag called `httponly` when forwarding the response to the client, for example: `Set-Cookie: NSC_iuuq_wj q=ffffffffc3a01f2445a4a423660; expires=Sun, 03-May-2015 15:14:35 GMT;path=/;httponly`.

The significance is that the cookie is not available to applications outside of the browser. This is a recommended approach from a security perspective, as this means even if a **Cross Site Scripting** (**XSS**) affected server is accessed by the User, the cookie can't be stolen. You need to however watch out for applications that require out-of-browser handling, a classic example being Java Applets or Client side scripts that need access to this cookie. The problem you may run into is that the requests generated outside of the browser will arrive at the NetScaler without a cookie and potentially end up on a different backend during load balancing, thus breaking the application.

You should also note that this flag exists as a tunable parameter also on the AAA vServer, which is also covered in this book, in a later chapter.

A related flag is the secure http flag, which tells the browser to use the cookie only in secure exchanges. CTX138055 shows a way of setting this using rewrite. So it goes by definition that you should only set this for SSL-based vServers, or you will be breaking the application since the cookies will never be returned.

Note that the articles I mention throughout the book can be found on the Citrix support site. The easiest way to get to them is `http://support.citrix.com/article/`.

Services or ServiceGroups

This choice usually comes down to how big the Server pool you manage is. A couple of servers are easy to manage using the services approach, but as you are starting several of them, you should consider using `ServiceGroups`. `ServiceGroups` present the following benefits:

- All settings are at the `ServiceGroup` level so adding new servers or removing them is faster, since you only need to provide Server and port details without repeating the parameters each time
- The resulting simplicity also means that you avoid any human errors that might lead to inconsistencies between the different services

Common LB issues

Now that you've learned how to choose the key options for our LB deployment, let's take a look at troubleshooting some of the common issues.

Troubleshooting – unable to access a newly created VIP

You've set up load balancing for the first time and tried to access the web page. Your browser appears to hang. Here's how you go about troubleshooting such issues. Start by checking whether the VIP and services are up. If the service is down, selecting **show service <servicename>** will show you why that service is down.

Some examples of what you might see are:

- No appropriate MIP or SNIP:

```
State: DOWN      Weight: 1        Passive: 0
Probes: 1030     Failed [Total: 18 Current: 18]
Last response: Failure - No MIP/SNIP available to send the monitor probe.
```

Resolution: Add a MIP or SNIP. Also make sure that the IP you add is from the right subnet, using a subnet calculator if you have to.

- The Server can't be reached:

```
Monitor Name: tcp-default
    State: UP        Weight: 1        Passive: 0
    Probes: 1057     Failed [Total: 39 Current: 1]
    Last response: Failure - Time out during TCP connection establishment stage
```

Resolution: This will take involvement from you as well as your server teams. Start by looking at a trace. Tracing on the NetScaler is introduced in *Chapter 9, Troubleshooting Tools*. If the server itself is running perfectly, a blocking Firewall rule might be the problem here.

Also, be sure that the monitor bound is of the right type; the port might be UP but you might need a monitor that runs specific queries to report an unavailable service accurately, especially for multi-tiered services. **ECV** (**Extended Content Verification**) monitors serve well here.

 It's not uncommon to land in a situation as a NetScaler Administrator, where the NetScaler shows a monitor time out, but the Server logs will not show any problems. This is one reason why the recommended way of approaching such issues is to get simultaneous traces — on the Client, on the NetScaler, and on the Server.

Troubleshooting application failures where VIP is UP

We've looked at troubleshooting a VIP being down. However, the vServer could be UP but you might see other issues when accessing it; this section talks about a troubleshooting approach for such issues:

- **Persistence issues**: If users report unusual behavior, such as no longer seeing items in their shopping baskets or seeing application errors, persistence could be a problem. If the situation allows, unbind all services except one and see if the issue still exists.

- **Application complexity**: This is also something to bear in mind; some applications might appear to be HTTP-based, but might have components/calls that use a different protocol. To rule out this being the problem, start with a TCP VIP or an ANY VIP first and observe all ports in use between the client and server. The application's documentation is a great way to get that information too. You can start going up a layer once this characteristic of the application is understood.

- **httponly cookie**: This is another area to watch out for; as we discussed while introducing it, any out-of-browser applications or programs will not have access to it if the cookie is marked httponly.

- **AppFirewall or rewrite/responder policies**: Check whether any AppFirewall or rewrite/responder policies are getting hit. Appfirewall can cause specific objects or buttons to fail if the necessary learnt rules are not deployed, or if the request matches the configured signature.

- **NetScaler HTTP protection features**: Lastly, it's also useful to know how the access to the VIP is being tested. Some enterprises may choose to use automated tools. This helps greatly with testing for scale, but also introduces the possibility that one of NetScaler's TCP/HTTP protection mechanisms are being triggered.

  One example I've encountered is when a customer was using a traffic load generator to test how a newly set up VIP would hold up. They noticed that the servers weren't getting much of the traffic. On deeper analysis, we realized that the traffic generated was pumping a lot of requests with a very small advertised window size (hence the _SW_ in the counter tcp_err_SW_ init_pktdrop in the following screenshot). This kind of behavior closely resembles a *Slow Read* attack, for which this protection was put in:

```
root@ns# nsconmsg -g tcp_err_SW -d current
Displaying performance information
NetScaler V20 Performance Data
NetScaler NS10.5: Build 54.9.nc, Date: Dec 15 2014, 13:17:00

reltime:mili second between two records Fri May  1 03:23:33 2015
  Index    rtime totalcount-val   delta rate/sec symbol-name&device-no&time
      0    56002          1995    1995     284 tcp_err_SW_init_pktdrop Fri May  1 03:24:29 2015
      1     7000          3990    1995     285 tcp_err_SW_init_pktdrop Fri May  1 03:24:36 2015
      2     7000          5985    1995     285 tcp_err_SW_init_pktdrop Fri May  1 03:24:43 2015
      3     7000          7980    1995     285 tcp_err_SW_init_pktdrop Fri May  1 03:24:50 2015
      4    28001          9975    1995     284 tcp_err_SW_init_pktdrop Fri May  1 03:25:18 2015
      5    49001         11970    1995     284 tcp_err_SW_init_pktdrop Fri May  1 03:26:07 2015
      6    56001         13965    1995     285 tcp_err_SW_init_pktdrop Fri May  1 03:27:03 2015
      7    63001         21945    7980    1140 tcp_err_SW_init_pktdrop Fri May  1 03:28:06 2015
      8     7000         25935    3990     570 tcp_err_SW_init_pktdrop Fri May  1 03:28:13 2015
```

Once this was understood, the tool was tweaked to instead resemble regular User traffic and the throughput issue was corrected.

Troubleshooting VIP performance issues

Performance issues manifest usually in the way of pages taking time to load or upload to or download from a site that is timing out. To troubleshoot these:

1. First, check what the direct access experience looks like and confirm that the issue is only seen when going via the NetScaler.

2. Obtain a trace. The key here again is simultaneous traces. Taking them simultaneously will save you time in the long run as you start questioning where in the path the bottleneck is.

Once you have the trace, look for the following:

- **MSS issues: MSS (Maximum Segment Size)** is the maximum size for a TCP segment that a receiver advertising the value can receive. The NetScaler can be configured to advertise different values but by default it advertises 1,460. If you are seeing that one of the entities is advertising a much smaller number here, it is something to consider as a cause for performance issues:

Time	Source	Destination	Info
291 24.882818198	192.168.1.18	192.168.1.55	52044→80 [SYN] Seq=0 Win=65535 Len=0 MSS=1460 WS=32 TSval
292 24.882829534	192.168.1.55	192.168.1.18	80→52044 [SYN, ACK] Seq=0 Ack=1 Win=8190 Len=0 MSS=1460

MSS will be shown on the SYN from Client and SYN/ACK from server right in the **Info** section, but you can also look this up from the **Options** section of the TCP Frame:

```
Options: (4 bytes), Maximum segment size
⊟ Maximum segment size: 1460 bytes
    Kind: Maximum Segment Size (2)
    Length: 4
    MSS Value: 1460
```

The **Options** part in the TCP handshake packets will also show you vital information, such as whether Window scaling is enabled and what the scale factor (multiplier) is. If the application experiencing delays involves large transfers, you can try increasing the scale factor so that the receive windows are expanded to accept more data per acknowledgement.

- **Networking issues**: If you are plugging more than one network interface into the same broadcast domain, ensure that you are not introducing a loop. This can very easily bring performance to its knees. Common issues are misconfigured or missing vlans, NIC flaps, or MBF-related issues. These are covered in greater detail in *Chapter 5. Networking*.

- **TCP Window issues**: Is it possible that the client, server, or the NetScaler running out of receive window? Usually, the Window size that each of the parties can receive will be 64 K to start with and decreases as it accumulates data that it needs to send, either onwards if it's the NetScaler, or to the application if it's the client or the server. If one of the parties is slow in consuming what is already sent to it, you could see **Zero Window** situations creeping in:

zero windows

Occasional zero windows are not a serious problem, as long as the receiver is able to quickly empty the receive buffer and send out a notification that it has free buffers to accept more data. The problem is when the zero window situation persists long enough that the sender has to give up, or if timeouts are getting hit. Take the following screenshot for example:

Here, SNIP has advertised a zero window to server, it cannot accept any further data, and the server is obliged to wait. If it thinks it has waited long enough, it will even send a probe to see whether the NetScaler is ready to accept more data (you can find such probes using the Wireshark filter, `tcp.analysis.zero_window_probe`). NetScaler on its part, waits for a packet from the client indicating that the client is ready to accept more data or that it has processed the data it has previously received. That confirmation arrives in the form of an ACK. Following this ACK, NetScaler SNIP sends out a TCP Window update, telling the server that is ready to accept more data. The key is whether this recovery happens fast enough, if it doesn't the performance will drop.

Also, a high number of zero windows from the client can cause the NetScaler to reset the connection in order to protect its memory from saturation as that kind of TCP pattern is characteristic of a known TCP attack (`sockstress`). This protection by the way is toggled using the command: `set ns tcpparam -limitedPersist ENABLED/DISABLED`.

- **Intermediate single packet drops**: A related issue is the situation where an intermediate device (such as a firewall) keeps dropping a particular packet seeing something suspicious about the packet. The difference compared to the earlier firewall issue we talked about is that this wouldn't be a simple 100% drop of packets, which actually is easier to spot. Instead, a large packet or simply an ACK from client or server is dropped continuously, which causes a retransmission loop until the connection fails.

These issues are best diagnosed by a trace and manually calculating SEQ and ACK numbers to find out whether each receiver is receiving and ACKing what the sender sends and whether that ACK is reaching the sender. Some amount of retransmissions or DupAcks are inevitable on any busy production network; however, if you are seeing a high number of them in the same TCP stream, that is a cause for concern.

Also, if you are seeing ICMP messages indicating that the packets are too large, please enable PMTUD in the list modes to avoid fragmentation or drop due to unable-to-fragment issues. We discussed PMTUD in the first chapter.

- **Surge queue building up on the service**: In the output that follows, we can see that the requests are ending up in the surge queue. In the following scenario, that I have set up to demonstrate such a situation, I have set the `MaxClients` parameter to `1`. This is telling the NetScaler not to send more requests to a service that is already processing one:

```
> stat lb vserver lbvip_http

Virtual Server Summary
                        vsvrIP    port    Protocol        State    Health    actSvcs
lbvip_http       192.168.1.205     80        HTTP           UP       100          2

          inactSvcs
lbvip_http           0

Virtual Server Statistics
                                            Rate (/s)                Total
Vserver hits                                     1456             45404293
Requests                                         1455             45404094
Responses                                        1455             45404093
Request bytes                                   119989           3723162112
Response bytes                                 1339037          41545267560
Total Packets rcvd                               1463             45407793
Total Packets sent                               2926             45592816
Current client connections                         --                  200
Current Client Est connections                     --                  200
Current server connections                         --                    1
Requests in surge queue                            --                  199
Requests in vserver's surgeQ                       --                    0
Requests in service's surgeQs                      --                  199
Spill Over Threshold                               --                    0
Spill Over Hits                                    --                    0
Labeled Connection                                 --                    0
Push Labeled Connection                            --                    0
Deferred Request                                    0                    0
Invalid Request/Response                           --                    0
Invalid Request/Response Dropped                   --                    0

Bound Service(s) Summary
                        IP    port        Type        State       Hits    Hits/s
ServiceA       192.168.1.61     80        HTTP           UP    20227569      730/s
ServiceB       192.168.1.62     80        HTTP           UP    20357609      725/s

             Req      Req/s       Rsp    Rsp/s  Throughp  ClntConn    SurgeQ
ServiceA  20227469     730/s  20227469   730/s         9       100       100
ServiceB  20357510     725/s  20357509   725/s         8       100        99

          SvrConn    ReuseP   MaxConn  ActvTran   SvrTTFB       Load
ServiceA     3497         0         1       100       135          0
ServiceB     3502         0         1       100       137          0
 Done
```

"Is the solution to immediately remove the `MaxClient` setting?" That depends. The value you configure here is to protect the servers from getting saturated and preventing an extremely degraded performance or worse, the server from crashing due to the load. So a deeper understanding of what the server can handle is needed (working with the Server vendor if needed) to choose an appropriate value.

- **NetScaler resource issues**: Check how the CPU and memory are doing. The NetScaler is a hardened appliance with a very well-tuned TCP stack and, as such, it can handle millions of connections before it starts becoming a bottleneck. Nevertheless, you can certainly hit situations where the resources on the NetScaler are saturated. These can be in the form of memory leaks or CPU spikes. Please check out *Chapter 8, Troubleshooting the NetScaler System* later in the book where I cover these in detail.

Troubleshooting VIP distribution issues

When you are bringing a new service or set of services into an existing load balancing environment, you would want to verify that the NetScaler is distributing load fairly evenly. There are multiple ways of doing this including looking at the service hits. I find it helpful, especially for troubleshooting, to look at `nsconmsg` outputs to see how this is happening.

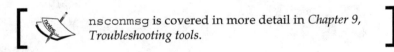

> `nsconmsg` is covered in more detail in *Chapter 9, Troubleshooting tools*.

In the following example, I have used the `-j` option to list the vServer name to help me narrow the output and using the `-s ConLB` command to set the debug level and the `distrconmsg` display (`-d`) option, I am able to see how the distribution evolves every 7 seconds.

What I can see in the following screenshot is that the VIP `205_vip` is using the least connections method for load balancing and SourceIP persistence and that all the hits are persistent. Also, it has two services `192:168.1.61:80` and `192.168.1.63:80`, and their respective hits. I started the second client with a delay, which is why `192.168.1.80` starts to be the only one to take load, given the persistence implication, before `192.168.1.63` starts to get some hits. The goal is to get this to be as even as possible:

```
root@ns# nsconmsg -s ConLb=3 -j 205_vip -d distrconmsg
Displaying Distribution of performance information
NetScaler V20 Performance Data
NetScaler NS10.5: Build 54.9.nc, Date: Dec 15 2014, 13:17:00


current time is Fri May  8 12:51:18 2015
--------------------------------------------------------------
VIP(192.168.1.205:80:UP LEASTCONNS): Hits(52270) Pers(SOURCEIP) PersHits(52270:100%)  E
S(192.168.1.63:80:UP) Hits(0:0%) PHits(0:0%) LbHits(0:0%)
S(192.168.1.61:80:UP) Hits(52270:100%) PHits:52270:100%) LbHits(0:0%)
VIP(192.168.1.205:0:Deviation(36960.5:141.421%))
--------------------------------------------------------------
CPU:7.8% MEM:170461630 UP:00.02:30:09 since:Fri May  8 10:21:09 2015


current time is Fri May  8 12:51:25 2015
--------------------------------------------------------------
VIP(192.168.1.205:80:UP:LEASTCONNS): Hits(101759) Pers(SOURCEIP) PersHits(101759:100%)
S(192.168.1.63:80:UP) Hits(1:0%) PHits(1:100%) LbHits(0:0%)
S(192.168.1.61:80:UP) Hits(101758:99%) PHits(101758:100%) LbHits(0:0%)
VIP(192.168.1.205:0:Deviation(71953.1:141.419%))
--------------------------------------------------------------
CPU:7.6% MEM:170410750 UP:00.02:30:16 since:Fri May  8 10:21:09 2015


current time is Fri May  8 12:51:32 2015
--------------------------------------------------------------
VIP(192.168.1.205:80:UP:LEASTCONNS): Hits(142905) Pers(SOURCEIP) PersHits(142905:100%)
S(192.168.1.63:80:UP) Hits(21539:15%) PHits(21539:100%) LbHits(0:0%)
S(192.168.1.61:80:UP) Hits(121366:84%) PHits(121366:100%) LbHits(0:0%)
VIP(192.168.1.205:0:Deviation(70588.3:98.791%))
```

Persistence, is the most common reason why you might see uneven distribution to the servers. This disparity coming from persistence can sometimes be much exaggerated due to all clients coming from NAT device and consequently having a single IP. This is why cookie insertion makes an excellent persistence method.

Another reason is using a load/response based method that changes distribution based on server capacity. Here's how to see those persistence entries:

```
> show persistentSessions
Type            SRC-IP                      DST-IP
SOURCEIP        192.168.1.151               192.168.1.61

SOURCEIP        192.168.1.35                192.168.1.61

SOURCEIP        192.168.1.51                192.168.1.63
```

This helps when you are trying to determine which server a particular client is being served from.

Why is the table empty when I configure cookie persistency?

If using cookie-based persistence, the client comes back with the LB cookie it was provided each time it places a request, so a persistence table is not necessary. Instead, use the `show lb vserver` output to identify which server the request will persist to:

```
1) 61_svc (192.168.1.61: 80) - HTTP State: UP    Weight: 1
       Persistence Cookie Value : NSC_205_wjq=ffffffffc3a01f2c45525d5f4f58455e445a4a423660
2) 63_svc (192.168.1.63: 80) - HTTP State: UP    Weight: 1
       Persistence Cookie Value : NSC_205_wjq=ffffffffc3a01f2e45525d5f4f58455e445a4a423660
```

Now, if you look at the header of a response and do a match, you can see that this response was served from `63_svc`:

```
HTTP/1.1 200 OK
Content-Type: image/png
Last-Modified: Sat, 18 Apr 2015 11:05:01 GMT
Accept-Ranges: bytes
ETag: "b07dcc83c779d01:0"
Server: Microsoft-IIS/7.5
Date: Fri, 08 May 2015 13:28:01 GMT
Content-Length: 184946
Set-Cookie: NSC_205_wjq=ffffffffc3a01f2e45525d5f4f58455e445a4a423660
```

Note that the cookie name can be changed from the default `NSC_vipname` format. This ability was specifically added for applications that required the cookie to have a specific name, for example, Lync 2013 needed the cookie to be called `MS-WSMAN`:

```
1) 61_svc (192.168.1.61: 80) - HTTP State: UP    Weight: 1
       Persistence Cookie Value : MS-WSMAN=ffffffffc3a01f2c45525d5f4f58455e445a4a423660
```

You can also dive a little deeper into the LB VIP's performance using the `-d oldconmsg` option. This will give you a ton of information to work with:

```
nsconmsg output with -d oldconmsg
```

```
root@ns# nsconmsg -s ConLb=2 -j 205_vip -d oldconmsg
Displaying debug performance information
NetScaler V20 Performance Data
NetScaler NS10.5: Build 54.9.nc, Date: Dec 15 2014, 13:17:00


current time is Fri May  8 14:02:07 2015
-------------------------------------------------------------------
NATSession : Free(6552)A(6553)InUse(1)
NATSession: Cur(Tcp[0] Udp[1] Icmp[0] Other[0])
NATSession: Op/s(Tcp[0] Udp[0] Icmp[0] Other[0])
Session: A:0 F:0 IUse:0 SEs: SIP:0 C:0 SSL:0 Svr:0 UserId:0 SIPDIP:0 DIP:0 SO:0
SSE: Conn (Srvr 0 Clnt 0) U:0
CM:  Conn (Srvr 0 Clnt 0) Sessions PCB 0 NATPCB 0
Z(SIP[4], C[0], SSL[0] Server[0] SIPDIP[0] DIP[0] SO[0])
Mon: Probes: 11385, Failed: 1118
VIP(192.168.1.205:80:UP:LEASTCONNS): Hits(5951793, 2826/sec) Mbps(30.86) Pers(COOKIE_INSERT) Err(5707566) SO(0) LConn_Best [1
      Pkt(7147/sec, 461 bytes) actSvc(2) DefPol(NONE) override(0) newlyUP(2)
      Conn: Clt(1999, 0/sec, OE[1999]) Svr(304) SQ(Total: 893 OnServer: 0 OnServices: 893)
      slimit_SO: (Sothreshhold: 0 [Ex: 0]  Consumed: [Ex: 0 Borrowed: 0 TotActiveConn: 1999] Available: 0
S(192.168.1.63:80:UP) Hits(1236173, 50/sec, P[1204294, 0/sec]) ATr(1:1) Mbps(0.69) BWlmt(2 kbits) RspTime(0.00 ms) Load(0) LC
, SI:0)
      Other: Pkt(153/sec, 489 bytes) Wt(1) Wt(Reverse Polarity)(10000)
      Conn: CSvr(1, 0/sec) MCSvr(720) OE(1) E(1) RP(0) SQ(0)
      slimit_maxClient: (MaxClt: 0 [Ex: 0]  Consumed: [Ex: 0 Borrowed: 0 TotActiveConn: 1] Available: 0)
      newlyUP_mode: YES, Pending: 4866, update: 0x143f4a, incr_time: 0x0, incr_count: 0
S(192.168.1.61:80:UP) Hits(4715620, 2775/sec, P[4236179, 0/sec]) ATr(1196:1196) Mbps(35.54) BWlmt(0 kbits) RspTime(492.66 ms)
96,I:1, B:1196, X:0, SI:0)
      Other: Pkt(20198/sec, 141 bytes) Wt(1) Wt(Reverse Polarity)(10000)
      Conn: CSvr(8154, 2774/sec) MCSvr(894) OE(1112) E(303) RP(0) SQ(893)
      slimit_maxClient: (MaxClt: 0 [Ex: 0]  Consumed: [Ex: 0 Borrowed: 0 TotActiveConn: 1112] Available: 0)
      newlyUP_mode: YES, Pending: 0, update: 0x143fd1, incr_time: 0x0, incr_count: 0
-------------------------------------------------------------------
CPU:6.1% MEM:182109182 UP:00.03:40:58 since:Fri May  8 10:21:09 2015
```

In the preceding screenshot, you can see the packets/sec, the weight of each service, the hits that each service is getting, the number of **active transactions** (**Atr**), traffic handled in Mbps, and in this particular test case, critically, the **Response time** (**RspTime**) which is 492.66 ms. We can see that the server is struggling a little bit, considering it's taking nearly half a second to respond to each request. Another, perhaps bigger indicator of trouble, is the surge queue that is building up SQ (893).

There are also some very useful connection level details you can learn from this screenshot:

- **CSvr(8154, 2774/sec)**: This is the number connections to the Service
- **MCSvr(894)**: This is the maximum number of connections it has handled at one time
- **OE(1112)**: This is the number of open established connections at one time
- **E(303)**: This is the number of established connections
- **RP(0)**: This is the number of connections in the reuse pool

What is the difference between established and open established?

Established, as the name would imply, are the connections that are active and traffic is being received on them. OPEN established are the ones that are in the TIME_WAIT state awaiting closure. There is a NetScaler zombie cleanup process that runs periodically and closes them to make room for newer connections. Any resets resulting from this type of closure will contain a window size of 9300.

Troubleshooting intermittent issues

If your users or application team reports that a VIP was unavailable for a brief period before automatically getting restored, here are a few possibilities that you need to look at:

- Was the traffic actually getting to the NetScaler? SNMP or the **Reporting** tab (covered in detail in *Chapter 2, Troubleshooting Core NetScaler Features*) of NetScaler are a great way to look this up. If you find that it never got to the NetScaler, consider:
  - Possible VLAN mismatches
  - Switch/firewall failures
  - DNS failures

- Did the Service Flap? The first place to look at will be the events to see if services or the VIP itself has flapped; you can do this by using the IP if it's unique, or using the IP and Port combination:

```
root@192_50_ns# nsconmsg -K /var/nslog/newnslog -d event | grep DOWN
MonServiceBinding_192.168.1.62:80_(tcp-default)(http-service-B): DOW
N; Last response: Failure - Time out during TCP connection establis
hment stage Mon May 25 17:16:43 2015
```

  In the preceding snippet, I can see the monitor failure that brought the service down. Notice that unlike with the earlier examples of nsconmsg, I am using the -K option and a newnslog file location. This is because we are doing a postmortem and want to look at historical data. If you leave it out, you will see only live data. You can also get a more detailed look at monitor states using the following:

  ```
  nsconmsg -K /var/nslog/newnslog -s ConMon=3 -d oldconmsg
  ```

- If the issue is still occurring, a trace would be even better (nstrace is covered in *Chapter 9, Troubleshooting Tools*) as it provides more insight than logs. As always, try and get simultaneous ones on NetScaler and the server to be able to effectively narrow this down.

- It is also worthwhile knowing if server maintenance was scheduled around that time. One such example would be scheduled snapshots of the server virtual machines, which will cause them to be unavailable over the network briefly.

- Surge queue can play a role here as well; if the server is loaded beyond configured capacity, the NetScaler will stop forwarding traffic to the servers until the established connections on that service comes down.

- Check whether there was a crash; you will find numbered folders under `/var/core/` with core dumps matching the timestamp of the issue and report them to techsupport. This has the potential of looking like a brief outage due to a failover that follows or in the case of a standalone because the unit reboots and starts serving traffic again. HA Failovers are covered in *Chapter 5, High Availability and Networking*.

SSL

We will now look at issues that can arise when load balancing SSL applications via the NetScaler. Let's start by looking at some considerations when deploying SSL, before discussing certificates and some essential Wireshark knowledge that you need in the SSL area. We will then apply this knowledge to troubleshoot some common issues before wrapping up the section with a discussion of SSL security best practices.

SSL deployment considerations

SSL is now ubiquitous. In fact, most public facing deployments simply cannot go into production without it. Using NetScaler to take the SSL processing load off the servers is referred to as *SSL offloading*. SSL offloading is great for performance because a NetScaler with its specialized SSL cards is optimized for handling SSL transactions, while your application servers typically are not.

> While the generic name SSL has stuck, SSL is no longer the choice for security and nor is TLS 1.0. The severity of the POODLE attack that impacts both protocols means that security standards mandate using TLS1.1, or better, even TLS1.2 now. All major browsers support these two versions. For the purpose of the chapter, we will use SSL since that is the name used in the field.

There are secondly those deployments (for example, in banks) where that encryption doesn't end at the NetScaler. The decryption happens at NetScaler, necessary policies applied, and traffic is then re-encrypted on its way to the server. This is called *End-to-End* encryption. Here, you still chose SSL as the protocol, but your backend servers are also added as SSL services instead of HTTP or whatever the application layer protocol is. While this deployment does lose some of the advantages of a proper SSL offload, the NetScaler value add of being able to apply HTTP processing, such as doing rewrites or being apply to inspect requests to weed out attacks remains.

A third kind of SSL deployment is where NetScaler doesn't understand the protocols natively but can still encrypt them, thus still providing SSL offload at the TCP level. Secure SMTP is a common example. For such deployments, ssl_TCP is the VIP of choice. Since you are terminating SSL and NetScaler can look into the SSL stream, a majority of the protection benefits are still available with ssl_TCP. However, connection multiplexing is lost.

Finally, there is SSL bridging where NetScaler plays no role in the SSL termination, it is entirely between the client and the server. All the NetScaler does in this case is connection-based load balancing between the different SSL enabled servers. One use case for SSL bridging is wanting client certificates to be sent all the way to the server in their original form. You do not even bind a certificate on the NetScaler for this deployment.

SSL bridging can also be used as a troubleshooting step, that is, if SSL offloading is not working, check whether bridging works. That will tell you that the focus needs to move to NetScaler's handling of SSL.

Certificates

SSL certificates exist in several formats. The most common formats that you encounter when working with NetScaler are PEM and PFX. The NetScaler supports binding PEM certificates to virtual servers, and it is a common format among open source systems, but you will also often stumble on PFX, especially when moving from IIS. In the most recent version, version 11.0, you can directly import PFX certificates without having to convert them, but it is nevertheless handy to know how to convert them using OpenSSL (included on the NetScaler) if you have used an use an earlier version:

```
root@ns# cd /nsconfig/ssl
root@ns# openssl pkcs12 -in iis-cert.pfx -out iis-cert.pem
Enter Import Password:
MAC verified OK
Enter PEM pass phrase:
Verifying - Enter PEM pass phrase:
root@ns#
```

Converting PFX server certificate to PEM using OpenSSL

You can also examine PEM certificates on the NetScaler without having to export them to your PC first. Let's quickly discuss the various sections of a certificate, as this becomes important when troubleshooting:

```
root@ns# cat iis-cert.pem
Bag Attributes
    Microsoft Local Key set: <No Values>
    localKeyID: 01 00 00 00
    friendlyName: 1e-74873c3a-ed25-4d43-af02-e77d16e69a74
    Microsoft CSP Name: Microsoft RSA SChannel Cryptographic Provider
Key Attributes
    X509v3 Key Usage: 10
-----BEGIN RSA PRIVATE KEY-----
Proc-Type: 4,ENCRYPTED
DEK-Info: DES-EDE3-CBC,573B974BA41CDF25

8qOCoZrjFVVtDIkethMIvapbTUL9VzO/wYZ0e3163gliS2iyFmAzSPVxX36cd6iz
glVO/75q5ZLniNjHvy2UD9pG9uWPWLcgb0J19Tco4dpOjqI5vWRGgfTCaWMrUAh0
vG53g0GR0VC+Oz0YeIdFk+H6w9dFRf+2M7/IjHJcPZ3kpxlbbo+BcPgBsSfzyBZ6
TL8JNCf2GFlfWsZglfoKrg0hikdO3EKqh/NBMU5cIlUErYYe5fpopTc8cLGyZcaL
5/jVWO35Wy577iZeQPPxQKiGSG7nbisT8vQYqxUElTYxsVuXxfG3WBUddmmXzQel
Fbm+GflfoiXb158iZIcaDYbdKCLSEp8JavMxCRWcsWXNJzB2MO5HUo4aEUf9UFxe
TObo9zENph5m1FlruQaWu9+Uh31dHFIeaI+5OxayGXjUyk3LH2U99AmntB0bP0eD
hbmit5kHJ/u4PwmR6tcvifeIdoxuMVpoWTd9isKhXCO5KGTIJsZagUf3n0EtaWrp
qo+0GQ54NrvOLPgNvAmykTB6AuvB2cTOmb/uKtsaefas3sDwEIpWY2UVOk4qrGN1
tlghPeQBhMxliexYslerEcmgR14/28BhcsfN9BSXRLEaM+zozMzjGJ7g0JIQ40k/
u9V1YFREag2YyILEe7GEY8vVxGnqt8ab5a63bLokKPlFch6bTMNRmj22IkfbyHDY
J99M9o7KB5L+XQ8MybNqoShFrDlb4biwzrJK9sQ7Enuhi+4iNHXip2sA0KHfHMcO
+4X7/zSzApHonOYBHhTOHZ1TaWS7rS4IpFSm48o+DGsrC91TLckwbg==
-----END RSA PRIVATE KEY-----
Bag Attributes
    localKeyID: 01 00 00 00
    friendlyName: vpn.xm.lab
subject=/C=FR/ST=IDF/L=Paris/O=xm.lab/OU=IT/CN=vpn.xm.lab
issuer=/DC=lab/DC=xm/CN=xm-XMDC-CA
-----BEGIN CERTIFICATE-----
MIIFITCCBAmgAwIBAgIKFGqx9wAAAAAABTANBgkqhkiG9w0BAQUFADA+MRMwEQYK
CZImiZPyLGQBGRYDbGFiMRIwEAYKCZImiZPyLGQBGRYCeG0xEzARBgNVBAMTCnht
```

PEM certificate with encrypted private key

In the screenshot, we see an encrypted private key followed by the certificate. The Proc-Type tells us the key is encrypted, and the DEK-Info tells us the encryption method used. The actual key then follows, demarcated by a BEGIN and END.

Note that, with the PEM format, the certificate and key can exist in the same file, but they don't necessarily have to. Also, the password protection that results in the encrypted form is optional. By contrast, in PFX, they always are in the same file and the file is always protected by a password.

You can run the same conversion with the -nodes option, in which case you will get a PEM file that doesn't have the encryption:

```
root@ns# openssl pkcs12 -in iis-cert.pfx -out server-cert-test.pem -nodes
Enter Import Password:
MAC verified OK
root@ns#
root@ns#
root@ns# cat server-cert-test.pem | more
Bag Attributes
    Microsoft Local Key set: <No Values>
    localKeyID: 01 00 00 00
    friendlyName: 1e-74873c3a-ed25-4d43-af02-e77d16e69a74
    Microsoft CSP Name: Microsoft RSA SChannel Cryptographic Provider
Key Attributes
    X509v3 Key Usage: 10
-----BEGIN RSA PRIVATE KEY-----
MIICXQIBAAKBgQCT2M34ZkIjuFFum5yCSYkWYIzvBszSh2e6bq7Q8h86LS9TKnur
pi+zfmNcu9JBIkgYZl8ao6UIWu9k8+HSd27yH879IUQaj485JrIP2UoXbOtQwWRz
```

Using Wireshark to examine the handshake

For the next few minutes, let's take a look at a sample trace and see how a *full* handshake unfolds.

SSL handshake

The following are the steps for SSL handshake:

1. The first packet that an SSL client sends after the TCP handshake is a Client Hello. This will tell you what SSL version the client is using, and whether they are reusing an SSL session (more on session reuse to follow) and what Ciphers it supports. The list of Ciphers is in the order that the client prefers:

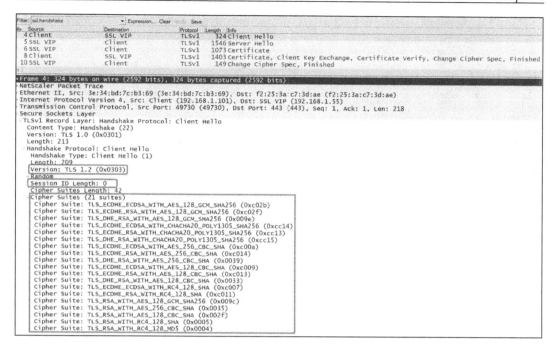

2. The first SSL packet from a server, as you've guessed, is the `Server Hello`. In this packet, the server indicates its version of TLS and next, see that it has chosen `TLS_RSA_WITH_RC4_128_MD5`, which is in the list that the client has provided in its `Client Hello`:

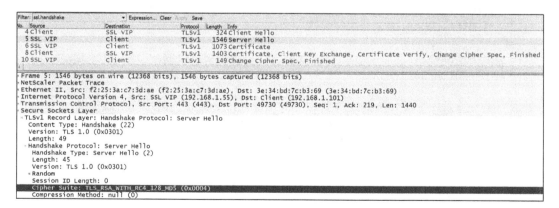

 Note that the Cipher chosen here, while commonly supported, is not the strongest. You can certainly tune this by creating a more tightly limited Custom Cipher group.

3. The Server Certificate exchange, along with details of CN, issuer, and validity is sent by the server. It is important that the trace captures this certificate exchange if it is to be decryptable:

4. In Client Certificate (Optional) the step that leads the client to provide its certificate is the presence of a certificate request in the previous step (Server Certificate Exchange):

```
TLSv1 Record Layer: Handshake Protocol: Multiple Handshake Messages
  Content Type: Handshake (22)
  Version: TLS 1.0 (0x0301)
  Length: 150
  Handshake Protocol: Certificate Request
    Handshake Type: Certificate Request (13)
```

5. In this step of Client Key Exchange, the Encrypted PreMaster key gets exchanged. How this key gets generated depends on the OS, but in general it uses a random number generator, taking some local characteristics into account:

```
No.  Source           Destination        Protocol  Length  Info
  4 Client            SSL VIP            TLSv1      324 Client Hello
  5 SSL VIP           Client            TLSv1     1546 Server Hello
  6 SSL VIP           Client            TLSv1     1073 Certificate
  8 Client            SSL VIP            TLSv1     1403 Certificate, Client Key Exchange, Certificate Verify, Change Cipher Spec, Finished
 10 SSL VIP           Client            TLSv1      149 Change Cipher Spec  Finished

▶Frame 8: 1403 bytes on wire (11224 bits), 1403 bytes captured (11224 bits)
▶NetScaler Packet Trace
▶Ethernet II, Src: 3e:34:bd:7c:b3:69 (3e:34:bd:7c:b3:69), Dst: f2:25:3a:c7:3d:ae (f2:25:3a:c7:3d:ae)
▶Internet Protocol Version 4, Src: Client (192.168.1.101), Dst: SSL VIP (192.168.1.55)
▶Transmission Control Protocol, Src Port: 49730 (49730), Dst Port: 443 (443), Seq: 219, Ack: 2408, Len: 1297
▼Secure Sockets Layer
 ▶TLSv1 Record Layer: Handshake Protocol: Certificate
 ▼TLSv1 Record Layer: Handshake Protocol: Client Key Exchange
    Content Type: Handshake (22)
    Version: TLS 1.0 (0x0301)
    Length: 134
  ▼Handshake Protocol: Client Key Exchange
    Handshake Type: Client Key Exchange (16)
    Length: 130
   ▼RSA Encrypted PreMaster Secret
     Encrypted PreMaster length: 128
     Encrypted PreMaster: 901a1b06a15591ed196e370b7b020d98436a7b4958b46da2...
 ▶TLSv1 Record Layer: Handshake Protocol: Certificate Verify
 ▶TLSv1 Record Layer: Change Cipher Spec Protocol: Change Cipher Spec
 ▶TLSv1 Record Layer: Handshake Protocol: Finished
```

The security of this PreMaster secret is paramount, which is why it gets encrypted with the server's public key so that only the server (which has the private key) can decrypt it.

6. Handshake finish step is the point at which the handshake ends. The finished messages indicate that the client and server are happy to move to encrypted (symmetric) data exchange. Now that we have some of the considerations out the way, let's look at how we approach SSL issues.

A session-reused handshake

Now, let's look at the version of the handshake that happens when the SSL session reuse is happening. Here, you see that the client already comes with a session ID from a previous session, and in the rather short SSL handshake that happens, the server certificate is not exchanged and no validation is done, and some computationally expensive steps are avoided by doing so:

```
Filter: ssl.handshake          ▼ Expression... Clear Apply Save
No.  Source           Destination        Protocol  Length  Info
  4 192.168.1.101     192.168.1.55       TLSv1      349 Client Hello
  5 192.168.1.55      192.168.1.101      TLSv1      243 Server Hello, Change Cipher Spec, Encrypted Handshake Message
  6 192.168.1.101     192.168.1.55       TLSv1      157 Change Cipher Spec, Encrypted Handshake Message

▶Frame 4: 349 bytes on wire (2792 bits), 349 bytes captured (2792 bits)
▶NetScaler Packet Trace
▶Ethernet II, Src: 3e:34:bd:7c:b3:69 (3e:34:bd:7c:b3:69), Dst: f2:25:3a:c7:3d:ae (f2:25:3a:c7:3d:ae)
▶Internet Protocol Version 4, Src: 192.168.1.101 (192.168.1.101), Dst: 192.168.1.55 (192.168.1.55)
▶Transmission Control Protocol, Src Port: 49419 (49419), Dst Port: 443 (443), Seq: 1, Ack: 1, Len: 243
▼Secure Sockets Layer
 ▼TLSv1 Record Layer: Handshake Protocol: Client Hello
    Content Type: Handshake (22)
    Version: TLS 1.0 (0x0301)
    Length: 238
  ▼Handshake Protocol: Client Hello
    Handshake Type: Client Hello (1)
    Length: 234
    Version: TLS 1.2 (0x0303)
   ▶Random
    Session ID Length: 32
    Session ID: bcdb48b9bcc61d251b705f96d008682cea9fcd78b69c5d82...
```

Session reuse is a great SSL performance technique. This is why it is enabled by default.

Session reuse and troubleshooting

As huge a benefit as session reuse is, it poses a problem when wanting to decrypt a trace. With the truncated handshake and the missing certificate, decryption will fail.

The recommendation around this is to disable SSL session reuse for the brief period that you are running the trace, and enable it again once the tracing is complete. If you forget to enable it, you will definitely see higher SSL card use or a higher CPU, based on your NetScaler platform, hence re-enabling it is important. The setting is managed from the SSL parameters tab for each VIP individually:

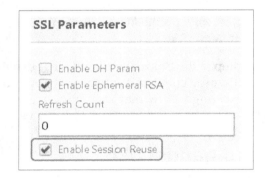

A second option is to completely close and restart the application.

Now that we looked at how the handshake works, let's take a look at how one goes about decrypting a trace in Wireshark.

Decrypting a trace using Wireshark

While troubleshooting SSL/TLS issues, you will find yourself often needing to look beyond the handshake and at the HTTP, or at other layer 7 level information. You can again use Wireshark for this purpose. To decrypt the trace:

1. Obtain the private key corresponding to the SSL VIP.
2. Click on **Edit** | **Preferences** | **Protocols** | **SSL**.

3. Click on the **RSA keys** list and create an entry; the following figure shows an example:

4. Click on **OK** all the way to the main window and you should now be able to see decrypted packets.

There is also a password field that needs to be filled in if the key is password protected. As an alternative, you can also use OpenSSL to decrypt the key even before getting to this step. The command is:

```
openssl rsa -in <encrypted key>  -out < decrypted output filename>
```

The quickest way to tell if the decryption worked is by using the filter `ssl && http`, as you can see the decrypted HTTP is in green in the following screenshot:

```
Filter: ssl && http                      ▼  Expression...  Clear  Apply  Save
No. Source               Destination          Protocol  Length  Info
747 192.168.1.101        192.168.1.55         HTTP      473 GET / HTTP/1.1
750 192.168.1.55         192.168.1.101        HTTP      1074 HTTP/1.1 200 OK  (text/html)
◄
▸ Frame 750: 1074 bytes on wire (8592 bits), 1074 bytes captured (8592 bits)
▸ NetScaler Packet Trace
▸ Ethernet II, Src: f2:25:3a:c7:3d:ae (f2:25:3a:c7:3d:ae), Dst: 3e:34:bd:7c:b3:69 (3e:34:bd:7c:b3:69)
▸ Internet Protocol Version 4, Src: 192.168.1.55 (192.168.1.55), Dst: 192.168.1.101 (192.168.1.101)
▸ Transmission Control Protocol, Src Port: 443 (443), Dst Port: 49730 (49730), Seq: 2451, Ack: 1883, Len: 968
▸ Secure Sockets Layer
▸ Hypertext Transfer Protocol
▸ Line-based text data: text/html
0000  48 54 54 50 2f 31 2e 31   20 32 30 30 20 4f 4b 0d   HTTP/1.1  200 OK.
0010  0a 43 6f 6e 74 65 6e 74   2d 54 79 70 65 3a 20 74   .Content -Type: t
Frame (1074 bytes) Decrypted SSL data (947 bytes)
```

Note that apart from an incomplete handshake being captured (due to a reused SSL session), a second case where Wireshark will fail to decrypt the trace is when protocols such as Diffie Hellman are used in the key exchange. In such cases, instead of the server's public and private keys, randomly generated keys are used that Wireshark doesn't have visibility into and thus the decryption fails.

If you are having trouble with decryption, look for clues in the SSL Debug file that you can choose under **Edit | Preferences | SSL**:

Secure Sockets Layer

RSA keys list   Edit...

SSL debug file

C:/keys/ssl-debug.txt   Browse...

☑ Reassemble SSL records spanning multiple TCP segments

☑ Reassemble SSL Application Data spanning multiple SSL records

What if I needed to share this key with the Citrix tech support for troubleshooting?

You will, on occasion, need to share the key with Citrix support for troubleshooting issues involving SSL. Citrix has strict measures in place around how this information is handled to avoid risk. However, sharing the key might not bode well with your security policy; luckily, it's easy to resolve this situation without adding to the risk by decrypting and exporting the session keys to share with Citrix.

With these session keys, Citrix (or any third-party you share the session keys with) can only decrypt a specific conversation. To do this using Wireshark first decrypt the trace as we've discussed. Then, navigate to **File | Export SSL Session Keys**.

The result will be a text file with the RSA Session ID and the Master Key that you can share with anyone that needs to be able to decrypt the session. The way this file will be used for decryption is by going to the *SSL Protocol Preferences* section of Wireshark and specifying it as the (Pre)-Master-Secret log filename.

> Note that when capturing the trace, it is important that you use the size 0 (unlimited size) option, as we discuss in *Chapter 9, Troubleshooting Tools*. If not, the trace will be truncated, which means the certificate is not fully captured and the trace will not be decryptable.

Now with the key concepts out of the way, let's look at some ways to approach troubleshooting SSL issues.

Troubleshooting SSL issues

If you have the possibility, create an equivalent HTTP VIP first for testing. If that works fine, we'll need to start looking at the SSL handshake using Wireshark.

Wireshark troubleshooting for SSL failures

Having verified that the HTTP version of the VIP works correctly, let's look at some potential failure areas:

- **Trust issues from unknown CA**: In the following example, we see that the handshake is failing because the NetScaler doesn't trust the certificate that is being presented by the client:

At this point, you will need to open the client certificate in the trace and see what **CA (Certificate Authority)** signed it. Once you note down the CA, check the SSL VIP configuration and see whether the CA has been specified in the list:

```
Secure Sockets Layer
  TLSv1 Record Layer: Alert (Level: Fatal, Description: Unknown CA)
    Content Type: Alert (21)
    Version: TLS 1.0 (0x0301)
    Length: 2
  Alert Message
    Level: Fatal (2)
    Description: Unknown CA (48)
```

Another way to catch this problem is by looking at SSL error counters. To do this, drop into shell and use the `nsconmsg -g ssl_err -d current` command:

```
root@192_50_ns# nsconmsg -g ssl_err -d current
Displaying performance information
NetScaler V20 Performance Data
NetScaler NS10.5: Build 54.9.nc, Date: Dec 15 2014, 13:17:00


reltime:mili second between two records Mon May 25 15:58:31 2015
  Index   rtime totalcount-val     delta rate/sec symbol-name&device-no
      0    7001             76         5       0 ssl_err_clientAuth_certCAnotfound
      1       0             73         5       0 ssl_err_clientAuth_unablegetissuercert
      2       0             82         5       0 ssl_err_ssl3_get_client_certificate
```

- **Trust issues from missing intermediate CA certificates**: Issues can also arise in the form of a missing certificate link. So if you are getting the certificate from an intermediate CA (which is very often the case), make sure you've linked these properly. You can do this from the **Certificates** section of the **SSL** tab once you have installed the intermediate CA certificate by selecting the server certificate and choosing **Link**:

Rather handily, NetScaler then looks at who signed this certificate (that is, the CA `int.xmx.lab`, in our case here) and presents its certificate for linking:

If there are multiple intermediate CAs, you will need to repeat this for all, working your way to the top of the chain, that is, the root CA. The result of this exercise is that when NetScaler presents the server certificate bound to the VIP, it also includes all intermediate CA certificates so that the client who might only know the root certificate will accept the server certificate by looking at the entire chain.

- **Client doesn't present a certificate with Client Cert Auth configured**: If the client doesn't present a certificate, while the NetScaler is expecting one due to client cert authentication configured, you will see the counter ssl_err_clientAuth_nocert increment.

```
root@192_50_ns# nsconmsg -g ssl_err -d current
Displaying performance information
NetScaler V20 Performance Data
NetScaler NS10.5: Build 54.9.nc, Date: Dec 15 2014, 13:17:00


reltime:mili second between two records Mon May 25 16:17:04 2015
   Index   rtime totalcount-val      delta rate/sec symbol-name&device-no
       0    7002             22          4       0 ssl_err_clientAuth_nocert
       1       0            106          4       0 ssl_err_ssl3_get_client_certificate
       2    7001             30          8       1 ssl_err_clientAuth_nocert
```

For the certificate to be presented correctly, the client browser needs, of course, to be set up with one, but as a troubleshooting step, also verify by looking for a certificate request (ssl.handshake.type == 13) from the NetScaler SSL VIP. The following is what it should look like:

```
⊕ Handshake Protocol: Certificate Request
⊕ Handshake Protocol: Server Hello Done
```

- **Protocol mismatches**: If the client and NetScaler cannot agree on the version of TLS to use, you will see a protocol version alert.

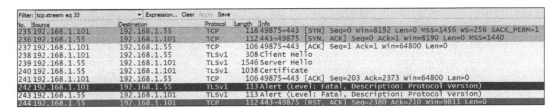

The counter `nsconmsg -g ssl_err` highlights this incompatibility.

SSL and TLS versions used can be managed from the SSL parameter tab of each SSL vServer.

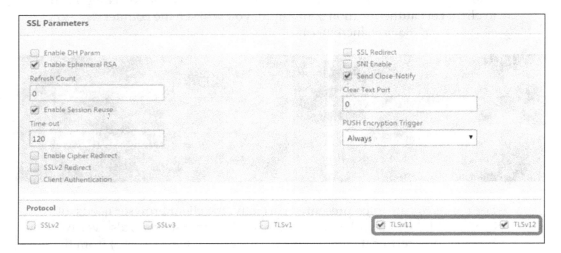

- **Cipher Mismatches**: If the protocols match but the server and client don't manage to find a common cipher, this will result in a handshake failure message in the trace.

No.	Source	Destination	Protocol	Length	Info
63	192.168.1.101	192.168.1.55	TCP	118	49955→443 [SYN] Seq=0 Win=8192 Len=0 MSS=1456 WS=256
64	192.168.1.55	192.168.1.101	TCP	112	443→49955 [SYN, ACK] Seq=0 Ack=1 Win=8190 Len=0 MSS=1
65	192.168.1.101	192.168.1.55	TCP	106	49955→443 [ACK] Seq=1 Ack=1 Win=64800 Len=0
66	192.168.1.101	192.168.1.55	TLSv1.2	308	Client Hello
67	192.168.1.55	192.168.1.101	TLSv1.2	113	Alert (Level: Fatal, Description: Handshake Failure)
68	192.168.1.55	192.168.1.101	TCP	112	443→49955 [RST, ACK] Seq=8 Ack=203 Win=9811 Len=0

```
Frame 67: 113 bytes on wire (904 bits), 113 bytes captured (904 bits)
NetScaler Packet Trace
Ethernet II, Src: f2:25:3a:c7:3d:ae (f2:25:3a:c7:3d:ae), Dst: 3e:34:bd:7c:b3:69 (3e:34:bd:7c:b3:69)
Internet Protocol Version 4, Src: 192.168.1.55 (192.168.1.55), Dst: 192.168.1.101 (192.168.1.101)
Transmission Control Protocol, Src Port: 443 (443), Dst Port: 49955 (49955), Seq: 1, Ack: 203, Len: 7
Secure Sockets Layer
  TLSv1.2 Record Layer: Alert (Level: Fatal, Description: Handshake Failure)
    Content Type: Alert (21)
    Version: TLS 1.2 (0x0303)
```

And here's the counter that goes when using `nsconmsg -g ssl_err -d current`:

```
reltime:mili second between two records Mon May 25 17:37:14 2015
   Index    rtime totalcount-val    delta rate/sec symbol-name&device-no
       0     7001              40       10       1 ssl_err_ssl3_get_client_hello
```

> You might have noticed that all traces that contain a failure seem to end with the same window size for the reset (9811). This is NetScaler's way of indicating to us, that the reset was sent due to a handshake failure.

SSL card failures

Card failures are fortunately very rare. But in case one happens, you will see a number of telltale signs. A card failure will:

- Result in an HA failover
- Show up in show node and `stat ssl` outputs
- Show you the counter `ssl_err_card_process_fail_rst` every time the device resets a connection it can't process due to the card being down
- Result in this reset having the window code 9820

SSL security concerns

SSL is such a vital component for customers, especially those bound by compliance laws that, keeping on top of the issues, is a constant effort and requires regular handling, what with new vulnerabilities being reported on a regular basis. Consider the following best practices to ensure you are well protected:

- Removing SSL and TLS 1.0 and moving to TLS 1.2 is a good option. Given the suite of SSLv3 vulnerabilities (for example, Poodle Attack) the goal should be to move to TLS, preferably TLS 1.2. NetScaler now supports TLS Versions 1.1 and 1.2, both on the frontend and the backend (backend support is currently only for MPX or SDX instances with an SSL card assigned at this point, not regular VPX).

  Note that sometimes, scanners report vulnerabilities purely based on the OpenSSL version used on NetScaler. It should be noted that OpenSSL while present on NetScaler, isn't actually used for SSL processing. For processing, Custom software is used. Also, the OpenSSL present on NetScaler is a locked down version, meaning code that is unnecessary or vulnerable is dropped.

- Avoid all RC4 Ciphers such as SSL3-RC4-MD5. There is now even an RFC (rfc7465) advocating against it. And avoid export Ciphers such as EXP-RC4-MD5. They are considered too weak and form the basis for attacks such as FREAK. Note that these ciphers have been removed from the default Cipher list for this very reason.

- Use the latest version of NetScaler, as security issues are taken pretty seriously and are among the first in line for the next build.

- Deny SSL renegotiation unless your application specifically needs it. You can do this using the following command:

```
Set ssl parameter -denySSLReneg ALL
```

You can also set this from the GUI under the advanced SSL parameters section of SSL, either setting to **ALL** or to a specific leg of the conversation:

Consider reading a couple of excellent blogs, written in this area by one of our consultants, that are a lot more comprehensive and explain how to get an A+ at https://www.ssllabs.com/ by following SSL security best practices. The short links are https://goo.gl/ WREk7y and https://goo.gl/00PH2C.

Engaging with Citrix

SSL vulnerabilities that are reported in the wild will likely have a **CVE** (**Common Vulnerabilities and Exposures**) ID associated with them. Try and identify the CVE of a vulnerability. The `https://cve.mitre.org/` website is a great place to find these.

If you have stumbled into a vulnerability on your own through your own testing, there are a couple of ways you can proceed:

- If you are using a scanner that reports a known vulnerability, first try with the latest version.

- If you see the same results with the latest build, note down the CVE and engage with `secure@citrix.com`. The `http://support.citrix.com/article/ctx140863` site contains more details around reporting vulnerabilities to Citrix.

Content switching

In this section, we will look at troubleshooting Content Switching. CS, as it is called in short, can be thought of as the single IP face of an infrastructure that is large and complex in the background. The idea is to have the CS vServer use Administrator configured rules to choose target LB vServers that each handle load balance for a particular type of content. The rules are the main value offered here as they can get very granular in identifying minute differences between two requests.

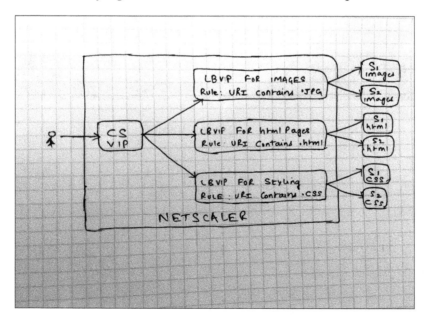

As such, troubleshooting CS in the vast majority of cases comes down to verifying two things:

- You have the right policies in place
- The LB vServers that are bound are up

Troubleshooting service unavailable errors

I have a CS VIP (`cs-vip`) that choses either the vServer `base-vip`, containing only HTML, or the vServer `image-vip`, containing only images by looking at the URL.

```
add cs vserver cs-vip HTTP 192.168.1.54 80 -cltTimeout 180 -Listenpolicy None
add cs policy base-policy -rule "http.REQ.URL.ENDSWITH(\"htm\")"
add cs policy images-policy -rule "http.REQ.URL.ENDSWITH(\"jpg\")||http.REQ.URL.ENDSWITH(\"png\")"
bind cs vserver cs-vip -policyName base-policy -targetLBVserver base-vip -priority 100
bind cs vserver cs-vip -policyName images-policy -targetLBVserver images-vip -priority 110
```

I try to access the VIP, and instead of the page with images that I expected to see, I land on a **Service Unavailable** error.

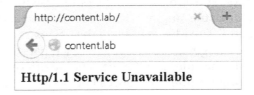

Now, let's investigate. As a first check, I verify that my VIP is active.

```
> show cs vserver
1)      cs-vip (192.168.1.54:80) - HTTP Type: CONTENT
        State: UP
```

Then, a quick look at a trace shows a 503 error. In http, all 500 series errors indicate a failure on the part of the server.

No.	Source	Destination	Protocol	Length	Info
57	192.168.1.101	192.168.1.54	HTTP	391	GET / HTTP/1.1
58	192.168.1.54	192.168.1.101	HTTP	295	HTTP/1.1 503 Service Unavailable

Filter: http   Expression... Clear Apply Save

Looking at the trace, however, the response is coming directly from the NetScaler, notice that there are no server side packets. This implies that NetScaler is the source of the 503 errors. This will happen when the NetScaler encounters a request for which there are no matching rules. Here, the base page / doesn't have an .htm, .jpg, or .png extension. The key is thus to have a rule for every occasion.

We might not be able to foresee every single extension there is on the site. So it is important to have a default LB vServer that catches all exceptions. I proceed to add a default LB vServer that catches this request, and now the page loads without an error.

Content switching timeout errors

We can also encounter content switching timeout errors that are not related to configuration.

From the error, I can already tell that this is a low-level failure, since the connection timed out. Logically, I proceed to check the status of my CS VIP, which shows no problems.

```
> show cs vserver cs-vip
        cs-vip (192.168.1.54:80)  - HTTP Type: CONTENT
        State: UP
```

In fact, I can even ping it:

```
C:\Users\rvt>ping content.lab

Pinging content.lab [192.168.1.54] with 32 bytes of data:
Reply from 192.168.1.54: bytes=32 time=2ms TTL=255
Reply from 192.168.1.54: bytes=32 time<1ms TTL=255
```

Given the experience from the previous issue, I verify the policies, which seem to be all okay, and proceed to take a trace. On filtering the trace with the Client IP, we see the problem. There is no response to the TCP connection requests.

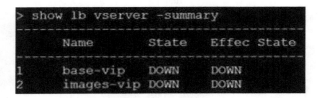

Since the CS vServer is up, we turn our attention to the backend servers for this CS VIP, that is, the LB vServers. Here, we see the problem, the VIPs are all down, including the `base-vip`, which is my catch-all.

```
> show lb vserver -summary
----------------------------------------
        Name        State    Effec State
----------------------------------------
1       base-vip    DOWN     DOWN
2       images-vip  DOWN     DOWN
```

So why is the content switching vServer not alerting us to this by changing its state to down? The answer to this puzzle lies in the -stateupdate parameter; by default, it is disabled.

Global Server Load Balancing

Global Server Load Balancing (**GLSB**) does for data centers what load balancing does for servers. It directs users to the best possible resource (best data center for a resource). Best here can mean, the closest, the healthiest, or the least loaded.

GSLB uses a proprietary protocol called **Metric Exchange Protocol** (**MEP**) to obtain the metrics needed for this decision. The result of GSLB processing is an **Address** (**A**) record in response to a DNS request that the client will then use to obtain the resource.

In this section, we'll look at what a typical first time flow looks like, what some of the considerations are for GSLB to work correctly, and then move on to troubleshooting.

GSLB flow

It is important to understand the several layers involved in a GSLB conversation to be able to troubleshoot it. Let's take a look at an example of a User wanting to launch the home page of web.xmx.lab, which belongs to the xmx.lab domain:

1. User accesses web.xmx.lab for the first time.

2. The DNS request for web.xmx.lab lands on the **local DNS (LDNS)** that the User's computer uses for DNS resolution.

3. LDNS doesn't know the answer to this request, so it looks up the addresses of the root servers it knows and contacts them for further direction.

4. The root will not know the address either, but let's say it knows the TLD server that is aware of all .lab domains. In this case, it will return this TLD server's address to the LDNS.

5. LDNS contacts the TLD, who in return provides the IP address of the DNS server authoritative for xmx.lab.

6. LDNS then contacts the authoritative name server for `xmx.lab` and this is the point at which GSLB comes into the picture. The authoritative name server, instead of directly providing an IP that represents `web.xmx.lab`, provides the IP addresses of the ADNS service of one of the several NetScalers participating in GSLB.

7. At this point, NetScaler, given its visibility into the various site metrics, decides what site IP is best to return and via the ADNS service, provides it to the client.

8. The client finally sends the actual request (HTTP, HTTPs, and so on) to this IP, considering it as the IP of `web.xmx.lab`.

Step 6 in the preceding flow can also use CNAMEs instead of the ADNS service IP. In this case, the Authoritative DNS will send CNAME records for one of the ADNS services and their corresponding IPs (glue records). The rest of the process is the same.

Metric Exchange Protocol

Understanding the exchange that happens between two (or many) NetScalers participating in GSLB is key for troubleshooting. Exchanging MEP packets is how NetScalers participating in GSLB communicate to each other about key statistics for each of the GLSB services, which in turn are the configured LB vServers and services that they represent. These statistics include:

- The state of the GSLB service
- Open connections
- Surge queue values
- The amount of requests being handled
- LDNS RTT information
- Persistency information

This will then allow the NetScaler receiving the DNS request to decide which target DNS IP to return.

MEP versus monitors

There are two means by which the local GSLB NetScaler monitors the status of remote sites. MEP is the best way to monitor remote sites, as it includes all this useful information allowing for intelligent GSLB decisions, but it isn't the only way. You can also bind monitors for this purpose. The best practice is to use the **Use Monitors when MEP** is down option. This way, you indicate a preference for MEP but will fall back to monitors should there be a problem with the MEP exchange.

RPC considerations

RPC settings give you control over MEP exchange. When you add a GSLB site, it will automatically result in an RPC node entry to give you control over how that site communicates.

You can view these entries using show rpcnode. In the following screenshot 1 is NetScaler HA related; it is for the NSIP. 2 and 3 are for MEP. The entry says that to reach site 192.168.1.51 (site IP), use the password shown and use any available source and use non-secure communication.

```
> show rpcnode
1)      IPAddress:   192.168.1.50 Password:   8a7b474124957776a0cd31b862cbe4d72b5cbd59868a136d4bdeb56cf03b28
SrcIP:  192.168.1.50
        Secure:  OFF
2)      IPAddress:   192.168.1.51 Password:   8a7b474124957776a0cd31b862cbe4d72b5cbd59868a136d4bdeb56cf03b28
SrcIP:  *
        Secure:  OFF
3)      IPAddress:   192.168.1.151 Password:   8a7b474124957776a0cd31b862cbe4d72b5cbd59868a136d4bdeb56cf03b28
 SrcIP:  *
        Secure:  OFF
```

It is a good practice especially if the communication between the sites is happening over the Internet to enable secure MEP, change the default password, and finally also set a specific source IP so that it sits well with your firewall rules.

```
> set rpcNode 192.168.1.151 -password Secure123$ -secure YES -srcIP 192.168.1.51
 Done
> show rpcNode 192.168.1.151
1)      IPAddress:  192.168.1.151 Password:  ed2a135565c27371a2de20 SrcIP:  192.168.1.51
    Secure:  ON
Done
```

In the preceding example, I am choosing the recommended settings and specifying that I want to use my SNIP, which is also my local site IP to talk to the remote sites.

Troubleshooting GSLB

Now with an understanding of the considerations, let's approach some of the common issues that NetScaler admins run into with GSLB and how to troubleshoot them.

DNS caching and GSLB

When troubleshooting GSLB, it is important to query the ADNS service directly to understand if the behavior is as expected or incorrect. There are several points in the GSLB path, where caching might mean you are not looking at the NetScaler's exact response. These are:

- End User application (for example, browser)
- The OS
- The LDNS
- Upstream DNS servers of the ISP

The amount of time ideally should be based on the TTL, but some devices will cache the entries for much longer as a way of reducing upstream DNS traffic. While you have limited possibilities for overriding the caches given that they are external entities, for troubleshooting at least, the best method would be to use nslookup or dig to query the ADNS directly.

```
C:\>nslookup
Default Server:  UnKnown
Address:  192.168.1.254

> server 192.168.1.51
Default Server:  [192.168.1.51]
Address:  192.168.1.51

> gslb.xmx.lab
Server:  [192.168.1.51]
Address:  192.168.1.51

Name:    gslb.xmx.lab
Address:  192.168.1.155

> gslb.xmx.lab
Server:  [192.168.1.51]
Address:  192.168.1.51

Name:    gslb.xmx.lab
Address:  192.168.1.55
```

Querying ADNS directly to verify gslb results

MEP down issues

If MEP is configured but shows as **Down**; this is either a network related issue (most common reason), or an RPC configuration issue.

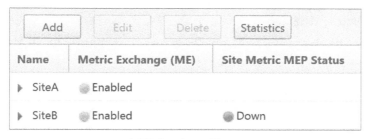

MEP showing as Down

Network considerations for MEP:

- MEP uses one of two ports based on secure/nonsecure:
    ◦ 3011 by nonsecure
    ◦ 3009 if set to secure

    These firewall rules need to allow bidirectional communication for these ports

- MEP connections are long-lived; intermediate devices should not attempt to tear this down

RPC related issues

The default configurations will never fail as such, but then, as we discussed, there are good reasons why you might want to adjust RPC configuration. While doing so though, ensure that the password settings match on both sides. The following `nsconmsg` command is handy when looking at MEP issues.

```
root@151ns# nsconmsg -g gslb -g rpc -d current
Displaying performance information
NetScaler V20 Performance Data
NetScaler NS10.5: Build 55.8.nc, Date: Jan 25 2015, 23:55:26


reltime:mili second between two records Sun May 31 19:37:13 2015
   Index   rtime totalcount-val       delta rate/sec symbol-name&device-no
       0    7001          11834          16       2 gslb_tot_gslb_msgs_rcvd
       1       0          12487          15       2 gslb_tot_gslb_msg_sent
       2    7000          11848          14       2 gslb_tot_gslb_msgs_rcvd
       3       0          12502          15       2 gslb_tot_gslb_msg_sent
```

The nsconmsg command for troubleshooting MEP

The output will tell you:

- Whether MEP is being sent and received; if it's being sent on one end but you don't see `gslb_tot_gslb_msgs_rcvd` going up on the other, it's time to take a trace and follow traffic on ports 3009 or 3011 depending on whether secure is enabled or disabled
- Whether there are any RPC related errors contributing to MEP failures

Troubleshooting proximity-based methods

Proximity-based methods use the location of the **Local DNS server** (**LDNS**) of a User as a guide to understand where the User should be directed to. Again, the closer the User is to the LDNS, the more accurate the decision, because the LDNS IP is all the NetScalers will see, not the actual Client IP.

There are two methods of Proximity:

- **Dynamic proximity**: This involves each GSLB partner NetScaler to calculate RTT values to the client as a means to determine what the best location for the User is. The ADNS service that fronts dynamic RTT counts on being able to use one of the three probes –ICMP, DNS, and TCP in that order. The SNIP will be the one initiating the connections. Using the time taken for the response, the RTT table is populated. What is learnt is also shared between the sites using MEP.

  The only troubleshooting step for this method is to verify that these protocols (or at least one of them) are able to pass through the firewalls so that RTT can be determined.

- **Static proximity**: This is more widely used than dynamic proximity. It involves the NetScaler referring to a database (`.csv` file) or custom location entries to identify what the best VIP for a client is. Note that in 11.0, owing to popular demand, Citrix now includes a built-in GeoIP database for this purpose.

```
root@151_ns# find / -name *.csv
/var/netscaler/inbuilt_db/Citrix_Netscaler_InBuilt_GeoIP_DB.csv
```

If static proximity is not working as it should, check the following:

- If you are using the database method, verify that it is correctly loaded with the `show locationFile` command, as follows:

```
> show locationFile
Location File IPv4: /var/netscaler/inbuilt_db/Citrix_Netscaler_InBuilt_GeoIP_DB.csv
Format: netscaler
 Done
```

- Query the file with the Client's IP using the `nsmap` command. This will tell you which site the NetScaler thinks the Client belongs to. This should explain any mismatch between where you expect the client to be directed to versus where they are actually being sent.

```
root@151_ns# nsmap -d -t
Enter IP address to test or q to exit: 2.2.2.2
2.2.2.2 2.2.2.0-2.2.3.255 "Europe"."FR"."*"."*"."*"."*" 2 east  49 north
```

- If you are using custom entries, ensure that the service IP (10.72.142.55 in the screenshot) falls within the boundaries of a specific location entry (IP from 10.72.142.1 IP to 10.72.142.75). This is how the NetScaler identifies which site lies in which location.

```
> show gslb site gslb-siteA
        gslb-siteA (10.72.142.51)        Site Type: LOCAL
        Metric exchange: ENABLED         Public IP: 10.72.142.51
        Network metric exchange: ENABLED        Persistence session exchange: ENABLED
        Trigger Monitors: ALWAYS

1)      gslb-local-serviceA (10.72.142.55:80) - HTTP     State: UP
 Done
> show location
1) IP from.....10.72.142.1      IP to.....10.72.142.75
Continent.Country.Region.City.ISP.Organization =
Europe.CH.*.*.*.*
```

In the absence of such an entry, you will see a round robin behavior which is suboptimal.

- Also bear in mind that custom entries and any DNS views have preference over the database entries. So search the configuration file to ensure that there isn't such an overriding configuration, which might explain the behavior you are seeing.

Summary

In this chapter, we looked at how to examine and troubleshoot uneven load balancing as well as performance issues when load balancing via the NetScaler. We then extended that learning to SSL, content switching, and global server load balancing, which are all application delivery features that many large enterprises rely on to deliver their applications at scale and in a globally distributed manner.

I hope the chapter has proven useful to you. In the next chapter, we will look at how to troubleshoot caching and compression, which are RFC standards-based features that help further optimize HTTP content delivery via the NetScaler.

3
Integrated Caching and Compression

In this chapter, we will look at Integrated Caching and Compression, two HTTP features that offer enormous performance benefits and help with loading pages faster. In the caching section, we will look at:

- The various caching terms employed (these aren't NetScaler specific)
- How cache policies are evaluated on the NetScaler
- What the exchange between a client and NetScaler looks like
- Guidance on what kind of content to cache and not cache
- How to monitor and troubleshoot caching

In the compression section, we will look at:

- Guidance on what content should and shouldn't be compressed
- What a compression-related exchange looks like
- How to monitor compression
- Troubleshooting considerations for compression

Integrated Caching

A good majority of content on the web is fairly static. Granted, the current nature of the web means that new content is created all the time, but it doesn't change with every request and some items, like the branding on a company's homepage, stay unchanged for years. Integrated Caching is an HTTP feature on the NetScaler that allows potentially massive savings on bandwidth and server CPU utilization by storing a copy of previously requested objects in its RAM and serving them to users over and over again as long as it is considered valid.

Let's look at some caching-related terms that we will use in this chapter:

- **Origin server**: This is the server in the backend that generates and owns the original content
- **Cache hit**: This means that a request that has landed on the NetScaler can be responded to with an object from the cache
- **Cache miss**: The request has to be sent to the origin server
- **Revalidation**: This is the NetScaler going back to the server to verify that the content is still fresh
- **Invalidation**: This is the action of marking cached content as stale

Understanding Integrated Caching on the NetScaler is in many ways the same as understanding what RFC2616 (The RFC for HTTP) says.

As such, it makes sense to understand the headers involved and what content should and shouldn't be stored.

Understanding HTTP headers as they relate to caching

Caching or more accurately web caching is an HTTP feature as we discussed. As such, it relies on certain HTTP headers to function correctly. This feature only works well because these headers and their behavior are described well in the RFC. Let's look at some of the headers involved. As you start to troubleshoot, these headers play a definitive role in determining whether caching is or isn't working as planned and what device, if any, is at fault. These headers are:

- Via: This is the most useful header when it comes to verifying that the NetScaler is participating in caching. This is of course configurable to help you determine from which of your several NetScalers the cached responses are originating:

```
General
    Request URL: http://10.72.142.75/
    Request Method: GET
    Status Code: ● 200 OK
    Remote Address: 10.72.142.75:80
Response Headers      view source
    Accept-Ranges: bytes
    Age: 1
    Connection: Keep-Alive
    Content-Length: 689
    Content-Type: text/html
    Date: Thu, 04 Feb 2016 14:55:20 GMT
    ETag: "90cd28b0c98cd1:0"
    Last-Modified: Fri, 21 Sep 2012 15:20:52 GMT
    Server: Microsoft-IIS/7.5
    Via: NS-CACHE-11.0
```

- If-Modified-Since: This is a request side header that the client uses to ask that a cache, like the NetScaler provide the full object if it has changed since the indicated date. In a large percentage of cases (talking about static objects here) those objects wouldn't have changed, which will result in a much smaller HTTP 304 response **Not Modified** instead of the much larger object.

- Cache-Control: This is a header that carries directives that *must* be obeyed by all caches between the User and the server. They allow the server to control whether the object can be cached or alternatively modified along the way.

```
Request Headers      view source
    Accept: image/webp,image/*,*/*;q=0.8
    Accept-Encoding: gzip, deflate, sdch
    Accept-Language: en-US,en;q=0.8
    Cache-Control: no-cache
    Connection: keep-alive
    Host: 10.72.142.75
    Pragma: no-cache
    Referer: http://10.72.142.75/
    User-Agent: Mozilla/5.0 (Windows NT 6.1; WOW64)
```

The main options are:

- ◦ no-cache: This means NetScaler should check the objects validity with server before serving hte object from cache.

- ◦ no-store: This option ensures that no intermediate devices (including NetScaler) cache the object. This is how sensitive items such as cookies should be treated.

- ◦ Private/public: This is used to indicate whether content is meant for a specific User or can be served to all users.

- ◦ no-transform: This tells intermediate caches not to transform (for example, compress) responses on their way to the User.

- ◦ max-age: The content must be revalidated if it is older than the indicated max-age.

- ◦ must-revalidate: Enforces revalidation strictly. It requires the cache to go back to check with the server as soon as it determines that the server-set expiry has reached (stale in caching terms). Proxy-revalidate is the same except that it's meant for proxies as is the case with the NetScaler.

 It is worth noting that NetScaler ignores all cache control headers in requests from clients; this behavior can be managed using the content group parameter ignoreReqCachingHdrs.

Evaluating cache policies

There are five possible actions for a cache policy. Apart from the obvious ones, CACHE, NOCACHE, and INVALIDATION, there are MAY_CACHE and MAY_NOCACHE. These are conditional and help to extend the decision making to include response side processing. To help digest this processing flow, let's take a look at a flow chart:

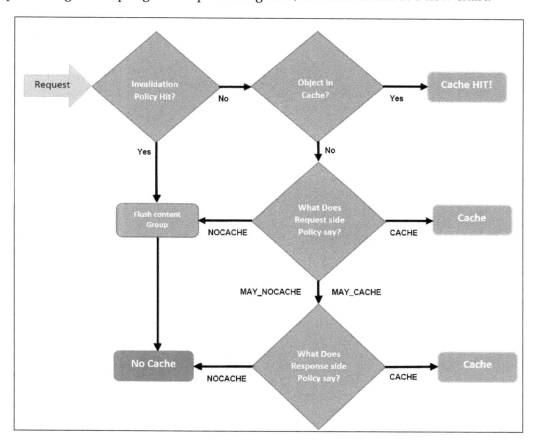

A sample cache response

Let's compare a response coming from the server with one that's being served from the NetScaler cache. Fiddler is an excellent tool for troubleshooting HTTP. Check it out at http://www.telerik.com/fiddler:

- Response direct from server:

```
HTTP/1.1 200 OK
Cache
  Date: Sat, 06 Feb 2016 11:29:40 GMT
Entity
  Content-Length: 689
  Content-Type: text/html
  ETag: "90cd28b0c98cd1:0"
  Last-Modified: Fri, 21 Sep 2012 15:20:52 GMT
Miscellaneous
  Accept-Ranges: bytes
  Server: Microsoft-IIS/7.5
  X-Powered-By: ASP.NET
```

- Response from NetScaler cache:

```
HTTP/1.1 200 OK
Cache
  Age: 1
  Date: Sat, 06 Feb 2016 11:21:57 GMT
Entity
  Content-Length: 689
  Content-Type: text/html
  ETag: "90cd28b0c98cd1:0"
  Last-Modified: Fri, 21 Sep 2012 15:20:52 GMT
Miscellaneous
  Accept-Ranges: bytes
  Server: Microsoft-IIS/7.5
  X-Powered-By: ASP.NET
Transport
  Connection: Keep-Alive
  Via: NS-CACHE-11.0: Paris_NS
```

Here are the observations we can make from the preceding screenshot:

- There is an Age header, which implies that the response came from a cache as only caches calculate and update this header's value.

- There is an Entity Tag (ETag) header that every cache (the ones in browsers included) relies on to validate cached objects. An ETag header is a hash or a fingerprint of an HTTP object. A change in ETag means that the cached object has changed at the server and hence should no longer be served from cache. NetScaler only inserts an ETag header if the server already didn't.

- There is the Via header we talked about earlier which helps identify which cache the request is coming from. This is a configurable value on NetScaler.

You could also add other Cache-Control directives when serving cached content from the NetScaler using the **Configure Cache Control** section that you will find within each content group:

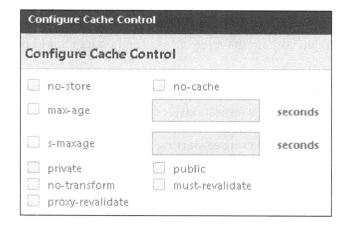

What kind of content should I cache and not cache?

Generally idempotent requests, that is, those that don't change the state of the server are cacheable (for example GET). The following are items you should *not* cache as they are generally meant for individual users:

- Cache-Control: no-cache
- Cache-Control: no-store
- Cache-Control: private items

Cookies should not be stored; having them served to multiple users could be a security disaster. Imagine users being shown each other's account. Thus, you will see that this setting to remove cookies is enabled by default. The NetScaler will for example, cache images but remove the cookies associated with them:

```
> show cache contentGroup DEFAULT | grep Cookies
          Remove Response Cookies: YES
```

PUT, POST, and DELETE must always go back to the server and they should result in invalidation of any cached data on intermediate caches.

Nonstorable HTTP response codes, as listed in the Citrix documentation, are as follows:

- 201, 202, 204, 205, 206 status codes
- All 4xx codes, except 403, 404, and 410
- 5xx status codes
- Responses that contain the Authorization header should not be cached

NetScaler's default caching behavior

NetScaler's caching behavior is entirely driven by policies. Hence, looking at the default policies is the best way to get an understanding of its default caching behavior. All the policies that you see starting with an underscore are default policies. These default policies being preconfigured on the NetScaler is of benefit as it saves the Administrator the time needed to mull over the HTTP RFCs to try and identify what is and what isn't a good practice.

Name	Expression	Actions
_nonGetReq	!HTTP.REQ.METHOD.eq(GET)	NOCACHE
_advancedConditionalReq	HTTP.REQ.HEADER("If-Match").EXISTS || HTTP.REQ.HEADER("If-Unmodified-Since").EXISTS	NOCACHE
_personalizedReq	HTTP.REQ.HEADER("Cookie").EXISTS || HTTP.REQ.HEADER("Authorization").EXISTS || HTTP.RE...	MAY_NOCACHE
_uncacheableStatusRes	! ((HTTP.RES.STATUS.EQ(200)) || (HTTP.RES.STATUS.EQ(304)) || (HTTP.RES.STATUS.BETWEEN(4...	NOCACHE
_uncacheableCacheControlRes	((HTTP.RES.CACHE_CONTROL.IS_PRIVATE) || (HTTP.RES.CACHE_CONTROL.IS_NO_CACHE) || (H...	NOCACHE
_cacheableCacheControlRes	((HTTP.RES.CACHE_CONTROL.IS_PUBLIC) || (HTTP.RES.CACHE_CONTROL.IS_MAX_AGE) || (HTT...	CACHE
_uncacheableVaryRes	((HTTP.RES.HEADER("Vary").EXISTS) && ((HTTP.RES.HEADER("Vary").INSTANCE(1).LENGTH > ...	NOCACHE
_uncacheablePragmaRes	HTTP.RES.HEADER("Pragma").EXISTS	NOCACHE
_cacheableExpiryRes	HTTP.RES.HEADER("Expires").EXISTS	CACHE
_imageRes	HTTP.RES.HEADER("Content-Type").SET_TEXT_MODE(IGNORECASE).STARTSWITH("image/")	CACHE
_personalizedRes	HTTP.RES.HEADER("Set-Cookie").EXISTS || HTTP.RES.HEADER("Set-Cookie2").EXISTS	NOCACHE

NetScaler Default Policies:

It is possible to deactivate these should you wish to, by unbinding them from the policy group, but it is not advised to do so without a very clear reason.

The NetScaler is largely RFC 2616 compliant. There are some deviations chosen considering industry practices for optimization but these are very minor. Two such deviations are:

- User attempts to bypass cache (using `Cache-Control:no-cache` and `max-age=0`) are ignored by default. This is to prevent DoS attempts by an attacker.

- Content with `Vary` header is not cached except for compressed responses. The NetScaler caches images by default, dropping any cookies if present.

Handling dynamic content

Dynamic content, that is, objects that change frequently, such as news, stocks, and weather updates, need extra care while handling. In theory, dynamic content is not to be cached at all and you will have servers setting such content with Cache-Control set to `no-cache`, `no-store`, and `must-revalidate` to discourage caching. While this helps content to always stay fresh, there are often performance and server offload benefits to be had from caching some of the dynamic content, albeit for a very short period of time.

It is very important when you are caching such dynamic content that you understand what part of it is User specific; anything that is User specific is strictly a no-no. Anything that can be normalized, for example, by dropping User specific info like cookies, can be cached.

Considerations for caching dynamic content

The following requirements are crucial when caching dynamic content:

- A solid understanding of how frequently the content changes.

- An understanding of what changes between requests, ID, or name while the rest of the response data remains the same. This type of data is called parameterized data and once identified correctly, you can cache one object per unique ID. Such as one for `UserID=1` and one for `UserID=2`. The way to handle such requests is by using cache selectors (hit parameters is also an option, but selectors are recommended).

How's my cache doing?

`show cache stats -detail` is an excellent command to understand how the hit ratio is at the current moment. Ideally, you would want to bring that as close as possible to 100 percent without breaking security or the application itself.

```
> show cache stats -detail

Integrated Cache Statistics - Detail


Integrated Cache Statistics - Summary
                                  Rate (/s)              Total
Hits                                    0                 8577
Misses                                  0                    1
Requests                                0                 8578
Hit ratio(%)                           --                  100
Origin bandwidth saved(%)              --                  100
```

Lower down in the output, you will be able to see what percentage of hits are 304 versus non-304. The HTTP header code 304 is sent in the response instead of a full (larger) response when a client indicates that they already have a certain object and are only checking whether there is a newer copy.

```
Hit Statistics
                                  Rate (/s)              Total
Non-304 hits                            0                 2313
304 hits                                0                 6264
Sql hits                                0                    0
Hits                                    0                 8577
304 hit ratio(%)                       --                   73
```

The images in the following table have been taken from a trace that compares how the two differ:

- For non 304 hit:

```
GET / HTTP/1.1
host: http.lbvip.com
Accept: */*

HTTP/1.1 200 OK
Age: 2179
Date: Sun, 19 Apr 2015 14:47:45 GMT
Connection: Keep-Alive
Via: NS-CACHE-10.0:   50
ETag: "c0ed4dfb27ad01:0"
Content-Type: text/html
Last-Modified: Sat, 18 Apr 2015 18:10:41 GMT
Accept-Ranges: bytes
Server: Microsoft-IIS/7.5
Content-Length: 689
```

- For 304 hit:

```
GET / HTTP/1.1
host: http.lbvip.com
If-Modified-Since: Sun, 19 Apr 2015 11:05:34 GMT
Accept: */*

HTTP/1.1 304 Not Modified
Connection: Keep-Alive
Date: Sun, 19 Apr 2015 14:47:45 GMT
Via: NS-CACHE-10.0:   50
Age: 2174
ETag: "c0ed4dfb27ad01:0"
```

You can see that they both come from the cache; that is evident from the Via header. Also, the object is the same in both cases going by the ETag value. The difference is that in the case of the 304 hit, the client helps to conserve bandwidth by requesting (conditionally, through the If-Modified-Since header) that the full response be given only if the object has changed since Sun, 19 Apr 2015 11:05:34 GMT. The bandwidth saved in this case is only 689 bytes, but we can easily see how this could be beneficial when it happens at scale. The caching term for Last-Modified, which is saved as a property of the object, is a validator.

When troubleshooting caching, I find it very useful to look at how the stats are changing over a few seconds of time; this is a good way to evaluate the new policy you've just put in place, or a setting you've just changed on the Content Group.

For this, you can use the -ntimes option, in the following example, where we ask for statistics to be shown three times (there will always be a 7 second difference between each output). It is handy to use Grep to make it easier to notice changes:

```
> show cache stats -detail -ntimes 3 | grep 304
```

Getting a closer look at objects in the cache

You can get a list of all objects by using the show cache object, which will help verify whether objects are getting cached in general or perhaps even search for a specific object. You can then take a closer look at the object by using its locator:

```
> show cache object
0x00000000e2b900000002   DEFAULT GET      //10.72.142.75:80/
0x0000000cc41d00000003   DEFAULT GET      //10.72.142.75:80/welcome.png
Done
> show cache object -locator 0x0000000cc41d00000003
        Integrated cache object statistics:
        Locator: cc41d00000003
        Response size: 0 bytes
        Response header size: 0 bytes
        Response status code: 200
        ETag: NONE
        Last-Modified: NONE
        Cache-control: NONE
        Date: Thu, 04 Feb 2016 14:55:20 GMT
        Contentgroup: DEFAULT
        Complex match: NO
        Host: 10.72.142.75
        Host port: 80
        URL: /welcome.png
        Destination IP: 10.72.142.75
        Destination port: 80
        Request time: 92276 secs ago
        Response time: started arriving 92276 secs ago
        Age: 92277 secs
        Expiry: 1454420069 secs left to expiry
```

Flushing versus expiring an object

When working with objects already in the cache, you might notice that there's two ways of dealing with an object that you no longer want to serve or consider stale. Flush directly deletes the object from cache. Expire would allow that object to be served but not before it's revalidated with the Server.

Flash cache

Flash cache is invaluable in the right situation and dangerous otherwise, so it needs a mention. An example of a *right situation* is when a large online event (for example, the Super Bowl) is expected to cause a sudden big surge in traffic that might place a hard-to-handle amount of load on the servers. The users are referred to as being part of a flash crowd (in caching terms). When Flash cache is enabled, the NetScaler forwards the first request to the server and queues the rest. Once the response is received, this is fanned out to all the users in the queue. So the performance benefit is obvious. The reason you need to be careful though is that even if the response is strictly not to be cached or shared, it is still served served to all users in the queue.

Troubleshooting caching issues

When troubleshooting caching, try to use a lightweight client that doesn't have its own cache; WFetch is an excellent example of one such tool:

1. The first troubleshooting step, especially if you find that caching is not working at all is the show cache parameter to see if memory is still at its default of 0, in which case NetScaler cannot cache any objects:

    ```
    > show cache parameter
            Integrated cache global configuration:
            Memory usage limit: 0 MBytes
            Memory usage limit (active value): 16 MBytes
            Maximum value for Memory usage limit: 794 MBytes
            Via header: NS-CACHE-11.0
    ```

    The Max memory limit shows as 794 MB; the NetScaler makes this calculation based on the total amount of memory available, setting aside memory that it needs to perform its usual functions. Also, where possible, always reboot NetScaler after making memory-related changes, especially when de-allocating memory assigned to cache. The de-allocation only happens at boot time.

2. Secondly, verify whether the necessary policies are getting hit. Start with a simple enough rule (I commonly use http.REQ.IS_VALID) to ensure there is a hit in any case before getting more specific.

3. Focus on any time differences between the server, NetScaler, and client. The object cannot be served from cache if its age is past max-age. Here's one way to find if that is what's happening.

```
> sh cache object -locator 0x0000001076500000065 | grep expired
        Expiry: Already expired
```

4. Check whether you are hitting any memory allocation failures. These are an indication that what you have allocated in step one is not sufficient.

```
> stat cache -detail | grep fail
Memory allocation failures                    696
```

5. Check whether the size of the object is larger than the max size configured on the Content Group. The default is only 80 K, which is fine for most deployments, but if your site has high resolution images, this default limit will easily get saturated.

6. Check whether there are any marker objects. In the following screenshot, the object, listheader_selected.png, is in the cache, however it isn't getting served from the cache yet as it is a marker object.

```
> sh cache object | grep listheader
0x0000000f4d820000019e  cache_test        GET      //192.168.1.55:80/ad
min_ui/common/css/ns/listheader_selected.png
```

We can determine this by examining the object using its locator. The reason for it being a marker object is that it hasn't been requested often enough, as the Reason clarifies.

```
> sh cache object -locator 0x0000000f4d820000019e | grep marker
        Negative marker cell: YES
        Reason marker created: Waiting for min hit
```

Compression

HTTP Compression, like caching, is a best practice that should be implemented in all Web Application deployments. Even with the fast links of today, there are performance benefits to be had, as compression can reduce size upwards of 70 percent. This size reduction in TCP terms means fewer packets and reduced round trip times.

Let's start by looking at what kind of content should and shouldn't be compressed:

- Content that should be compressed:
  - Any response that is text based is a good candidate for compression. HTML, CSS, JS, and XML, which are all items that you find on most web pages, fall into this category
  - MS Office documents

- Content that shouldn't be compressed:
  - Any response that is already compressed should not be compressed; this only adds to the size of the response.
  - Images and other binary data should not be compressed for the same reason. Most image formats on the web are already compressed.

The NetScaler's default compression behavior

Go to the **Compression** section, click on **policies**, and select the option to show built-in compression policies:

Name	Expression	Response Action
ns_cmp_content_type	ns_content_type	COMPRESS
ns_cmp_msapp	(ns_msie && (ns_msword || ns_msexcel || ns_msppt))	COMPRESS
ns_cmp_mscss	(ns_msie && ns_css)	COMPRESS
ns_nocmp_mozilla_47	ns_mozilla_47 && ns_css	NOCOMPRESS
ns_nocmp_xml_ie	(ns_msie && ns_xmldata)	NOCOMPRESS
ns_adv_cmp_content_type	HTTP.RES.HEADER("Content-Type").CONTAINS("text")	COMPRESS
ns_adv_cmp_msapp	HTTP.REQ.HEADER("User-Agent").CONTAINS("MSIE") ...	COMPRESS

Some of these use custom expressions in the policy (for example, `ns_content_type`). When you're not sure, for example, what the expression is actually looking for, you can navigate to **AppExpert | Expressions | classic**:

Impact of using Compression

Compression, while it is a recommended feature and a great performance optimization, is a hit on the CPU when done at volume. This is one reason to consider tuning your policies, by applying the best practices around what is and isn't a good candidate for compression.

The default configuration already bypasses compression if the CPU is at 100 percent:

```
> show cmp parameter | grep CPU
          CPU load at which to bypass compression: 100%
```

Verifying and monitoring Compression

Statistics similar to those for caching are available by using `Compression Statistics - Detail`:

```
> stat cmp -detail

Compression Statistics - Detail


HTTP Compression Statistics
                                         Rate (/s)              Total
HTTP compression requests                        0                  2
Compressible bytes received                      0               1934
Compressible packets received                    0                  3
Compressed bytes transmitted                     0               1135
Compressed packets transmitted                   0                  2
                                             Value
HTTP Bandwidth saving (%)                    41.31
HTTP compression ratio                        1.70
```

The output will also show errors, should anything go wrong with compression.

```
Decompression Errors
                                        Rate (/s)              Total
Wrong data                                   0                     0
Less Data                                    0                     0
More Data                                    0                     0
Memory failures                              0                     0
Unknown                                      0                     0
```

In my experience, however, while troubleshooting this feature, I found the most value for my time by looking at header traces and the flow, so let's look at them for a better understanding.

Understanding the packet flow

Compression only works if the client explicitly says to the NetScaler that it is capable of working with compression. It does so using the Accept-Encoding header. This header also specifies what type of compression it can work with; gzip and deflate are the common ones you'll find most sites using.

The following header snippet demonstrates what a request will look like:

```
Request Headers        view source
   Accept: text/html,application/xhtml+xml,application/xml;
   Accept-Encoding: gzip, deflate, sdch
   Accept-Language: en-US,en;q=0.8
   Connection: keep-alive
   Host: 10.72.142.55
   User-Agent: Mozilla/5.0 (Windows NT 6.1; WOW64) AppleWeb
```

The response will look like this:

- With Compression off:

```
Response Headers        view source
   Accept-Ranges: bytes
   Content-Length: 689
   Content-Type: text/html
   Date: Sun, 26 Apr 2015 13:20:23 GMT
   ETag: "90cd28b0c98cd1:0"
   Last-Modified: Fri, 21 Sep 2012 15:20:52 GMT
   Server: Microsoft-IIS/7.5
```

- With Compression on:

```
Response Headers
  Accept-Ranges: bytes
  Cache-Control: private
  Content-Encoding: gzip
  Content-Length: 456
  Content-Type: text/html
  Cteonnt-Length: 689
  Date: Sun, 26 Apr 2015 10:57:09 GMT
  ETag: "90cd28b0c98cd1:0"
  Last-Modified: Fri, 21 Sep 2012 15:20
```

The `Content-Encoding: gzip` header is how the NetScaler communicates to the client that what it is serving is compressed content and that it is compressed using the `gzip` algorithm. You will also notice that the original `Content-Length` header (`Cteonnt-Length`) is now jumbled. That's because NetScaler has to calculate the new `Content-Length` given the different size due to compression.

While other compression algorithms are available, the recommended one is `gzip` since virtually every browser supports it.

Troubleshooting considerations

Here are some of the things to look at if you suspect Compression, which generally is a very safe feature, to be a potential source of the problem:

- If a browser is not able to load specific objects, try disabling `Appfw` and Compression where possible as a test to rule these out. If you have the possibility to test by recreating a TCP VIP instead of HTTP, doing so will help rule out the role of compression in the issue.

- If you need to disable Compression during a test, don't disable the feature. In fact, even if you do, the disabling will not take effect; once enabled, it needs to be turned off at the service.

- Related to the preceding point, also note that once you enable the feature, all services created from that point will have compression turned on by default.

Summary

In this chapter, we looked at why Caching and Compression are beneficial, how these features behave when enabled on the NetScaler, what the traffic flows look like, what the dos and don'ts are and how to approach troubleshooting these features.

If you can find the time, also give RFC 2616 a read, it is an excellent resource not just for this chapter but for understanding the many interesting intricacies of the HTTP protocol.

Any deployments that use HTTP based VIPs should be using Caching and Compression because they have the potential to offer a huge performance benefit and greatly reduced server load when processing traffic at volume.

AAA for Traffic Management

4

The authentication feature for Web Applications in NetScaler goes by the name of **AAA for Traffic Management (AAA for TM)**. Authentication is a critical area on NetScaler, as more and more enterprises continue to make their services available over the Internet. In this chapter we will cover the following topics, including troubleshooting:

- Lightweight Directory Access Protocol (LDAP)
- Remote Authentication Dial-In User Service (RADIUS)
- Certificate authentication
- NTLM and Form Based Authentication (FBA)
- Kerberos, which is fast and quite mature in the enterprise
- SAML

Authentication is one of those areas where knowing the flow that one should expect to see in a trace goes a long way in helping with troubleshooting. The observations made from looking at a successful authentication can serve as a baseline and help in detecting the main point of failure. Once at this point, we can then turn our attention to the individual failures and the reasons for them. As such, we will spend a good part of this chapter looking into the flow of packets, explaining each step and the important things to look at as we go along.

AAA for TM functions in one of two ways from a User experience perspective:

- Using a HTTP 401 type of authentication, where the User sees a dialog box prompting them for credentials.
- Using FBA, where the User will be redirected to a login page. FBA is used for apps which have their own logon page. **Outlook Web App (OWA)** is the most common example.

In both cases, SSO is optionally possible so that the dialog box or the form presented by the application is autocompleted by NetScaler, by using credentials it obtains from the User as part of the initial authentication.

Regardless of the choice of User experience chosen by the Administrator, the underlying protocol handling remains the same. Let's start looking at these protocols and the associated flows one by one.

Lightweight Directory Access Protocol

LDAP is very popular both as a directory service and for authentication and authorization. It provides an excellent level of flexibility in identifying whether a User exists, whether the credentials are correct, and what groups the User is a part of (this is called group extraction).

The ports used for LDAP are as follows:

- **TCP 389**: Standard LDAP
- **TCP 636**: Encrypted LDAP
- **TCP 3268**: Global catalog, unencrypted
- **TCP 3269**: Global catalog, encrypted

Authentication flow

The following Wireshark snapshot shows what the exchange between NetScaler and the LDAP server should look like:

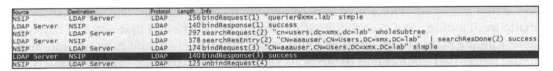

Source	Destination	Protocol	Length	Info
NSIP	LDAP Server	LDAP	156	bindRequest(1) "querier@xmx.lab" simple
LDAP Server	NSIP	LDAP	140	bindResponse(1) success
NSIP	LDAP Server	LDAP	297	searchRequest(2) "cn=users,dc=xmx,dc=lab" wholeSubtree
LDAP Server	NSIP	LDAP	378	searchResEntry(2) "CN=aaauser,CN=Users,DC=xmx,DC=lab" | searchResDone(2) success
NSIP	LDAP Server	LDAP	174	bindRequest(3) "CN=aaauser,CN=Users,DC=xmx,DC=lab" simple
LDAP Server	NSIP	LDAP	140	bindResponse(3) success
NSIP	LDAP Server	LDAP	125	unbindRequest(4)

LDAP

The steps here are as follows:

- `bindRequest`: Here, the NetScaler is authenticating itself to the LDAP server
- `bindResponse`: If the method used (usually **SASL – Simple Authentication and Security Layer**) and the credentials provided are both okay, the LDAP server responds with a *success*
- `searchRequest`: At this point, NetScaler runs through the User authentication; it starts by verifying if the username provided exists

- `searchResEntry`: The LDAP server confirms the existence of a User in its database
- `bindRequest` with User credentials: The NetScaler provides the LDAP identifier for the User and the password for the LDAP server to confirm they match
- `bindResponse`: The server confirms they are indeed correct
- `unbindRequest`: NetScaler terminates the LDAP exchange

Troubleshooting LDAP

There are two things you can do to troubleshoot LDAP:

- Take a trace on the NetScaler and compare it to the screenshot we've reviewed to see where the flow deviates or breaks.
- Take a look at the very handy `aaad.debug` file using `cat /tmp/aaad.debug` from the `shell`. `aaad.debug` is a pipe-based file which is most useful to look at when you can have a test User log in at the same time. We will revisit this file at various times in the chapter as it is relevant to all types of authentication.

Running `cat` on `aaad.debug` will start by showing who the authenticating User is:

```
root@15lns# cat /tmp/aaad.debug
Thu Jul 16 23:28:36 2015
 /home/build/rs_105/usr.src/netscaler/aaad/naaad.c[786]: process_kernel_socket_call to authenticate
user :aaauser, vsid :9594
Thu Jul 16 23:28:36 2015
 /home/build/rs_105/usr.src/netscaler/aaad/naaad.c[2654]: start_cascade_auth starting cascade authentication
Thu Jul 16 23:28:36 2015
 /home/build/rs_105/usr.src/netscaler/aaad/ldap_drv.c[106]: start_ldap_auth Starting LDAP auth
Thu Jul 16 23:28:36 2015
 /home/build/rs_105/usr.src/netscaler/aaad/ldap_drv.c[1058]: get_svr_name Server name length 13, name <192.168.1.90">
Thu Jul 16 23:28:36 2015
 /home/build/rs_105/usr.src/netscaler/aaad/ldap_drv.c[125]: start_ldap_auth attempting to auth aaauser @ 192.168.1.90"
```

The query used to look for the User is shown as follows:

```
ns_ldap_search Searching for <<(& (sAMAccountName=aaauser) (objectClass=*))>> from base <<cn=users,dc=xmx,dc=lab>>
```

The output should conclude with *sending accept*, which indicates that the authentication attempt was successful. A *sending reject* would indicate the contrary:

```
send_accept sending accept to kernel for : aaauser
```

RADIUS protocol

In NetScaler environments, RADIUS is commonly used for two-factor authentication, and is the protocol to choose when integrating with **One Time Password (OTP)** servers.

The ports used by Radius are as follows:

- **UDP 1812**: Authentication
- **UDP 1813**: Radius Accounting
- **UDP 1645 and 1646**: Legacy ports for the same purpose that some servers might use

Authentication flow

When authenticating, the exchange will start with an access-request from the NetScaler to the RADIUS server. To this, the server can respond with one of three responses, given as follows:

- **Access-Accept**: All is good and the User is through
- **Access-Reject**: Either the RADIUS server parameters, such as the secret, are not configured correctly, or the User credentials are incorrect
- **Access-Challenge**: This is what you will see when using an OTP solution, the NetScaler has received a prompt for additional credentials

The following is a screenshot of a successful RADIUS (**Access-Accept**) authentication:

Troubleshooting RADIUS authentication

`aaad.debug` again proves handy in the case of RADIUS troubleshooting:

```
netscaler/aaad/radius_drv.c[727]: continue_radius_auth attempting to auth aaauser @ 192.168.1.30
```

The IP, shown in the preceding screenshot following @, will be that of the radius server. This will then be followed by the result, such as `sending accept` or `sending reject`:

```
netscaler/aaad/radius_drv.c[1938]: process_radius radius accepts : aaauser

netscaler/aaad/radius_drv.c[1940]: process_radius extracted group string :(null)

netscaler/aaad/naaad.c[1965]: send_accept sending accept to kernel for : aaauser
```

If the server settings are misconfigured, you will see something like the following screenshot. The `4003` indicates that the server did not respond in a timely fashion:

```
netscaler/aaad/radius_drv.c[2021]: process_radius rad_continue_send_request:No valid RADIUS responses received

netscaler/aaad/naaad.c[2203]: send_reject_with_code Rejecting with error code 4003

netscaler/aaad/naaad.c[2230]: send_reject_with_code Not trying cascade again

netscaler/aaad/naaad.c[2232]: send_reject_with_code sending reject to kernel for : aaauser
```

Error code 4003 is just one of several possibilities. The following table, taken from one of the Citrix blogs, covers a more complete list of error codes:

Error Code	Definition
4001	Invalid credentials
4002	Login not permitted
4003	Server timeout
4004	System error
4005	Socket error talking to authentication server
4006	Bad (format) for username
4007	Bad (format) for password
4008	Password mismatch (when entering new password)
4009	User not found
4010	Restricted login hours
4011	Account disabled
4012	Password expired
4013	No dial-in permission (RADIUS-specific)
4014	Error changing password
4015	Account locked

Source: Enhanced Authentication Feedback on `https://www.citrix.com/blogs/`

The enhanced authentication feedback is an option to show the RADIUS error to the end User as part of the authentication process, but this is not enabled by default as it might provide too much information, in general to an attacker regarding what is failing. You can enable this using the following command:

```
> set aaa parameter -enableEnhancedAuthFeedback YES
Done
```

Client Certificate Based Authentication protocol

Client Certificate Based Authentication provides a strong level of security by means of two factors. Also, increasingly (with XenMobile and WorxMail scenarios), it is seen as a key enabler for SSO. The typical use case is that User devices will be provided the certificate to present automatically when accessing certain services. The client side application or browser presents the certificate, which allows the username to be extracted and either prefilled, or used for SSO to the Service.

The ports used by this protocol are typically TCP 443 or TCP 8443. The User will get prompted for a certificate by the service or NetScaler vServer. For browsers, the User experience will be similar to the following screenshot, as the browser checks with the User if it's okay to respond to the certificate request with the User's certificate:

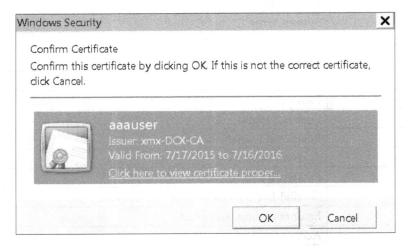

The NetScaler can be set up by using a certificate profile, such as the following, to extract the username from the appropriate field and prepopulate the login form to make it easier for the User to authenticate.

The following screenshot shows one setup to extract the uPN of the User present in the Subject Alternative Name field of the certificate, so that the User doesn't have to remember this. This setting is available when creating an authentication profile of type certificate, as shown in the following screenshot:

The result is that the AAA for TM login page presented to the User has the username prefilled and the User just needs to put in their password:

Client versus Server Certificates

Let's focus for a moment on what is different between a Client Certificate and a Server Certificate. In the following table we have them side by side for comparison and you can see that the `issued to` and `purpose` differ. Client Certificates are issued to individual users instead of an FQDN or a domain.

Server Certificate	Client Certificate
The following screenshot shows how a Server Certificate looks like:	The following screenshot shows how a Client Certificate looks like:

At the outset, this is very similar to the exchange we saw in the SSL chapter with no Client Authentication in place. Except that here (in the highlighted packet `472`), the client also presents its certificate.

Authentication Flow when using Client Certificates

Consider the following Wireshark screenshot:

There is a key step that the server needs to take that tells the client that it has to present its certificate: `Certificate Request`. You can find this using the filter `ssl.handshake.type==13`:

If we look deeper into this packet, we will see that while requesting a certificate, the server also presents the distinguished name of the CA that it expects those certificates to be coming from:

```
Handshake Protocol: Certificate Request
  Handshake Type: Certificate Request (13)
  Length: 72
  Certificate types count: 2
  Certificate types (2 types)
  Distinguished Names Length: 67
  Distinguished Names (67 bytes)
    Distinguished Name Length: 65
      Distinguished Name: (id-at-commonName=xmx-DCX-CA,dc=xmx,dc=lab)
```

This will help the client choose which certificate it needs to send in case it has many. In the absence of this detail it will present all its certificates. The `certificate verify` that we see in the same packet is to indicate to the server that it also has the private key to this certificate:

```
Handshake Protocol: Certificate Verify
  Handshake Type: Certificate Verify (15)
  Length: 258
  Signature with client's private key
    Signature length: 256
    Signature: 226598ccc288033ed47b10d60c57a59bb85fe18abf0e7b08...
```

This is an important authentication step; without this confirmation, the certificate is not considered suitable for authentication, as it does not necessarily *belong* to the User presenting it.

On receiving the Client Certificate, the NetScaler checks three things:

- The NetScaler compares the signature on the certificate with the public key of the bound CA
- It also checks that the certificate is still valid by looking at the date
- CRL/OCSP checks are done to ensure it's not revoked

If any of these fails, the authentication will fail. A common configuration issue is that the CA certificate is not bound to the SSL vServer, or is not the correct one. The following screenshot shows what that failure looks like:

```
241 192.168.1.155    192.168.1.101    TLSv1 Certificate
246 192.168.1.101    192.168.1.155    TLSv1 Certificate, Client Key Exchange, Certificate Verify
247 192.168.1.155    192.168.1.101    TLSv1 Alert (Level: Fatal, Description: Unknown CA)
252 192.168.1.101    192.168.1.155    TLSv1 Client Hello
253 192.168.1.155    192.168.1.101    TLSv1 Server Hello
254 192.168.1.155    192.168.1.101    TLSv1 Certificate
257 192.168.1.101    192.168.1.155    TLSv1 Certificate, Client Key Exchange, Certificate Verify
258 192.168.1.155    192.168.1.101    TLSv1 Alert (Level: Fatal, Description: Unknown CA)
```

 The aaad.debug file for Client Certificate Authentication issues.

You can approach this either with a trace, or by looking at the ssl_err_clientAuth counters:

```
root@151ns# nsconmsg -g ssl_err_clientAuth -d current
Displaying performance information
NetScaler V20 Performance Data
NetScaler NS10.5: Build 55.8.nc, Date: Jan 25 2015, 23:55:26


reltime:mili second between two records Fri Jul 11 17:22:11 2015
  Index   rtime totalcount-val    delta rate/sec symbol-name&device-no
      0    7001            14        2       0 ssl_err_clientAuth_certCAnotfound
      1       0            14        2       0 ssl_err_clientAuth_unablegetissuercertlocally
      2    7000            16        2       0 ssl_err_clientAuth_certCAnotfound
      3       0            16        2       0 ssl_err_clientAuth_unablegetissuercertlocally
```

Other items to consider here are:

- Time/date on the NetScaler, server or client being incorrect can cause the certificate to incorrectly be identified as expired.

- CRL or OCSP checks failing. If OCSP is in use, ensure that the NetScaler can talk to the OCSP server. Given how critical a failure here is, you can use the -trustResponder on the OCSP responder as a workaround while you work to identify the root cause and corrective measure.

 SSL handshake failures in the trace are generally flagged by the NetScaler by resetting the connection using a Window Size of 9811.

NTLM SSO (401 Based Authentication)

NTLM (NT LAN Manager) is a Microsoft protocol which is still very frequently used in web server authentication scenarios, especially within an enterprise. It is enabled by the use of LDAP (invariably Active Directory). When used for authentication in front of servers that use NTLM, enabling SSO on the NetScaler makes very good sense.

When NTLM SSO fails via the NetScaler, the usual User experience will be that they see two 401 dialog boxes followed by a 403 error.

NTLM Authentication flow

NTLM is a challenge-based protocol. The exchange involves the server challenging the client to prove its identity in order to be able to see the resource it is requesting.

The following screenshot is an exchange between the NetScaler SNIP and a web server that has NTLM Authentication enabled. You can filter this communication using `http || ntlmssp`:

Number	Source	Destination	Protocol	Info
373	SNIP	SERVER	HTTP	GET / HTTP/1.1
378	SERVER	SNIP	HTTP	HTTP/1.1 401 Unauthorized (text/html)
379	SNIP	SERVER	HTTP	GET / HTTP/1.1 , NTLMSSP_NEGOTIATE
380	SERVER	SNIP	HTTP	HTTP/1.1 401 Unauthorized , NTLMSSP_CHALLENGE (text/html)
381	SNIP	SERVER	HTTP	GET / HTTP/1.1 , NTLMSSP_AUTH, User: XMX\aaauser
384	SERVER	SNIP	HTTP	HTTP/1.1 200 OK (text/html)

tcp.stream eq 42 && (http || ntlmssp) ▾ Expression... Clear Apply Save

Now let's examine each of the steps in more detail:

1. First, NetScaler forwards the client's request for an object, and instead of the usual **200OK** receives a **401 Unauthorized** from the server. Thus, it knows that authentication is in place. The **401 Unauthorized** response also contains the **WWW-Authenticate: NTLM** header, which indicates what authentication mechanism is in place:

```
GET /welcome.png HTTP/1.1
Host: lb.xmx.lab
Connection: keep-alive
Accept: image/webp,*/*;q=0.8
User-Agent: Mozilla/5.0 (Windows NT 6.1; Win64
Referer: http://lb.xmx.lab/
Accept-Encoding: gzip, deflate, sdch
Accept-Language: en-US,en;q=0.8

HTTP/1.1 401 Unauthorized
Content-Type: text/html
Server: Microsoft-IIS/7.5
WWW-Authenticate: NTLM
Date: Sat, 18 Jul 2015 12:26:08 GMT
Content-Length: 1293
```

2. NetScaler then responds to this challenge for credentials by sending information about itself and a number of negotiate flags that clarify to the server what versions of NTLM it can speak. In NTLM lingo, this is called a Type1 message:

```
Authorization:        NTLM T1RMTVNTUAABAAAAF4II4AAAAAAAAAAAAAAAAAAAA=\r\n
NTLM Secure Service Provider
  NTLMSSP identifier: NTLMSSP
  NTLM Message Type: NTLMSSP_NEGOTIATE (0x00000001)
 Negotiate Flags: 0xe0088217
  Calling workstation domain: NULL
  Calling workstation name: NULL
```

3. Upon receiving the Type1 message from NetScaler, the server responds with a Type2 message. This response will contain two important details – that of the target domain and a challenge:

```
NTLM Secure Service Provider
  NTLMSSP identifier: NTLMSSP
  NTLM Message Type: NTLMSSP_CHALLENGE (0x00000002)
  Target Name: XMX
  Negotiate Flags: 0xe2898215
  NTLM Server Challenge: b0287088c1d97b8b
```

4. Here, the NetScaler uses the challenge it received in the previous message to construct its next request, which will contain everything needed for the authentication to succeed:

```
Domain name: XMX
User name: aaauser
Host name: NETSCALER
Session Key: 7ceb084ee75a6757ba0a4d803030204b
Negotiate Flags: 0xe2088211
```

5. The server, happy with the authentication details, responds with **200OK** and the requested resource.

Troubleshooting NTLM

Traces and counters combined with the `aaad.debug` prove sufficient in most cases to troubleshoot NTLM issues. Consider the following four step approach to troubleshoot them:

1. Obtain a trace while you have the User login. Since NTLM is web-based, you can also use a HTTP tracing tool such as Fiddler to see what response codes the server is sending. Also check that the **WWW-Authenticate: NTLM** header is indeed sent by the server to ensure the right protocol is being used.

2. Look for the SSO-related counters in the following screenshot at the time of the issue. You can use the shell command `nsconmsg -g sso -d current` to see if success or failure ones are going up. The following screenshot shows a successful exchange:

```
root@151ns# nsconmsg -g sso -d current
Displaying performance information
NetScaler V20 Performance Data
NetScaler NS10.5: Build 55.8.nc, Date: Jan 25 2015, 23:55:26


reltime:mili second between two records Sat Jul 18 14:17:07 2015
  Index    rtime totalcount-val    delta rate/sec symbol-name&device-no
      0    21002              6        3       0 svpn_tot_sso_cache_miss
      1        0              6        3       0 svpn_tot_sso_true_401_triggers
      2        0              6        3       0 svpn_tot_sso_successes
      3        0              6        3       0 svpn_tot_sso_ntlm_negotiate_tokens_inserted
      4        0              6        3       0 svpn_tot_sso_ntlm_rcvd_401_challenge
      5        0              6        3       0 svpn_tot_sso_ntlm_auth_tokens_inserted
      6        0              6        3       0 svpn_tot_401_in_sso_init
      7        0              6        3       0 svpn_tot_401_in_sso_progress
```

3. Look at the `aaad.debug` info to identify reasons for the failure.

4. Load balancing can sometimes be an issue if you are pointing to a VIP for authentication and if the handshake is incorrectly being broken up and sent to different servers. If you are seeing this, consider configuring persistence such as Source IP or Cookie.

Form-based Authentication

Form-based authentication is suited to applications that present a login form instead of a dialog box. This sort of authentication configuration makes sense when the application itself is form-based.

Form-based Authentication makes most sense when used with SSO. The typical configuration uses a `SuccessRule` parameter, which is a means for NetScaler to detect if the SSO was successful or not. If the `SuccessRule` criterion is met, NetScaler presents the final page, such the User's mailbox, when the application is OWA. If it is not met, NetScaler passes the login page as is to the User so that they can manually enter the credentials – say, when the credentials for SSO are not the same as for NetScaler authentication.

Please take a look at CTX128197 (`http://support.citrix.com/article/CTX128197`) for an article which shows you how to configure form-based SSO for exchange 2010 through NetScaler.

Authentication flow

Let's take a look at the flow as it should happen:

1. The client sends the GET for a resource; in the case of OWA it will be /owa.

2. NetScaler checks to see if authentication is configured and if an Authentication Cookie (NSC_TMAA or NSC_TMAS if secured) is already present in the request. If it is, the User doesn't need to authenticate again and is taken straight to the service.

3. Since the User is connecting for the first time, they won't have the Cookie. NetScaler then looks at the configuration to see if form-based authentication is configured.

4. Since the configuration contains form-based authentication, NetScaler will respond with a script. This script will contain the details of the AAA VIP to go to, to authenticate. Following is what the script looks like. It contains the details of the AAA vServer that the User needs to go to:

```
GET /owa HTTP/1.1
Host: owa.xmx.lab
Connection: keep-alive
Accept: text/html,application/xhtml+xml,application/xml;q=0.9,image/webp,*/*;q=0.8
User-Agent: Mozilla/5.0 (Windows NT 6.1; Win64; x64) AppleWebKit/537.36 (KHTML, like Gecko)
Accept-Encoding: gzip, deflate, sdch
Accept-Language: en-US,en;q=0.8

HTTP/1.1 200 OK
Set-Cookie: NSC_TASS=xyz;Path=/;expires=Wednesday, 09-Nov-1999 23:12:40 GMT
Set-Cookie: NSC_TMAP=xyz;Path=/;expires=Wednesday, 09-Nov-1999 23:12:40 GMT
Connection: close
Content-Length: 735
Cache-control: no-cache, no-store
Pragma: no-cache
Content-Type: text/html

<html><head><META HTTP-EQUIV="Content-Type" CONTENT="text/html; charset=UTF-8"><style type="
onLoad='document.forms[0].submit();'><form action="https://aaa.xmx.lab/cgi/tm" method="post"
name=loc value="aHR0cDovL293YS54bXgubGFiL293YQ=="><input type=hidden name=localdate value=""
span><input id="Continue" type="submit" value="Continue"><span id="Trailing phrase after Con
language="javascript">var date = new Date();document.forms[0].localdate.value = date.getTime
```

5. The result of executing the preceding script will be a redirection to a page where they can log in (/cgi/login):

```
POST /cgi/login HTTP/1.1
Host: aaa.xmx.lab
Connection: keep-alive
Content-Length: 29
Cache-Control: max-age=0
Accept: text/html,application/xhtml+xml,application/xml;q=0.9,image/webp,*/*;q=0.8
Origin: https://aaa.xmx.lab
User-Agent: Mozilla/5.0 (Windows NT 6.1; WOW64) AppleWebKit/537.36 (KHTML, like Gecko) Chrom
Content-Type: application/x-www-form-urlencoded
Referer: https://aaa.xmx.lab/vpn/tmindex.html
Accept-Encoding: gzip, deflate
Accept-Language: en-US,en;q=0.8
Cookie: NSC_TASS=aHR0cHM6Ly9vd2EueG14LmxhYi9vd2E%3D

login=aaauser&passwd=AAApwd12HTTP/1.1 302 Object Moved
Location: https://owa.xmx.lab/owa
Set-Cookie: NSC_TMAA=879fba361fd83696ab895c95b676807c;HttpOnly;Path=/;Domain=xmx.lab
Set-Cookie: NSC_TMAS=c6f06d8ac23e01493a333fac3ac95892;Secure;HttpOnly;Path=/;Domain=xmx.lab
```

6. Once on this page, the User types in their credentials and the authentication vServer authenticates the User. As part of the authentication, if SSO is configured it also tries to authenticate to the backend server, such as OWA, to see if the credentials are accepted, and if they are, looks to see if the response contains the success criteria. Reviewing CTX128197, we know that the criterion is for cadata cookie to be larger than 70 characters:

```
POST /owa/auth.owa
HTTP/1.1
Host: owa.xmx.lab
Connection: keep-alive
Accept: text/html,application/xhtml+xml,application/xml;q=0.9,image/webp,*/
*;q=0.8
User-Agent: Mozilla/5.0 (Windows NT 6.1; Win64; x64) AppleWebKit/537.36 (KHTML,
like Gecko) Chrome/43.0.2357.134 Safari/537.36
Referer: http://owa.xmx.lab/owa/auth/logon.aspx?url=http://owa.xmx.lab/owa/
&reason=0
Accept-Language: en-US,en;q=0.8
Cookie: PBack=0; OutlookSession=812eb9f1b5f345ab8cce7dce500bf324
Accept-Encoding: identity
Content-Type: application/x-www-form-urlencoded
Content-Length: 140

username=xmx%5Caaauser&password=Freebsd12&isUtf8=1&=Sign
+in&trusted=0&forcedownlevel=0&flags=0&destination=http%3A%2F%2Fowa.xmx.lab%2Fowa
%2FHTTP/1.1 302 Moved Temporarily
Content-Length: 0
Location: http://owa.xmx.lab/owa/
Server: Microsoft-IIS/7.5
X-OWA-Version: 14.2.247.5
Set-Cookie: sessionid=450c7f5b-952a-487d-b36d-9f66ea3d5334; path=/
Set-Cookie: cadata="0zwrxj6hpIhihB+XNtNQ4kSDR6Mn4ilCy+xefq6K3vguDRG1qWQFj6KDpa4+/
GFIeCKEUucRKMUDzHjVmZjp3ngK7wvVOXkdsK/Q8wIrRa8U="; HttpOnly; path=/
Set-Cookie: sessionid=450c7f5b-952a-487d-b36d-9f66ea3d5334; path=/; path=/
```

7. When this condition is met, NetScaler obtains the OWA mail homepage itself and presents it to the User. In the process it also increments the SSO counters as successful.

8. If SSO is not configured, the User will see the OWA login page instead.

The following steps detail how to troubleshoot form-based authentication:

1. DNS needs to work correctly for the redirect to the AAA URL to work, and so do certificates, on the LB vServer, but also on the authentication vServer. So, check to see if the users can resolve and access the LB vServer and the AAA vServer without any errors.

2. If you are still unable to get to the AAA page, try adding the site to the list of trusted sites.

3. If SSO is failing (as earlier, use `nsconmsg -g sso -d current` from shell to check if it is):

    1. Check first if the SSO policy is getting hits.

    2. Take a trace and check if cookies TMAA/TMAS are getting inserted.

    3. Is rewrite enabled and are the policies getting hits? Also, check that the PBack cookie for OWA is getting inserted.

    4. Is the success rule correct? This will be different for different apps. The correct way to determine what that should be for your custom application is it to take a trace and identify a cookie that gets consistently set following a successful login.

    5. Did you set a high enough value for `responsesize`? Look at a successful response's content-length to determine the right value.

Kerberos authentication

Kerberos, which started off as an MIT project, has grown in popularity to the point that it is now the default choice for enterprise authentication in a domain-based environment. It is considered to be fast (especially given the ability to cache and reuse tickets) and secure from a credential handling perspective, given that the User does not need to send the password over the network to authenticate. It is also open in a real sense, so as long as you can put the necessary keytabs (think of it as a key) in place, you can have a mixed Windows and Linux environment authenticating in perfect harmony.

Kerberos is a complex protocol (especially when you come across it for the first time), so to take this step by step, we will take a quick look at the components that need to be in place, and the flow, before looking at troubleshooting and a quick configuration checklist. This will give us a good base before we dive into the communication flow.

Kerberos parties

Kerberos authentication in the context of NetScaler involves the following three parties:

- The users/clients
- The **KDC (Key Distribution Center)** which has two subcomponents:
    - **Authentication Service (AS)** that looks for the User and returns a Ticket Granting Ticket, which you can in turn use to get session tickets.
    - **Ticket Granting Service (TGS)** that provides those session tickets
- The NetScaler AAA vServer that authenticates the users, talks to the KDC, and obtains tickets on behalf of the users.

Kerberos uses TCP port 88.

Configuration checklist

Here's a quick checklist of the items that need to be in place for KCD to function properly:

- On the Active Directory Server:
    - AD account representing the NetScaler as a system User that can obtain tickets for other users
    - Keytab for this NetScaler User
    - Constrained delegation enabled for the NetScaler system account
    - List of resources that the end User can delegate to NetScaler for authentication
- On the Web Server:
    - Kerberos enabled on the site
    - Best practice is to have NTLM enabled as fallback

- On the NetScaler:
  - ○ Authentication on the LB VIP. The server is added on the NetScaler with its domain/hostname – this is very important. The domain controller should also be able to resolve the hostname correctly:

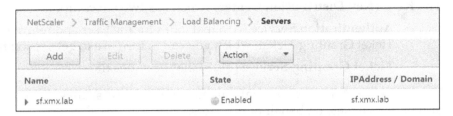

- Authentication vServer with authentication and session/traffic policies

Kerberos deployment options

There are a couple of choices available for implementing Kerberos:

- **Impersonation versus Delegation**: To impersonate a User in the impersonation scenario, NetScaler needs the credentials of the User. It then uses these User credentials to obtain tickets on behalf of the User. In the case of delegation, the User provides just the username to the NetScaler, which has a delegation-capable account on AD created for it and can do the rest. The ability to get tickets this way is very powerful because it means the User can, for example, just send a certificate and NetScaler can SSO the User by obtaining tickets on behalf of the User.

- **Kerberos with and without Protocol Transition**: Kerberos can be deployed end to end if all machines accessing the resource are part of a domain and can talk to the KDC. More common, however, is the scenario of users coming in externally, using a different authentication mechanism (such as Client Certificates, or LDAP or SAML), and then have the NetScaler talk Kerberos in the backend. This is called **Protocol Transition** (S4USELF).

Authentication flow

The following trace snapshot, taken on a client, shows the exchange that needs to happen so that end-to-end Kerberos authentication (in other words, without Protocol Transition) can work:

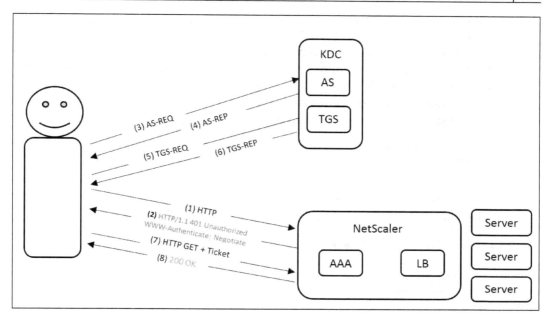

The flow as it happens:

- The client tries to access a page hosted via the NetScaler.

- NetScaler challenges the client, and on seeing the possibility to *negotiate* (that is, see the negotiate header), which indicates Kerberos is available, the client chooses to use it, since it's the preferred authentication mechanism. The following is how that negotiated response looks:

```
GET / HTTP/1.1
Accept: application/x-ms-application
Accept-Language: en-US
User-Agent: Mozilla/4.0 (compatible;
Media Center PC 6.0)
Accept-Encoding: gzip, deflate
Host: kcdvserver.rvt.krb
Connection: Keep-Alive

HTTP/1.1 401 Unauthorized
WWW-Authenticate: Negotiate
WWW-Authenticate: NTLM
```

- The client then requests a TGT from the KDC using the AS-REQ request.

- The AS component of the KDC provides the TGT in the response AS-REP. A session key is also provided in this response. This TGT is something you can see on the client machine and this is handy for troubleshooting.

- The client still needs a ticket for the specific service it's trying to access. It sends a `TGS-REQ` for this purpose to the TGS component of the KDC. This will contain the clients TGT it obtained in the previous step along with something called an **authenticator**. This is basically an encrypted form of the client's name and the current time stamp. The presence of this timestamp helps offer protection against replay attacks.

- The TGS responds with a service ticket along with a session key.

- The client now sends the same request but, to prove it has authenticated, presents the service ticket and again, an authenticator (see the following figure).

- The NetScaler, which is fronting the server, is happy to let the client through this time and provides the resource requested (**200 OK**).

Here's a screenshot of Kerberos in action:

Number	Source	Destination	Protocol	Info
1120	Client	NetScaler VIP	HTTP	GET / HTTP/1.1
1121	NetScaler VIP	Client	HTTP	HTTP/1.1 401 Unauthorized (text/html)
1125	Client	KDC	KRB5	AS-REQ
1126	KDC	Client	KRB5	KRB Error: KRB5KDC_ERR_PREAUTH_REQUIRED
1133	Client	KDC	KRB5	AS-REQ
1134	KDC	Client	KRB5	AS-REP
1142	Client	KDC	KRB5	TGS-REQ
1144	KDC	Client	KRB5	TGS-REP
1149	Client	NetScaler VIP	HTTP	GET / HTTP/1.1
1151	NetScaler VIP	Client	HTTP	HTTP/1.1 200 OK (text/html)

```
GSS-API Generic Security Service Application Program Interface
 OID: 1.3.6.1.5.5.2 (SPNEGO - Simple Protected Negotiation)
 Simple Protected Negotiation
 negTokenInit
  mechTypes: 4 items
  mechToken: 608205c206092a864886f71201020201006e8205b1308205...
  krb5_blob: 608205c206092a864886f71201020201006e8205b1308205...
   KRB5 OID: 1.2.840.113554.1.2.2 (KRB5 - Kerberos 5)
   krb5_tok_id: KRB5_AP_REQ (0x0001)
  Kerberos
   ap-req
    pvno: 5
    msg-type: krb-ap-req (14)
    Padding: 0
    ap-options: 20000000 (mutual-required)
    ticket
     tkt-vno: 5
     realm: RVT.KRB
    sname
    enc-part
   authenticator
```

Kerberos authentication with Protocol Transition

In order for end-to-end Kerberos to work, the client needs to be able to reach the KDC. This will not be possible in most environments, either because there are external users or partners in the mix, or simply because security policies require not exposing the KDC directly to all users. This is where Protocol Transition comes into the picture. Let's now turn our attention to the flow for this scenario. For the purpose of this section, I have set up LDAP in the frontend, with Kerberos in the backend.

Here, NetScaler authenticates the users with whatever authentication policy is bound to the AAA vServer but then uses Kerberos in the backend to obtain service tickets for those authenticated users. The following image demonstrates the flow:

```
GET / HTTP/1.1
Host: owa.xmx.lab
User-Agent: Mozilla/5.0 (Windows NT 6.1; WOW64; rv:39.0)
Accept: text/html,application/xhtml+xml,application/xml;q
Accept-Language: en-GB,en;q=0.5
Accept-Encoding: gzip, deflate
Connection: keep-alive

HTTP/1.1 401 Unauthorized
Content-Type: text/html
Server: Microsoft-IIS/7.5
WWW-Authenticate: Negotiate
X-Powered-By: ASP.NET
Date: Sun, 19 Jul 2015 16:24:56 GMT
Content-Length: 1293
```

The flow goes like this:

- The User requests the page
- With LDAP authentication being configured on the frontend, LDAP exchange takes place and the User is authenticated
- The User tries to request the page again, providing the AAA cookie
- Now NetScaler tries to obtain the page for the User
- When it contacts the server, it sees that Kerberos is enabled on the server in the form of a **WWW-Authenticate: Negotiate** challenge
- At this point, it uses the username from the earlier authentication to get the ticket on behalf of the User
- With the Kerberos authentication complete, NetScaler requests the page again
- It receives the response
- This response is forwarded to the User.

Here's a filtered trace snapshot that demonstrates the complete flow:

- `dcx.xmx.lab` is the KDC
- `exx.xmx.lab` is the web server that the client is trying to get to

Note that there are no `AS-REQ`/`AS-REP` packets in the NetScaler to KDC exchange. This is because a TGT, once obtained, can be reused for several hours, and such a reuse is happening here:

Number	Source	Destination	Protocol	Info
231	Client	NS VIP	HTTP	GET / HTTP/1.1
232	NS VIP	Client	HTTP	HTTP/1.1 401 Unauthorized (text/html)
290	Client	NS VIP	HTTP	GET / HTTP/1.1
327	NS SNIP	exx.xmx.lab	HTTP	GET / HTTP/1.1
332	exx.xmx.lab	NS SNIP	HTTP	HTTP/1.1 401 Unauthorized (text/html)
361	NS IP	dcx.xmx.lab	KRB5	TGS-REQ
364	dcx.xmx.lab	NS IP	KRB5	TGS-REP
373	NS SNIP	exx.xmx.lab	HTTP	GET / HTTP/1.1
381	exx.xmx.lab	NS SNIP	HTTP	HTTP/1.1 200 OK (text/html)
382	NS VIP	Client	HTTP	HTTP/1.1 200 OK (text/html)

There are a couple of important points to note here:

- NSIP is the default source IP for external authentication requests going from the NetScaler.
- You can either leave the necessary firewall ports open for the NSIP to be able to talk to the KDC, or use an LB vServer with Netprofiles to specify which IP to use for this communication.

Troubleshooting Kerberos

Here are some steps you should consider when troubleshooting Kerberos:

- Ensure port 88 is open to the KDC.
- Ensure the backend servers providing the content are configured to negotiate Kerberos. The following screenshot shows what you might ideally set on IIS on the server under authentication:

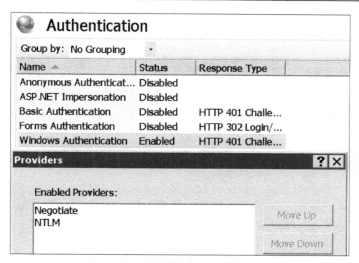

Kerberos with fallback to NTLM

- DNS plays a vital role in Kerberos, so ensure that it's properly working by trying to resolve the various entities.
- Check that the User and the resources are in the same Kerberos realm. If different, there are limitations on S4U depending on the AD domain and forest functional levels (2012R2 introduced some new cross-domain S4U functionality), but down-level domains may fail when the User and resource are not in the same domain.
- Ensure that delegation is configured correctly, that is:
    ◦ The Service Account has delegation enabled
    ◦ The Service Account is trusted for delegation
    ◦ If you are performing constrained delegation, verify that the necessary services are in the list
    ◦ For Protocol Transition to work, check **Use any authentication protocol**

The following is what I have used for the test I performed for my Windows-based Kerberos environment:

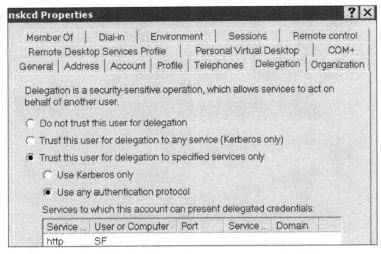

Configuration on AD allowing NetScaler system to trust "nskcd" to perform delegation on behalf of users to the HTTP service on the server

Focus on `aaad.debug` and `nskrb.debug`, as these are the most useful outputs to look at when troubleshooting Kerberos authentication. The screenshots that follow show a successful protocol transition from LDAP to Kerberos:

1. We start first by looking at the `aaad.debug` output (`cat/tmp/aaad.debug`) to see if the frontend authentication has been successful and that protocol transition has happened (S4U) before moving our attention to `nskrb.debug` (`cat/tmp/nskrb.debug`).

2. The following screenshot shows LDAP authentication starting for the protocol transition case:

```
cat /tmp/aaad.debug
5:27:24 2015
/rs_105/usr.src/netscaler/aaad/naaad.c[499]: main timer 1 firing...
5:27:36 2015
/rs_105/usr.src/netscaler/aaad/naaad.c[786]: process_kernel_socket call to authenticate
r, vsid :10239
5:27:36 2015
/rs_105/usr.src/netscaler/aaad/naaad.c[2654]: start_cascade_auth starting cascade authentication
5:27:36 2015
/rs_105/usr.src/netscaler/aaad/ldap_drv.c[106]: start_ldap_auth Starting LDAP auth
5:27:36 2015
/rs_105/usr.src/netscaler/aaad/ldap_drv.c[1058]: get_svr_name Server name length 12, name <dcx.xmx.lab>
5:27:36 2015
/rs_105/usr.src/netscaler/aaad/ldap_drv.c[125]: start_ldap_auth attempting to auth aaauser @ dcx.xmx.lab
```

3. In the following screenshot we see LDAP authentication succeed:

```
105/usr.src/netscaler/aaad/ldap_common.c[397]: ns_ldap_check_result ldap_result found expected result LDAP_RES_BIND
:36 2015
105/usr.src/netscaler/aaad/ldap_drv.c[761]: receive_ldap_user_bind_event Bind OK.
:36 2015
105/usr.src/netscaler/aaad/naaad.c[2933]: unregister_timer releasing timer 16
:36 2015
105/usr.src/netscaler/aaad/naaad.c[1965]: send_accept sending accept to kernel for : aaauser
:36 2015
105/usr.src/netscaler/aaad/naaad.c[805]: process_kernel_socket get_s4u received 118 bytes for s4u_req

:36 2015
105/usr.src/netscaler/aaad/krb_drv.c[105]: start_get_s4u starting get_s4u
```

4. At this point, take a look at `nskrb.debug`. The following screenshot shows NetScaler obtaining TGT for `aaauser`:

```
Sat Jul 25 17:51:48 2015
 nskrb.c[353]: ns_process_kcd_req user non-enterprise username aaauser@XMX.LAB
Sat Jul 25 17:51:48 2015
 nskrb.c[364]: ns_process_kcd_req tgt ticket cachename is /var/krb/tgt_nskerbero
slb.XMX.LAB_XMX.LAB
Sat Jul 25 17:51:48 2015
 nskrb.c[365]: ns_process_kcd_req delegated cachename is /var/krb/s4u_aaauser_XM
X.LAB_nskerberoslb.XMX.LAB_XMX.LAB
Sat Jul 25 17:51:48 2015
 nskrb.c[366]: ns_process_kcd_req tgs cachename is /var/krb/tgs_aaauser_XMX.LAB_
sf.xmx.lab_XMX.LAB
Sat Jul 25 17:51:48 2015
 nskrb.c[840]: ns_kinit got TGT in cache, kinit returning

Sat Jul 25 17:51:48 2015
 nskrb.c[1209]: ns_kgetcred kgetcred cache file /var/krb/s4u_aaauser_XMX.LAB_nsk
erberoslb.XMX.LAB_XMX.LAB  contains ticket for host/nskerberoslb.XMX.LAB@XMX.LAB
```

5. NetScaler gets the service ticket for `aaauser` to the service `sf.xmx.lab`, as shown in the following screenshot:

```
Sat Jul 25 17:51:48 2015
 nskrb.c[1299]: ns_kgetcred krb5_get_creds returned 0, svcname HTTP/sf.xmx.lab@X
MX.LAB, impersonate str NULL, deleg /var/krb/s4u_aaauser_XMX.LAB_nskerberoslb.XM
X.LAB_XMX.LAB outcache /var/krb/tgs_aaauser_XMX.LAB_sf.xmx.lab_XMX.LAB

Sat Jul 25 17:51:48 2015
 nskrb.c[1043]: ns_serialize_creds client name in creds: aaauser@XMX.LAB

Sat Jul 25 17:51:48 2015
 nskrb.c[1056]: ns_serialize_creds client name in creds:len 15 aaauser@XMX.LAB

Sat Jul 25 17:51:48 2015
 nskrb.c[1067]: ns_serialize_creds server name in creds:len 23 HTTP/sf.xmx.lab@X
MX.LAB

Sat Jul 25 17:51:48 2015
 nskrb.c[1079]: ns_serialize_creds keytype is 18, keylen is 32
```

6. Compare and look for any errors reported in this output if you are having a problem. A common one that comes up is KDC_ERR_S_PRINCIPAL_UNKNOWN, which means there is a duplicate SPN and the server is, as a result, unsure which key to use to decrypt the request. There is a list of these errors available at the Microsoft site: https://technet.microsoft.com/en-us/library/bb463166.aspx. You will need the SETSPN tool to troubleshoot these on the server.

   ° A further validation of success or failure would be done with the means of counters:

```
root@151ns# nsconmsg -g kcd -d current
Displaying performance information
NetScaler V20 Performance Data
NetScaler NS10.5: Build 55.8.nc, Date: Jan 25 2015, 23:55:26


reltime:mili second between two records Sat Jul 25 17:55:48 2015
   Index   rtime totalcount-val      delta rate/sec symbol-name&device-no
       0   42004              2          1       0 aaa_kcd_tgt_cache_hits
       1       0              2          1       0 aaa_kcd_s4u2self_cache_hits
       2       0              3          1       0 aaa_kcd_tot_kcd_success
       3       0              9          3       0 sso_tot_kcd_pe_cache_hits
```

   ° If you are seeing no action in the aaad.debug file, verify that your authentication policies are configured correctly.

   ° If you see entries in aaad.debug but S4U does not happen, verify that the client is not somehow falling back to NTLM by taking a trace and looking at the **WWW-Authenticate** header.

○ Another way to troubleshoot KCD step by step is to do it manually via the shell, using `kgetcred`. This will allow you to do a baseline verification by taking any browser or client machine particularities out of the picture. In the following screenshot, the individual steps are highlighted:

```
root@151ns# CACHE IS EMPTY
root@151ns# nskrb klist -c /tmp/krb5cc_0
nskrb: No ticket file: /tmp/krb5cc_0
root@151ns#
root@151ns# GETTING A TGT for the NetScaler Account
root@151ns# nskrb kinit nskcd@XMX.LAB
nskcd@XMX.LAB's Password:
root@151ns#
root@151ns# CACHE NOW HAS TICKET
root@151ns# nskrb klist -c /tmp/krb5cc_0
Credentials cache: FILE:/tmp/krb5cc_0
        Principal: nskcd@XMX.LAB

  Issued                Expires               Principal
Jul 25 18:24:00 2015  Jul 26 04:24:00 2015  krbtgt/XMX.LAB@XMX.LAB
root@151ns#
root@151ns# GET TGT for user using NetScaler delegation account
root@151ns# nskrb kgetcred -c /tmp/krb5cc_0 --out-cache=/tmp/imper_cache
--impersonate=aaauser@XMX.LAB nskcd@XMX.LAB
root@151ns#
root@151ns# verify TGT successfully otained
root@151ns# /netscaler/nskrb klist -c /tmp/imper_cache
Credentials cache: FILE:/tmp/imper_cache
        Principal: aaauser@XMX.LAB

  Issued                Expires               Principal
Jul 25 18:25:28 2015  Jul 26 04:24:00 2015  nskcd@XMX.LAB
root@151ns#
root@151ns# GET Service Ticket for user using delegation
root@151ns# nskrb kgetcred --delegation-credential=/tmp/imper_cache --out
-cache=/tmp/kcd_cache http/sf@XMX.LAB
root@151ns#
root@151ns# verify Service Ticket successfully obtained
root@151ns# /netscaler/nskrb klist -c /tmp/kcd_cache
Credentials cache: FILE:/tmp/kcd_cache
        Principal: aaauser@XMX.LAB

  Issued                Expires               Principal
Jul 25 18:27:59 2015  Jul 26 04:24:00 2015  http/sf@XMX.LAB
```

○ Look for Kerberos logs on the KDC; these can be very helpful too. To do this, head over to event viewer on the Active Directory Server and look for Kerberos logon attempts. Some of the event IDs to look for are listed in the following screenshot:

Date and Time	Event ID	Task Category
7/26/2015 8:26:30 PM	4672	Special Logon
7/26/2015 8:26:17 PM	4769	Kerberos Service Ticket Operations
7/26/2015 8:26:17 PM	4768	Kerberos Authentication Service
7/26/2015 8:26:17 PM	4769	Kerberos Service Ticket Operations
7/26/2015 8:26:17 PM	4769	Kerberos Service Ticket Operations
7/26/2015 8:26:17 PM	4768	Kerberos Authentication Service

Logon entries in event viewer

○ Kerberos logon attempts will show up as special logons; expanding one of them will show Kerberos-level details such as the following:

SubjectUserSidS-1-5-21-3614084837-668173954-446922676-1110
SubjectUserNameaaauser
SubjectDomainNameXMX
SubjectLogonId0x66948
PrivilegeListSeSecurityPrivilege SeTakeOwnershipPrivilege SeLoadDriverPrivilege
SeImpersonatePrivilege

Security Assertion Markup Language

Security Assertion Markup Language (**SAML**) is an XML based AAA mechanism which is starting to take off as a prominent way of doing web-based SSO between different enterprises (or partners). The main reason for its success is that it takes away the complexity of handling authentication from the enterprises that actually provide the service. This advantage is especially amplified in the case of multi-tenanted environments and means that the two different environments can evolve at their own speeds.

SAML, conceptually, has three entities:

• The User with their browser.

• A **Service Provider** (**SP**), who is responsible for providing the resource, such as a web page.

- An **Identity Provider** (**IDP**), who is responsible for confirming to the SP that a User is who they say they are and, when needed, providing additional attributes about the User that the SP can then use to make a decision on granting access to the service. The messaging units (formatted in XML) used to present this information are called assertions.

The glue that holds this model together is the trust between the SP and the IDP. That trust uses a couple of concepts that we'll discuss briefly: **Certificates** and **Canonicalization**.

Certificates in SAML

SAML's distributed model crosses enterprise boundaries. So, having a way to trust messages between the parties responsible for the service – the NetScaler, the IDP, and the SP, is key.

X.509 certificates were the model chosen to establish this trust, as the certificate model had already proved itself in the Internet world. The NetScaler, IDP, and SP each encrypt and sign their messages using their public keys. Thus it is important that the CA certificates (whether they are self-signed or signed by a public CA) are trusted by the receiving parties.

Canonicalization in SAML

Canonicalization is an XML signatures concept. Two XML documents can be physically different (for example, when viewed on an editor), and yet be semantically the same. This poses a challenge for mechanisms such as SAML, which rely on XML signatures for message validation. The problem originates from the fact that when the two physically different messages are encrypted and signed, the resulting signature hashes will be different. Thus the validation will fail at the verifying party and as a result the SSO will fail.

Canonicalization is a technique where the signing party generates a second version of the message, called the canonicalized version. This is done using techniques and algorithms followed by the various parties for compatibility. The canonicalized version only cares about specific parts of the message that are important, and not the entirety. Once signed this way, the receiving party, who also knows how to create a canonicalized version, does so before calculating the digest for validation.

The troubleshooting section lists some counters that help identify SSO failures resulting from certificate or message validation failures.

Depending on the deployment choice, there are two possible flows for SSO:

- SP Initiated SSO
- IDP Initiated SSO

Let's look at what these are and the associated flows.

SP Initiated SSO

Here, the SSO process is initiated by NetScaler. The LB vServer acts as the Service Provider associated AAA vServer acting as the SP.

Please check out Citrix blog 174193098 for an example of how to set this up; it will serve as a handy base deployment using just a free IDP, a NetScaler, and any regular web server. Now let's look at the flow to expect when using such a deployment:

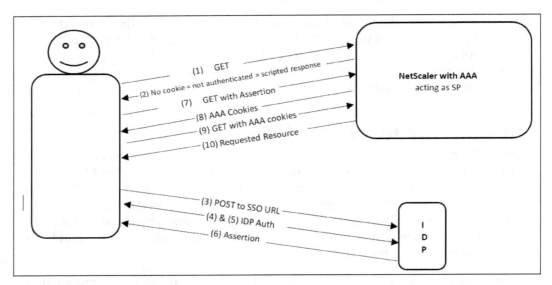

Something to remember when looking at traces is that there is no communication between the NetScaler and the IDP here. There is an implicit trust between the two parties, achieved through the binding of appropriate certificates.

The following Wireshark screenshot shows what the exchange looks like between the User and the NetScaler VIP:

Source	Destination	Protocol	Info
User	NetScaler LB VIP	HTTP	GET / HTTP/1.1
NetScaler LB VIP	User	HTTP	HTTP/1.1 200 OK (text/html)
User	NetScaler LB VIP	HTTP	POST /cgi/samlauth HTTP/1.1 (application/x-www-form-urlencoded)
NetScaler LB VIP	User	HTTP	HTTP/1.1 302 Object Moved
User	NetScaler LB VIP	HTTP	GET / HTTP/1.1
NetScaler LB VIP	User	HTTP	HTTP/1.1 200 OK (text/html)

Let's deconstruct the steps:

1. The client sends a GET for the page it wants to access.

2. Since there are no AAA cookies in that request, NetScaler realizes that this is an unauthenticated User and instead of responding with the requested page, responds with a form script, which, when executed on the User's browser, redirects them to the IDP SSO URL to authenticate:

```
<META HTTP-EQUIV="Content-Type" CONTENT="text/html; charset=UTF-8"><style type="text/css">body{ visibility: hi
nent.forms[0].submit();'><form action="https://fedweb.xmx.lab/simplesaml/saml2/idp/SSOService.php" method="post">
WxwOkF1dGhuUmVxdWVzdCB4bWxuczpzYW1scD0idXJuOhc2lzOm5hbWVzOnRjOlNBTUw6Mi4wOnByb3RvY2
```

The NetScaler meanwhile saves the information about the GET it received in its local state information to resume when the User returns.

3. The User, as a result of step 2, does a POST to the IDP at the SSO URL, this POST also includes the referer and origin headers:

```
POST /simplesaml/saml2/idp/SSOService.php HTTP/1.1
Cache
  Cache-Control: max-age=0
Client
  Accept: text/html,application/xhtml+xml,application/xml;q=0.9,image/webp,*/*;q=0.8
  Accept-Encoding: gzip, deflate
  Accept-Language: en-US,en;q=0.8
  User-Agent: Mozilla/5.0 (Windows NT 6.1; Win64; x64) AppleWebKit/537.36 (KHTML, like Gecko) Chrome/44.0.2403.125
Entity
  Content-Length: 4548
  Content-Type: application/x-www-form-urlencoded
Miscellaneous
  Origin: http://lb.xmx.lab
  Referer: http://lb.xmx.lab/
```

4. The User gets prompted for credentials.

5. The User provides credentials and gets authenticated.

6. This will result in another form script (similar to the one from NetScaler earlier), which will provide the User the assertion and where to POST that assertion. This script is saying to the User: "go back to the SP and provide this assertion to get access to your resource":

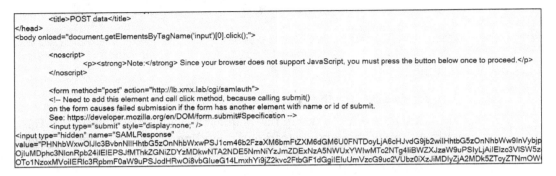

```
            <title>POST data</title>
</head>
<body onload="document.getElementsByTagName('input')[0].click();">

        <noscript>
                <p><strong>Note:</strong> Since your browser does not support JavaScript, you must press the button below once to proceed.</p>
        </noscript>

        <form method="post" action="http://lb.xmx.lab/cgi/samlauth">
        <!-- Need to add this element and call click method, because calling submit()
        on the form causes failed submission if the form has another element with name or id of submit.
        See: https://developer.mozilla.org/en/DOM/form.submit#Specification -->
        <input type="submit" style="display:none;" />
<input type="hidden" name="SAMLResponse"
value="PHNhbWxwOlJlc3BvbnNlIHhtbG5zOnNhbWxwPSJ1cm46b2FzaXM6bmFtZXM6dGM6U0FNTDoyLjA6cHJvdG9jb2wiIHhtbG5zOnNhbWxww9InVybjp
OjluMDphc3NlcnRpb24iIElEPSJfMThkZGNiZDYzMDkwNTA2NDE5NmNiYzJmZDExNA5NWUxYWlwMTc2NTg4liBWZXJzaW9uPSIyLjAiIAElzc3VISW5z
OTo1NzoxMVoilERlc3RpbmF0aW9uPSJodHRwOi8vbGlueG14LmxhYi9jZ2kvc2FtbGF1dGgiIEluUmVzcG9uc2VUbz0iXzJiMDlyZjA2MDk5ZTcyZTNmMOW
```

7. The User will POST the assertion to LB VIP, with `/cgi/samlauth` appended to the path.

8. This will result in a redirect once again to the LB VIP, but this time with the all essential AAA cookies that prove the User is authenticated:

```
User              NetScaler LB VIP    HTTP    POST /cgi/samlauth HTTP/1.1  (application/x-www-form-url
NetScaler LB VIP User             HTTP    HTTP/1.1 302 Object Moved

    Set-Cookie: NSC_TMAA=701ce5a2d67c0de74a3a0b30b78c765a;HttpOnly;Path=/;Domain=xmx.lab\r\n
    Set-Cookie: NSC_TMAS=ea8cbf7f7c746d30b13e0518e2a307ab;Secure;HttpOnly;Path=/;Domain=xmx.lab\r\n
```

9. The User now acts on this redirect and asks for the same resource as in step 1, but with the cookies.

10. The NetScaler, having verified the cookies, returns the requested resource.

IDP initiated SSO

In the case of IDP initiated SSO, the User, instead of going to the resource (SP) first, lands on the IDP at a URL configured for SSO.

The User doesn't need to know how to create this URL by themselves. It will be provided to them as a result of accessing a simpler landing page – such as a web-based CRM, embedded with this URL, crafted for SSO. This URL will contain a couple of important parameters:

- The SP's identity

- The URL that the User is actually trying to get to, via the RelayState parameter:

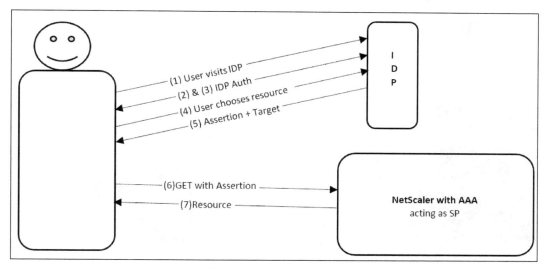

Flow for IDP initiated Auth

In the following example I am using a simple web page with an embedded URL to simulate an IDP initiated scenario. Here, unlike with the SP initiated scenario, the User learns of the SP via the IDP. The following fiddler trace shows the full exchange from the perspective of the User's machine:

	Host	URL	Resu
1	flights.lab	/confirmbooking	301
2	flights.lab	/confirmbooking/	200
3	flights.lab	/confirmbooking/click_to_confirm.png	200
4	Tunnel to fedweb.xmx.lab:443		200
5	fedweb.xmx.lab	/simplesaml/saml2/idp/SSOService.php?spentityid=lb.xmx.lab&RelayState=http://lb.xmx.lab	302
6	fedweb.xmx.lab	/simplesaml/module.php/core/loginuserpass.php?AuthState=_a5f9db74a20fc6dfdb17fd7e7...	200
7	fedweb.xmx.lab	/simplesaml/resources/script.js	200
8	fedweb.xmx.lab	/simplesaml/resources/default.css	200
9	Tunnel to fedweb.xmx.lab:443		200
10	fedweb.xmx.lab	/simplesaml/resources/icons/experience/gtk-dialog-authentication.48x48.png	200
11	Tunnel to fedweb.xmx.lab:443		200
12	fedweb.xmx.lab	/simplesaml/resources/icons/ssplogo-fish-small.png	200
13	fedweb.xmx.lab	/simplesaml/resources/header-bkg.png	200
14	fedweb.xmx.lab	/simplesaml/resources/icons/favicon.ico	200
15	fedweb.xmx.lab	/simplesaml/module.php/core/loginuserpass.php?	200
16	lb.xmx.lab	/cgi/samlauth	302
17	lb.xmx.lab	/	200
18	lb.xmx.lab	/welcome.png	200

Fiddler trace taken on Client for IDP initiated Authentication

Verifying a successful exchange using counters

You can verify that your SAML SSO setup works by using the `nsconmsg` command: `nsconmsg -g saml -d current`. A successful authentication will result in the `saml_assertion_verify_success` counter going up:

```
root@151ns# nsconmsg -g saml -d current
Displaying performance information
NetScaler V20 Performance Data
NetScaler NS10.5: Build 55.8.nc, Date: Jan 25 2015, 23:55:26


reltime:mili second between two records Thu Jul 30 20:12:48 2015
  Index    rtime totalcount-val      delta rate/sec symbol-name&device-no
      0    14001             6          1       0 saml_assertion_verify_success
      1        0             6          1       0 saml_tot_dht_put_success
      2        0             6          1       0 saml_tot_dht_get_notfound
```

Troubleshooting

Here are some areas you should focus on if your SAML SSO isn't working:

- SAML, like Kerberos, is quite strict about time being correct, so verify date and time on the various devices and use NTP as a best practice.

- Ensure that DNS is working correctly. The client must be able to successfully resolve and contact both the SP and the IDP.

- Verify that the certificates that represent each entity are trusted by the others.

- If users might report **404 page not found** errors when accessing the page, verify that the SAML redirect URL is configured correctly on the profile.

- Canonicalization, as we discussed, is a critical piece in this integration, to ensure that validation works correctly. To identify if you are running into canonicalization issues, look for the following counters going up:

    ○ `saml_assertion_parse_fail`

    ○ `saml_signature_verify_fail`

    ○ `saml_canonicalize_fail`

    ○ `saml_digest_verify_fail`

The syntax would be:

```
nsconmsg -g <one of counters above > -d current
  e.g. nsconmsg -g saml_canonicalize_fail -d current
```

- Look up the ns.log (/var/log/ns.log) while reproducing the issue. There is a good level of detail here around requests and errors for users authenticating using SAML. In the following screenshot we see that the authentication failed because a signed assertion was expected, but instead was received without any signing info:

```
Jul 30 21:13:33 <local0.err> 192.168.1.150 07/30/2015:19:13:33 GMT 151ns 0-PPE-0 :
AAATM Message 1655 0 :   "Unsigned Assertion seen"
Jul 30 21:13:33 <local0.err> 192.168.1.150 07/30/2015:19:13:33 GMT 151ns 0-PPE-0 :
AAATM Message 1656 0 :   "Verification of SAML assertion resulted in failure 917509
"
```

Summary

In this all-important chapter we looked at the authentication capabilities of the NetScaler. We covered the protocols that enterprises use most commonly and examined the packet flows involved, the deployment options, and troubleshooting techniques for each.

In the next chapter we will look at Networking and High Availability issues.

5
High Availability and Networking

NetScaler is a high performance network device, expected to be able to handle several gigabytes of traffic per second while being highly available given how critical enterprise applications are. To ensure optimal performance, NetScaler is generally integrated very tightly into the network, and where there is such integration involved, there is naturally a potential for issues during the deployment stage. Such issues are the focus of this chapter.

The two main areas we'll look at in this chapter are:

- High Availability issues
- Networking issues

High Availability

For many environments that use it, NetScaler becoming unavailable means losing access to a fleet of web applications, and even access to the corporate network in the case of NetScaler Gateway deployments. So it is little wonder that, when NetScaler is deployed in an enterprise, it is always deployed in **High Availability (HA)** pairs.

In a properly set up HA pair environment, the standby NetScaler, which we refer to as the secondary in this chapter, jumps into action within milliseconds of detecting a failure and announces its intention to become the primary. If the network is fast in adapting itself to the change of ownership, traffic gets restored within seconds of the failure.

There are several other ways of providing High Availability via NetScaler – HA over INC, Route Health Injection, and Clustering. The focus of this section is on the way that more than 90% of deployments use it, which is High Availability in Active-Standby over layer 2 connectivity.

In the next few pages, we will look at the various facets of HA before diving into troubleshooting.

Ports used for High Availability

NetScaler HA relies on a set of services which in turn use specific ports. Heartbeats are sent over UDP port 3003. Propagation and synchronization use TCP ports 3008 and 3009 or 3010 and 3011. The following is a list of the ports when RPC is enabled and when it is not enabled:

- If secure RPC is enabled:
  - 3008 for synchronization
  - 3009 for propagation

- If secure RPC is not enabled:
  - 3010 for synchronization
  - 3011 for propagation

For file synchronization for certificates, TCP port 22 is used.

RPC communication can be secured (secure RPC) using the set rpcnode command. By default, it is unsecured, so TCP ports 3010 and 3011 are the ones used.

Configurations kept independent in High Availability

Setting up High Availability only requires a single line of configuration on each node add `ha node <node ID> <IP Address>` (the node IDs don't need to be unique).

- NSIPs
- Interface configurations
- Hostnames

 Any configuration changes made outside of these areas should be done only on the primary. The risk with not following this is that the command run on the secondary will not be propagated, and hence will be lost during the next sync/propagation.

HA pairing requirements

For High Availability to function properly, the following must be the same on both devices:

- Version and build
- Hardware (for MPX, SDX)
- License

Setting up and verifying High Availability

Setting up High Availability only requires an add ha node entry per node. For example on one node is greater than add ha node 1 10.72.142.70. And on the other it is greater than add ha node 1 10.72.142.50. (Node IDs don't need to be unique.)

If everything goes well the result should look like this. The key areas of the output are highlighted:

```
> show node
1)      Node ID:        0
        IP:     192.168.1.50 (192_50_ns)
        Node State: UP
        Master State: Primary
        Fail-Safe Mode: OFF
        INC State: DISABLED
        Sync State: ENABLED
        Propagation: ENABLED
        Enabled Interfaces : 1/1
        Disabled Interfaces : None
        HA MON ON Interfaces : 1/1
        Interfaces on which heartbeats are not seen : None
        Interfaces causing Partial Failure: None
        SSL Card Status: NOT PRESENT
        Hello Interval: 200 msecs
        Dead Interval: 3 secs
        Node in this Master State for: 0:0:2:40 (days:hrs:min:sec)
2)      Node ID:        1
        IP:     192.168.1.60
        Node State: UP
        Master State: Secondary
        Fail-Safe Mode: OFF
        INC State: DISABLED
        Sync State: SUCCESS
        Propagation: ENABLED
        Enabled Interfaces : 1/1
        Disabled Interfaces : None
        HA MON ON Interfaces : 1/1
        Interfaces on which heartbeats are not seen : None
        Interfaces causing Partial Failure: None
        SSL Card Status: NOT PRESENT

Local node information:
        Critical Interfaces: 1/1
```

The SSL card status NOT PRESENT, in the preceding output, is not a problem in a VPX which may or may not have an SSL card. But any instance where card is present and shows DOWN needs immediate attention.

Troubleshooting HA Failovers

HA Failover-related issues are generally considered to be very serious. There are broadly of four types:

- HA node state issues
- Heartbeats not being seen
- New primary not handling traffic
- Sync and propagation issues

Let's take a look at these one by one.

HA Node state issues

Sometimes when you do a `show node`, you might see the status **Not UP**. This means the node is not ready to process traffic, if it were to become primary. This can be because of the following reasons:

- Critical interfaces are down
- The SSL card is down
- High Availability is disabled (on the remote node)
- The unit is still booting up or rebooting

There is a very handy list of the various node states and what they mean in article CTX118519. I sourced the following tables from the article as they will greatly help with understanding what the Node state is complaining about.

Node States seen on Primary:

Value	Meaning
INIT	The appliance is initializing.
UP	The appliance is working as expected.
PARTIAL_FAIL	One or more interfaces on which HAMON ON is configured are not working.
COMPLETE_FAIL	All the interfaces of the appliance are not working.
DISABLE	The HASTATUS of the node is disabled.

Node States seen on Secondary:

Value	Meaning
INIT	This is the receipt of the message stating that the peer is initializing.
UP	This is the receipt of the message stating that the peer is working as expected.
PARTIAL_FAIL	This is the receipt of the message stating that one or more interfaces of the peer on which HAMON ON is configured are not working.
UNKNOWN	If the appliance is not working, then the peer stat is unknown.
DOWN	The monitoring failed on all links of the peer node.

Source: Citrix Knowledge Base

Heartbeats not being seen

Heartbeats, which use UDP port 3003, are used by each NetScaler in the pair to let the peer know how they are doing. You can spot them in a Wireshark trace by using the filter udp.port==3003, as shown by the following screenshot:

```
udp.port==3003              ▼  Expression...  Clear  Apply  Save
     Source        Destination      Length  Info
  1 Primary        Secondary          366 TEI:52  S  P,  func=SREJ,  N(R)=48
  5 Secondary      Primary            366 TEI:52  S  P,  func=SREJ,  N(R)=48
  6 Primary        Secondary          366 TEI:52  S  P,  func=SREJ,  N(R)=48
  7 Secondary      Primary            366 TEI:52  S  P,  func=SREJ,  N(R)=48
  8 Primary        Secondary          366 TEI:52  S  P,  func=SREJ,  N(R)=48
  9 Secondary      Primary            366 TEI:52  S  P,  func=SREJ,  N(R)=48
 10 Primary        Secondary          366 TEI:52  S  P,  func=SREJ,  N(R)=48
 17 Secondary      Primary            366 TEI:52  S  P,  func=SREJ,  N(R)=48
 18 Primary        Secondary          366 TEI:52  S  P,  func=SREJ,  N(R)=48
 27 Secondary      Primary            366 TEI:52  S  P,  func=SREJ,  N(R)=48
 56 Primary        Secondary          366 TEI:52  S  P,  func=SREJ,  N(R)=48
 73 Secondary      Primary            366 TEI:52  S  P,  func=SREJ,  N(R)=48
```

The default rate of heartbeats is 5 per interface per second. This can be changed by adjusting the Hello Interval:

```
> set ha node 1 -helloInterval 500 -deadInterval 5
```

The dead interval specifies when a secondary unit should take over. The default is 3 seconds. In other words, missing 15 heartbeats in succession on an interface marked as critical will result in a Failover. In the following screenshot, pay attention to interfaces causing partial failure in the show node output:

```
> show node
1)          Node ID:       0
            IP:     10.72.142.50 (prodlb-a)
            Node State: UP
            Master State: Secondary
            Fail-Safe Mode: OFF
            INC State: DISABLED
            Sync State: SUCCESS
            Propagation: ENABLED
            Enabled Interfaces : 1/1 1/2
            Disabled Interfaces : None
            HA MON ON Interfaces : 1/1
            Interfaces on which heartbeats are not seen : 1/1 1/2
            Interfaces causing Partial Failure: 1/1
            SSL Card Status: NOT PRESENT
            Hello Interval: 200 msecs
            Dead Interval: 3 secs
            Node in this Master State for: 1:11:17:42 (days:hrs:min:sec)
```

This will list any interfaces that NetScaler deems as critical, but doesn't see heartbeats on. In the above image, the node is in a secondary state after failing over because it's not seeing heartbeats on 1/1, which has HA monitoring enabled on it.

NetScaler will also complain about missing heartbeats on interfaces that are enabled but not plugged in. A common misconception about heartbeats is that they are only sent on interfaces with HAMON enabled, which isn't true. Heartbeats are sent on all enabled interfaces and are expected on all enabled interfaces. So, the correct way to remedy the heart beats not seen error on an unused interface is to disable the interface.

 Disabling unused interfaces is a NetScaler best practice. It helps reduce clutter in node state information during troubleshooting.

The shell command `nsconmsg -g ha_tot_pkt -d current` shows you the number of heartbeat packets sent and received, as shown in the following screenshot:

```
root@60ns# nsconmsg -g ha_tot_pkt -d current
Displaying performance information
NetScaler V20 Performance Data
NetScaler NS10.5: Build 58.11.nc, Date: Jul 14 2015, 13:28:13


reltime:mili second between two records Fri Aug 14 00:13:13 2015
  Index    rtime  totalcount-val    delta rate/sec symbol-name&device-no
      0     7002          106607       35        4 ha_tot_pkt_rx
      1        0          105666       35        4 ha_tot_pkt_tx
      2     7002          106642       35        4 ha_tot_pkt_rx
      3        0          105701       35        4 ha_tot_pkt_tx
      4     7001          106678       36        5 ha_tot_pkt_rx
      5        0          105736       35        4 ha_tot_pkt_tx
      6     7002          106686        8        1 ha_tot_pkt_rx
```

Using nsconmsg to verify HA heartbeat exchange

 Sometimes the heartbeats are not received because the peer unit has crashed. If this crash happens on the primary, a Failover will result. Crashes are discussed in the *Chapter 8, System-Level Issues*.

Identifying Failovers in events

When a Failover does happen, you can identify timelines and why the Failover happened by looking at the events. There are various ways to get this information:

- By looking at the `/var/log/ns.log` file
- By navigating to **GUI | Diagnostics | Manage Logs | View events**:

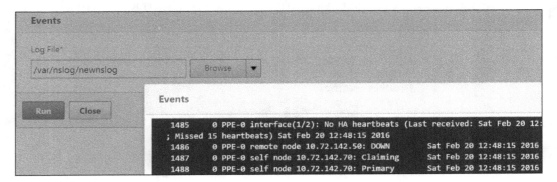

- By using the `nsconmsg` command:

```
nsconmsg -K /var/nslog/newnslogs -d event
```

- Furthermore, you can then grep for `node` to filter out HA-related events, as shown in the following screenshot:

```
root@rvtns# nsconmsg -d event | grep node
1486    0 PPE-0 remote node 10.72.142.50: DOWN       Sat Feb 20 12:48:15 2016
1487    0 PPE-0 self node 10.72.142.70: Claiming     Sat Feb 20 12:48:15 2016
1488    0 PPE-0 self node 10.72.142.70: Primary       Sat Feb 20 12:48:15 2016
1499    0 PPE-0 remote node 10.72.142.50: INIT        Sat Feb 20 12:49:26 2016
1501    0 PPE-0 remote node 10.72.142.50: UP          Sat Feb 20 12:49:27 2016
```

VLAN issues causing heartbeat failures

VLAN issues are a common reason for heartbeats to not be seen. Let's look at some important points about VLANs in the context of heartbeats:

- Heartbeats are by default sent untagged and use the NSVLAN, which by default is 1.

- The untagged command is important to note, as it means that for heartbeats to work properly by default, the switch needs to accept untagged traffic, and some switches might be set up not to do so.

- If untagged packets are not accepted on the switch, the packets will need to be tagged using the -tagall ON interface command. But with tagall ON, the heartbeats will be tagged with VLAN 1 by default. Switches in general drop packets tagged with VLAN 1. This leaves us with two choices to achieve a working configuration:

    ○ **Option 1**: You can change the default VLAN of the interfaces by using the set nsconfig -nsvlan command (the change needs a reboot):

```
> set ns config -nsvlan 100 -ifnum 1/1
Warning: The configuration must be saved and the system rebooted
> show nsconfig | grep 1/1
        NetScaler IP Vlan: 100 Tagged: YES Bound Ports: 1/1
```

    ○ **Option 2**: You can change the membership of the interface by binding a different VLAN (for example 100) without the tagged option. Then you set the tagall option on the interface, as shown in the following screenshot:

```
> add vlan 100
Done
> bind vlan 100 -ifnum 1/1
Done
> set interface 1/1 -tagall ON
Done
```

New primary doesn't take over traffic after Failover

There are several reasons why this issue could happen:

- ARP issues
- stay secondary being set
- Health issues
- Split brain

Let's discuss them in more detail.

ARP issues

When a secondary NetScaler becomes the primary, it has to inform the upstream devices that it is now responsible for all of the VIPs. It does so by sending out gratuitous ARPs at a rate of two per VLAN per interface per second, as shown in the following screenshot. Note that the opcode of these GARPs is set to request by default:

```
Filter: arp.isgratuitous          ▼ Expression... Clear Apply Save
Time                    Source           Destination      Length Info
22:22:57.633883540      192.168.1.189    Broadcast        94 Gratuitous ARP for 192.168.1.182 (Request)
22:22:57.633883752      192.168.1.189    Broadcast        94 Gratuitous ARP for 192.168.1.183 (Request)
22:22:57.633883988      192.168.1.189    Broadcast        94 Gratuitous ARP for 192.168.1.183 (Request)
22:22:57.633884231      192.168.1.189    Broadcast        94 Gratuitous ARP for 192.168.1.183 (Request)
22:22:57.633884467      192.168.1.189    Broadcast        94 Gratuitous ARP for 192.168.1.183 (Request)
22:22:57.633884683      192.168.1.189    Broadcast        94 Gratuitous ARP for 192.168.1.184 (Request)
22:22:57.633884941      192.168.1.189    Broadcast        94 Gratuitous ARP for 192.168.1.184 (Request)
22:22:57.633885178      192.168.1.189    Broadcast        94 Gratuitous ARP for 192.168.1.184 (Request)
22:22:57.633885421      192.168.1.189    Broadcast        94 Gratuitous ARP for 192.168.1.184 (Request)
22:22:57.633885635      192.168.1.189    Broadcast        94 Gratuitous ARP for 192.168.1.185 (Request)
22:22:57.633885871      192.168.1.189    Broadcast        94 Gratuitous ARP for 192.168.1.185 (Request)
22:22:57.633886117      192.168.1.189    Broadcast        94 Gratuitous ARP for 192.168.1.185 (Request)
22:22:57.633886385      192.168.1.189    Broadcast        94 Gratuitous ARP for 192.168.1.185 (Request)
» Frame 211: 94 bytes on wire (752 bits), 94 bytes captured (752 bits)
» NetScaler Packet Trace
» Ethernet II, Src: 192.168.1.189 (c6:84:c6:e4:a6:62), Dst: Broadcast (ff:ff:ff:ff:ff:ff)
» Address Resolution Protocol (request/gratuitous ARP)
   Hardware type: Ethernet (1)
   Protocol type: IP (0x0800)
   Hardware size: 6
   Protocol size: 4
   Opcode: request (1)
   [Is gratuitous: True]
   Sender MAC address: 192.168.1.189 (c6:84:c6:e4:a6:62)
   Sender IP address: 192.168.1.61 (192.168.1.61)
   Target MAC address: Broadcast (ff:ff:ff:ff:ff:ff)
   Target IP address: 192.168.1.61 (192.168.1.61)
```

The problem usually arises with firewalls, or IDS or IPS devices, that might not like GARP and hence drop these announcements. There are two ways to deal with this problem:

- Try with a different GARP opcode. Some devices prefer the opcode reply to request. You can set this by using the below command.

  ```
  > set l2param -garpReply ENABLED
  ```

- The use of **VMACs (Virtual MACs)** will keep the MAC address constant. Upstream devices thus do not need to know that the MAC address has changed, which is where the regular GARP-based method runs into delays or fails. The Failover as a result using this method is much faster.

  Note, however, that for VMACs to work the switches need to support them as well, since the switch suddenly sees the MAC address move to a different port, and this might be disallowed by default on some switches. CTX121681 covers VMAC configuration in detail.

Stay secondary being set

There is a HA misconfiguration and the backup node was set to `stay secondary`, in which case it will never attempt to become the primary.

Both nodes unhealthy

If the new primary itself has some HA node issues and it sees itself as less than healthy, the Failover might not happen when needed. You can avoid this situation by enabling the `failsafe` setting. The command to do this will be:

```
>set ha node -failsafe ON
```

Enabling `failsafe` mode will ensure that even if both devices fail the HA health check, at least one of them will assume the primary role.

Split brain issues

The term "split brain" is used to describe a situation where both devices in the HA pair are trying to become primary because neither device receives heartbeats from the other, yet both are active on the network. Neither node handles traffic because there are constant Failovers.

The troubleshooting to employ here is the same as for heartbeats not being seen. For example, correct the VLAN settings on the NetScaler and the switch.

Depending on the severity of the impact to service, you might want to take one node immediately off the network as a first step while you try to resolve the configuration issue.

Synchronization and propagation issues

Synchronization and propagation are very important aspects of High Availability. If they don't function, the NetScalers could end up with different configurations, which will lead to a service impact when a Failover does happen.

The following is a list of reasons that can lead to synchronization and propagation failures:

- The ports needed, 3008/3009/3010/3011, are blocked. However, this is generally rare, given that the pair are generally only separated by a switch.

- The versions or hardware don't match. This condition can be identified in the show node output. The AUTO DISABLED part indicates that there is a mismatch:

```
> sh node
1)      Node ID:       0
        IP:      192.168.1.50 (192_50_ns)
        Node State: UP
        Master State: Secondary
        Fail-Safe Mode: OFF
        INC State: DISABLED
        Sync State: AUTO DISABLED
        Propagation: AUTO DISABLED
        Enabled Interfaces : 1/1
```

This is the reason why you should always have the primary and secondary on the same version, except momentarily when upgrading software, when one of the nodes will have to be on newer code.

- RPC settings are used by each NetScaler to authenticate to its peer during HA and GSLB exchanges. If in doubt, do a quick comparison of the RPC node entries on the two NetScalers. You can do this using the >show rpcnode command on each NetScaler in the High Availability pair and compare the settings on primary and secondary.

Networking issues

To make the most of a NetScaler investment, it is utilized mostly for its layer 4 to layer 7 magic, while relying on an external router or firewall for routing. The NetScaler integration with the network is thus mainly at layer 2. The issues in this area are key, both from a reachability and performance perspective, when working with NetScaler, and are the main focus of this section. The topics we will cover specifically in this section are:

- Interface error conditions and interface buffer issues
- Network loops and VLAN issues
- Unsupported SFPs
- Channeling issues

We will also look at a couple of source IP-related issues before wrapping up.

NetScaler packet handling

Before we dive into more specific points, let's quickly discuss how NetScaler makes its packet handling decisions. NetScaler in its default configuration listens to packets in what is referred to as **promiscuous mode**. In this mode, it accepts all packets whether or not they are intended for one of its MAC addresses. This behavior is necessary so NetScaler can support modes such as L2 mode, where it behaves like a switch. After picking up all packets it can see on the network, NetScaler drops those packets not addressed to it in software if L2 mode is disabled.

> While promiscuous mode for listening is always on, L2 mode itself is disabled by default and there should be a very good reason for you to change that setting, such as a deployment very specifically asking for it. Unless considered carefully, L2 mode can introduce the risk of a loop by collapsing broadcast domains.

The following diagram taken from Citrix eDocs is extremely helpful in demonstrating the decision path that NetScaler follows when trying decide between processing and dropping a packet:

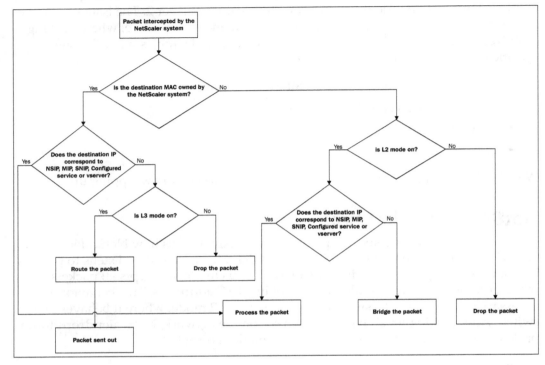

Source: Citrix eDocs

With this understanding of the decision process, let's take a look at some layer 2 issues.

Error conditions that contribute to packet drops

We've talked about how NetScaler picks up all packets it can see on the network before dropping those that don't fit its configured mode. A question that comes up often is around the Drops field in the show interface output. It is customary in networking to use interface drops as a measure of how healthy an interface is. However, in the case of NetScaler, for the reasons we've discussed, this field doesn't really help as we will most likely see a large count here, as L2 is disabled by default. So in the screenshot that follows, you can ignore the Drops counter that's showing a huge value:

```
> show interface 1/1
1)      Interface 1/1 (NetScaler Virtual Interface) #0
        flags=0xe060 <ENABLED, UP, UP, HAMON, 802.1q>
        MTU=1500, native vlan=1, MAC=4e:98:83:95:10:ac, uptime 287h31m10s
        LLDP Mode: NONE

        RX: Pkts(2699381) Bytes(466007827) Errs(0) Drops(1079694) Stalls(0)
        TX: Pkts(1506188) Bytes(460982602) Errs(0) Drops(0) Stalls(0)
        NIC: InDisc(0) OutDisc(0) Fctls(0) Stalls(0) Hangs(0) Muted(0)
        Bandwidth thresholds are not set.
```

However, there are several others in this screenshot that warrant attention if seen going up. Here's a quick description of what each of these indicate:

- **InDisc and OutDisc**: The Disc part signifies discards. These going up indicates that the interface had to discard packets; this could well be because the interface has run out of buffers. We will talk about buffer issues shortly.

- **Fctls**: This means NetScaler has received some flow control pause frames from the peer interface. It is generally an indication of integration issues with the connected switch or NIC congestion.

- **Stalls**: These indicate that packets in the buffer are unable to get out within a certain amount of time in one of the directions (RX or TX). They could be due to physical or software issues; you need to work with Citrix support for such cases. If stalls happen often enough, the interface will be reset.

- **Hangs**: NIC states are polled periodically to see if they are responsive. If the NIC doesn't respond to this polling, it is considered a hang. Citrix support needs to be engaged for such cases.

- **Mutes**: This is very likely because of a network loop resulting from the lack of a necessary broadcast domain such as a VLAN. When the MAC address that represents a server or a peer NetScaler IP is constantly seen on more than one interface within the same VLAN, one of the interfaces is disabled temporarily to stop the loop condition; at this point the mutes count is increased. We will also talk about loops in a moment.

NIC buffer issues

A NetScaler interface always has a finite buffer, which operates in a **FIFO (First in-First Out)** fashion. Running out of buffer space means an NIC has to drop packets. Due to the nature of TCP, any sustained dropping of packets will severely impact performance.

This situation can be identified by using the counter `-g nic_err_rx_nobufs`, as shown in the following screenshot. Here the `0/1` and `0/2` interfaces are running out of buffers:

```
root@ns#nsconmsg -K newnslog -g nic_err_rx_nobufs -d current
Displaying performance information
NetScaler V20 Performance Data
NetScaler NS10.1: Build 127.10.nc, Date: Jun 23 2014, 07:57:42
reltime:mili second between two records Thu Feb 12 19:39:45 2015
  Index   rtime totalcount-val    delta rate/sec symbol-name&device-no&time
      0  315000         18568         1       0 nic_err_rx_nobufs interface(0/1)
      1  336007         18569         1       0 nic_err_rx_nobufs interface(0/1)
      2   42001         64703         1       0 nic_err_rx_nobufs interface(0/2)
      3  329006         18570         1       0 nic_err_rx_nobufs interface(0/1)
      4   14001         18571         1       0 nic_err_rx_nobufs interface(0/1)
      5   21000         18572         1       0 nic_err_rx_nobufs interface(0/1)
```

NIC reporting no buffers when trying to receive a packet

The most common reasons why this could happen are:

- Management NICs are being used for production traffic. The interfaces `0/1` and `0/2` are meant to handle management traffic, which is generally low in volume. They are also missing some of the driver optimizations present on the `1/x` and `10/x` interfaces and hence are not suitable for handling production traffic.

- There is a mismatch between incoming and outgoing bandwidth. To resolve this issue, consider adding interfaces with more bandwidth (such as `10/x` interfaces) or creating an LA channel, which also provides redundancy. This needs to be done in the direction where the `Disc` counters are going up.

- The NetScaler is having a CPU crunch or a CPU tight loop, due to which all incoming packets are getting queued and are waiting for processing. If you are seeing resource usage shoot up, you need to work with Citrix to identify the underlying reason.

Network loops

When two interfaces from NetScaler are plugged into the same switch and are not part of a channel, they will effectively be in the same broadcast domain, and naturally a network loop will occur. This situation can be detected using the following command:

```
nsconmsg -g nic_tot_bdg_mac_moved -d current
```

```
root@ns#nsconmsg -g nic_tot_bdg_mac_moved -d current
Displaying performance information
NetScaler V20 Performance Data
NetScaler NS10.5: Build 55.8.nc, Date: Jan 25 2015, 23:55:26

reltime:mili second between two records Tue Aug 11 08:49:42 2015
  Index  rtime totalcount-val      delta rate/sec symbol-name&device-no
     0   10580             2          2       0 nic_tot_bdg_mac_moved interface(0/1)
     1       0             2          2       0 nic_tot_bdg_mac_moved interface(1/2)
     2    7002             3          1       0 nic_tot_bdg_mac_moved interface(0/1)
     3       0             3          1       0 nic_tot_bdg_mac_moved interface(1/2)
     4    7002             5          2       0 nic_tot_bdg_mac_moved interface(0/1)
     5       0             5          2       0 nic_tot_bdg_mac_moved interface(1/2)
```

A resolution to this would be to use VLAN techniques to separate out the broadcast domains. For production interfaces, you can also consider bundling the interfaces into a channel.

VLAN issues

While the VLAN implementation on NetScaler is pretty much standards-based, and as a topic is usually well understood, configuration issues are still relatively common. They sometimes arise because application delivery controllers, such as NetScaler, often require an uncommon overlap between networking-level and application-level skillsets.

Let's start with a quick review of VLANs, touching on areas that we didn't look at when discussing them in the context of High Availability, and then we'll delve into troubleshooting:

- VLANs are used to break down L2 domains.
- VLANs can be proprietary (Cisco ISL) or standards-based (such as 802.1Q, or simply dot1Q). NetScaler uses 802.1Q.
- VLAN tags are how frames are identified as being part of a particular VLAN.
- Any packet that doesn't contain a VLAN tag is assumed to belong to the Native VLAN of the interface picking up the packet.
- For VLANs to work correctly, either the packets need to be tagged with the right VLAN or the interface accepting the packet must have its native VLAN set to the correct one. Otherwise, it will drop the packet.
- When an interface is bound to a VLAN without the -tagged configuration option, the interface's native VLAN changes to the most recent bound VLAN. This is how you change an interface's native VLAN on NetScaler.

- To find out what VLAN a particular packet belongs to when looking at a trace (taken in `nstrace` format), expand the `NetScaler Packet Trace` node:

```
Frame 42: 138 bytes on wire (1104 bits), 138 bytes captured (1104 bits)
NetScaler Packet Trace
  Operation: NEW_RX (0xab)
  Nic No: 0
  Activity Flags: 0x0000
  SendCwnd: 0
  RTT: 0
  tsRecent: 0
  httpAbortTrackCode: connection is trackable (0)
  Source Node: 0
  Destination Node: 0
  Cluster Flags: 0x00 (None)
  Core Id: 0
  Vlan: 1
```

NetScaler format trace showing VLAN and other custom info

If NetScaler is dropping packets due to VLAN mismatches on the incoming packets, the `nic_err_vlan_promisc_tag_drops` counters go up. You can use the following command to detect this situation: `nsconmsg -g nic_err_vlan_promisc_tag_drops -d` current:

```
root@ns# nsconmsg -g nic_err_vlan_promisc_tag_drops -d current
Displaying performance information
NetScaler V20 Performance Data
NetScaler NS10.5: Build 55.8.nc, Date: Jan 25 2015, 23:55:26


reltime:mili second between two records Wed Apr 22 08:49:42 2015
  Index   rtime totalcount-val     delta rate/sec symbol-name&device-no
      1       0          90979        12        1 nic_err_vlan_promisc_tag_drops interface(1/1)
      2       0          91001        22        3 nic_err_vlan_promisc_tag_drops interface(1/1)
      3       0          91201        29        4 nic_err_vlan_promisc_tag_drops interface(1/1)
```

Unsupported SFPs

If a newly installed SFP constantly shows its status as DOWN, it is possible that the SFP is not being recognized. Verify that the interfaces are indeed Citrix-provided ones.

It is tempting to reuse SFPs from a decommissioned device, such as a switch; however, there will be compatibility issues in doing so. To ensure performance stays top notch, Citrix develops custom driver code that integrates tightly with specific tested interface models. Thus, when an interface that the code is not written for is plugged in, it can result in poor performance and also in error conditions, and is hence unsupported.

If the interface is instead a DAC cable, verify that it is a Citrix-approved one. CTX137259 lists the currently supported ones, which are as follows:

```
10GBASE-CU SFP+ Cable 1 Meter, passive P/N
10GBASE-CU SFP+ Cable 3 Meter, passive P/N
10GBASE-CU SFP+ Cable 5 Meter, passive P/N
```

Unsupported NICs can be identified by looking at `dmesg.boot`:

```
10/2: Ethernet address: 00:fe:cd:33:8b:d7
ix1: <Intel(R) PRO/10GbE PCI-Express Network Driver, Version -
ix1: ixgbe bus speed = 5.0Gbps and PCIe lane width = 8
ix1: IXGBE_PHYSICAL_LAYER_SFP_PLUS_CU
SFP+/SFP, vendor CISCO-TYCO    , part number 1-2053783-2
SFP+/SFP, vendor CISCO-TYCO    , part number 1-2053783-2
   10G 0x00 1G 0x00 CT 0x04
 [*** Unsupported SFP+/SFP type!]
```

While on the topic of SFP compatibility, the following text taken from the Citrix documentation is also good to note:

"While the SFP and SFP+ ports share the same physical dimensions, the 1GE SFP transceivers are not compatible to the SFP+ ports, and the 10 GE SFP+ transceivers are not compatible to the SFP ports. Do not install a 10 GE SFP+ transceiver in a 1 GE SFP port, and vice versa. The size of the socket enables you to install 1 GE SFP as well as 10 GE SFP+ transceivers. However, the NIC does not recognize the mismatched transceiver, the interface is not available, and the port LED lights are not switched on."

Link aggregation issues

On NetScaler, there are two ways of aggregating multiple interfaces, manual aggregation and LACP. Issues with aggregation most commonly arise in LACP environments. This could be either due to a mismatch in channel settings, or due to the switch/NetScaler not negotiating **LACPDUs (Link Aggregation Control Protocol Data Units)** or LACP messages as it should. The starting point for these issues should be to look at the LACPDU counters. In the following screenshot taken from a healthy environment, we see LACPDUs exchanged periodically:

```
root@ns#nsconmsg -g tx_lacp -g rx_lacp -s disptime=1 -d current | grep "(1/4)"
   5887    84015       14627        1        0 nic_tot_rx_lacpdus interface(1/4) Fri Aug 14 13:02:01 2015
   5879    84015       14609        1        0 nic_tot_tx_lacpdus interface(1/4) Fri Aug 14 13:02:01 2015
   5881    28006       14610        1        0 nic_tot_tx_lacpdus interface(1/4) Fri Aug 14 13:02:29 2015
   5887    28006       14628        1        0 nic_tot_rx_lacpdus interface(1/4) Fri Aug 14 13:02:29 2015
   5889    28006       14613        1        0 nic_tot_tx_lacpdus interface(1/4) Fri Aug 14 13:04:00 2015
```

LACPDUs sent and received on NetScaler

For an SDX, always remember to configure LACP from the SVM. This is the current recommendation and replaces the older one of configuring LACP directly on NetScaler instances themselves.

USIP networking issues

We talked about USIP in our opening chapter. When enabled, it preserves the client's source IP address (instead of substituting it with the SNIP) all the way to the server. If strategically used, this can increase the throughput of NetScaler by bypassing it on its return. **Direct Server Return** (CTX110501) is a configuration that uses USIP for this benefit. USIP does however pose two challenges that we need to be aware of:

- When USIP is enabled one of the following needs to be done:
  - NetScaler needs to be present in the return path to proxy the response
  - The server needs to use the VIP as its source IP if it is indeed going back to the client using Direct Server Return

  If neither is in place, any firewall, or the client itself, which is not expecting to see the Server's source IP, will drop the connection. If you are seeing issues where the application doesn't launch with USIP enabled, but works otherwise, take a trace on the Client and Server to verify that the return packets to the client match the VIP IP.

- A second problem with USIP is that of performance scalability. NetScaler can reuse TCP connections to the Server, as we discussed in the *Load balancing* section *Chapter 2, Traffic Management Features*. To be able to perform this optimization, NetScaler maintains a reuse pool where it keeps these *warm* optimized TCP connections, which can then be used agnostically for different clients. The use of USIP fragments the reuse pools, thereby reducing how much reuse is achievable.

So USIP should be considered only if the deployment is one that really needs it, such as in the case of Direct Server Return deployments.

Network issues from blocked source IPs

For a lot of enterprises, NetScaler straddles the external and internal environments. It sits in the DMZ, potentially behind a firewall and almost certainly in front of another. It is very well understood that the NSIP is used to manage NetScaler. A little less obvious is that NSIP (and not the SNIP) is also the default source IP used to access authentication Servers. This can pose problems since network security policies don't allow management IPs such as the NSIP to be able talk to backend servers such as the authentication Servers.

There are two ways to mitigate this challenge:

- Replace the LDAP server with an LB vServer that load balances the server. With this configuration, the source IP used changes to SNIP instead of NSIP.

- Use network profiles to specify the IPs you want to use to talk to certain servers. You can even specify a range of addresses using an IPSET to control exactly what IPs you want to talk to which Services/Servers.

In the following example, we are telling NetScaler which three IPs (3 SNIPs in this case) to use to talk to a service configured for authentication. This way you can always have NetScaler choose its IPs carefully, in order to play well with your firewall rules.

```
> add ipset snips_for_auth
 Done
> bind ipset snips_for_auth 10.72.142.51
 Done
> bind ipset snips_for_auth 10.72.142.52
 Done
> bind ipset snips_for_auth 10.72.142.53
 Done
> add netProfile netprofile_for_auth -srcIP snips_for_auth
 Done
> set service auth_service -netProfile netprofile_for_auth
 Done
```

When multiple SNIPs are available for balancing, NetScaler round robins the SNIPs that match the server subnet, so the firewalls should allow these multiple SNIPs; or you can use NetProfiles to tighten which of them get used.

Summary

In this chapter, we started with a look at NetScaler High Availability, which is key to ensuring that key services continue to be available despite a system-level issue on NetScaler. We looked at how the functionality works, which ports it uses, situations where High Availability can pose problems due to nodes not being able to see each other, and how to detect and remedy such situations.

In the second half of the chapter, we discussed how NetScaler handles packets it sees on the network, before focusing on layer 2 issues, which form the bulk of the network issues seen with NetScaler. We then concluded the chapter by touching on a couple of source IP-related areas and how to resolve them.

I hope this chapter has been useful to you. Please join me in the next as we look at troubleshooting the Application Firewall feature on NetScaler.

6
Application Firewall

While network-based attacks rely on vulnerabilities in transport layer protocols such as TCP or even lower level protocols, Web application attacks target vulnerabilities that are specific to the application, such as the input it accepts. Because this application-level visibility is missing in **Standard Network Firewalls**, they cannot offer sufficient fine-grained protection. This is where **web Application Firewalls** come in.

Application Firewall or **AppFirewall**, which is how it is commonly referred to, is available either as a standalone product, as an option with NetScaler Enterprise Edition or is included when purchasing NetScaler Platinum Edition. We will use the term AppFirewall everywhere in the chapter for easier reading.

 Payment Card Industry Data Security Standard (PCI-DSS) is a security standard that is aimed to certify whether your e-commerce infrastructure is secure enough for your customers to use for transactions. Web Application Firewalls are specified as Requirement 6.6 of the PCI-DSS standard, which lists that either proactive code reviews (non-trivial due to the personnel requirements) or a properly configured AppFirewall as a mandatory requirement.

While this book is about troubleshooting, application attacks are a new subject for many and hence knowing some of that background information and how it applies to NetScaler is crucial for troubleshooting.

To help you make the most of this chapter by covering this background info, we will use the following order for the topics:

- Deployment considerations
- HTTP changes that occur when using AppFirewall
- Application attacks and how AppFirewall protects against them
- Troubleshooting

Deployment considerations

While you can stand up a basic AppFirewall deployment quickly, things are far from plug and play and you shouldn't move to production without adequate testing. This topic discusses some of the considerations you should think about during your planning phase.

Deploying AppFirewall involves the following steps:

1. Enabling AppFirewall.
2. Creating an AppFirewall profile that specifies the protections that will be enabled.
3. Creating a policy to narrow down what types of requests need to be scanned.
4. Choosing a bind point to specify which VIPs will use these protections.

Creating a suitable profile and policy requires a thorough understanding of the application that you are protecting and the service that it is required to provide. Working with the developers of your applications is key to getting this configuration correct. Questions you should ask are:

- What kind of application am I trying to protect from malicious User input?
- The following points influence the profile type:
    - Is it an HTML based application?
    - Is it a Web service that typically involves XML?
    - Is it a Web 2.0 application that contains a bit of both (for example, xhtml or REST-based services)?

- Do you need a basic profile or an advanced profile? Choosing basic or advanced changes the protections that are enabled by default. The protections that get enabled by default when choosing an advanced profile turn on a behavior called **Sessionization**. Sessionization introduces AppFirewall cookies and hidden form fields for tracking. The protections that turn on sessionization are:
  - Start URL with URL closure
  - Cookie consistency
  - Form field consistency
  - Cross site request forgery

  So if you require these four protections, start with an advanced profile.

- Positive and negative security models. You need to consider whether you want to handcraft the protection for your applications or if you want to use signatures. In AppFirewall terms, handcrafting the protections you will apply by inspecting all possible valid User interactions and writing rules for them is known as using a positive security model. While this is a daunting task due to the number of combinations possible, the learning feature greatly alleviates the effort involved by silently monitoring and discovering requests that you can then commit at the click of a button.

  Using signatures on the other hand is the negative security model. This model has the advantage of allowing you to benefit from a widely applied knowledge of past and current vulnerabilities. Also, getting the latest protection is as simple as clicking on the update version button from the GUI:

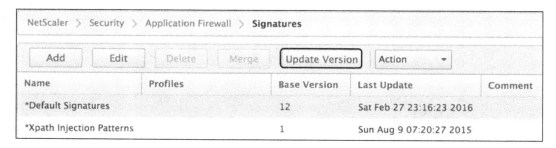

The source of these signatures is snort, which is a leading and trusted open source intrusion protection system. The recommended practice is to use a hybrid model where you apply specific rules you have learned but complement it by turning on signatures suitable for the Web application.

HTTP changes that occur when using AppFirewall

AppFirewall needs to modify packets in order to detect any sort of tampering. In addition to this, enabling certain protections requires AppFirewall to drop parts of the Server response (such as credit cards and other sensitive data) or alternatively transform them (such as keywords) so that special characters are rendered harmless. In this section, let's examine these changes:

- One of the first changes you will notice if using features that require sessionization is that AppFirewall adds session cookies to the application's own cookies.

```
Basic Profile                                Advanced Profile
GET /WebGoat HTTP/1.1                         GET /WebGoat HTTP/1.1
Host: 192.168.1.55                            Host: 192.168.1.55
Connection: keep-alive                        Connection: keep-alive
Accept: text/html,application/xhtml+xml,      Accept: text/html,application/xhtml+xml,application/xml;q
Upgrade-Insecure-Requests: 1                  Upgrade-Insecure-Requests: 1
User-Agent: Mozilla/5.0 (Windows NT 6.1;      User-Agent: Mozilla/5.0 (Windows NT 6.1; WOW64) AppleWebK
Accept-Language: en-US,en;q=0.8               Accept-Encoding: gzip, deflate, sdch
Accept-Encoding: identity                     Accept-Language: en-US,en;q=0.8

                                              HTTP/1.1 302 Found
HTTP/1.1 302 Found                            Server: Apache-Coyote/1.1
Server: Apache-Coyote/1.1                     Location: http://192.168.1.55/WebGoat/
Location: http://192.168.1.55/WebGoat/        Transfer-Encoding: chunked
Transfer-Encoding: chunked                    Date: Sat, 05 Sep 2015 14:48:48 GMT
Date: Sat, 05 Sep 2015 14:26:29 GMT           Set-Cookie: citrix_ns_id=IU7AJvGtDAgXvhUo6KCaakof8jkA000
```

AppFirewall Session Cookie when using Advanced Profiles

- When **Advanced Protections** are enabled, AppFirewall also removes caching headers so that instead of a conditional response, a full response is received. This is needed to allow AppFirewall to understand the context of the data being exchanged and drop the response if needed. This does however mean that you will see more requests to the backend servers when using **Advanced Protections**.

 Note that images are exempt from this behavior.

- When forwarding the Server's response back to the client, the Content Length header is dropped. Instead a new Transfer-Encoding: chunked header is added. This is a process called chunking, and indicates to the client that the exact size of the response is not known in advance. This step is necessary because the AppFirewall might have to introduce changes of its own to the response (such as drop sensitive data in the response), thereby impacting the size of the response. In such cases, the end of data is indicated by a zero-sized chunk:

Server Response	What is forwarded to User
GET /WebGoat/login.mvc HTTP/1.1 Host: 192.168.1.55 Connection: keep-alive Accept: text/html,application/xhtml+xml,application Upgrade-Insecure-Requests: 1 User-Agent: Mozilla/5.0 (Windows NT 6.1; WOW64) App Accept-Language: en-US,en;q=0.8 Cookie: JSESSIONID=E66D4230EE74695CD6E5C191D455BE29 Accept-Encoding: identity HTTP/1.1 200 OK Server: Apache-Coyote/1.1 Pragma: no-cache Expires: Thu, 01 Jan 1970 00:00:00 GMT Cache-Control: no-cache Cache-Control: no-store Content-Type: text/html;charset=ISO-8859-1 Content-Language: en-US Content-Length: 3188 Date: Sun, 13 Sep 2015 16:15:49 GMT	GET /WebGoat/login.mvc HTTP/1.1 Host: 192.168.1.55 Connection: keep-alive Accept: text/html,application/xhtml+xml,appli Upgrade-Insecure-Requests: 1 User-Agent: Mozilla/5.0 (Windows NT 6.1; WOW6 Accept-Encoding: gzip, deflate, sdch Accept-Language: en-US,en;q=0.8 Cookie: JSESSIONID=E66D4230EE74695CD6E5C191D4 HTTP/1.1 200 OK Server: Apache-Coyote/1.1 Pragma: no-cache Expires: Thu, 01 Jan 1970 00:00:00 GMT Cache-Control: no-cache Cache-Control: no-store Content-Type: text/html;charset=ISO-8859-1 Content-Language: en-US Date: Sun, 13 Sep 2015 16:15:49 GMT X-Expires-Orig: Thu, 01 Jan 1970 00:00:00 GMT Transfer-Encoding: chunked

 Citrix article CTX131488 is an excellent source for more on this topic; I highly encourage reading it as it is quite comprehensive in explaining the packet changes involved.

Configuring logging

Logs are crucial when troubleshooting AppFirewall issues. For AppFirewall to log any requests when one of the configured protections receives a hit, logging needs to be enabled for that specific protection. These logs are written to /var/log/ns.log. In the interest of preserving them for longer than the NetScaler logging process permits, you can also consider sending them to a syslog server through a syslog policy.

Logging works independent of blocking. To explain this, consider the following screenshot:

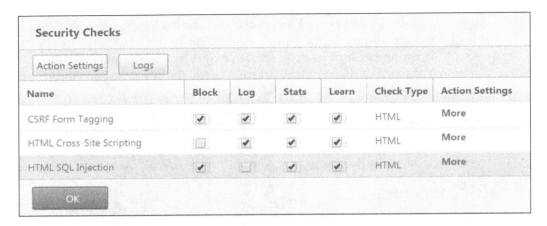

As a result of this configuration:

- CSRF violations will both be blocked and all blocking will be logged
- XSS attacks will not be blocked but you will still see log entries to warn you
- SQL injection attacks will be blocked silently (not useful if you are trying to troubleshoot)

 Note that AppFirewall also supports **CEF** (**Common Event Format**) logging, a popular open standard for logging. Using CEF logging helps when you want to use third-party applications to aggregate your logs. The command is `set AppFirewall settings CEFLogging ON`.

Application attacks and AppFirewall protections

This section is a quick review of some of the important web application attacks, how they work, and what AppFirewall does to protect against them. This knowledge is invaluable since it helps to better understand log entries when troubleshooting.

We will just use the terms **User**, **Attacker**, **AppFirewall**, **Website**, and **Server** in our examples to keep it simple.

Note that these attacks and AppFirewall's capability to protect against them can be demoed using WebGoat, which is a deliberately vulnerable site, provided by OWASP. It is free and extremely handy for picking up this knowledge hands on.

Cross-site scripting

Modern Web pages require scripts to function for rich functionality. **Cross-site scripting (XSS)** is an attack that targets Web pages that accept scripted input without properly validating them. Here is an example of one such attack:

1. `http://example.com/` is an e-commerce site that also happens to have a page for comments: `http://www.example.com/comments`.

2. `http://example.com/` does not validate User input when comments are posted.

3. Attacker posts scripted content (for example, JavaScript) on this comments page.

4. The script when executed, sends the session cookie of the User to a remote server managed by the Attacker.

5. A number of unsuspected users visit the site.

6. All users visiting the comments page are vulnerable to XSS and have their cookies sent to a remote server owned by the Attacker.

7. Attacker then uses these cookies to impersonate the victims.

To protect against XSS attacks

NetScaler AppFirewall when used in front of a Web server, scans all requests looking for potentially risky tags, such as the tag `<script>`, which indicates that the input is a script. When such a tag is found, depending on the configuration in the profile, it can either block or transform the request to render it harmless.

The following screenshot shows one such blocked attempt:

```
PFW APPFW_XSS 767 0 :  192.168.1.90 894-PPE0 rxSb4SCSFgcVKTbf8suwWAPlwaEA000 advanced-pro
file http://192.168.1.55/WebGoat/attack?Screen=28&menu=900 Cross-site script check failed
 for field address1="Bad tag: script" <blocked>
```

With regards to how unsafe tags are determined, there exists a predefined list. This list can be seen by navigating to **Application Firewall | Signatures | Default Signatures**. This list can be modified to suit your Web page's functionality by creating a copy of the original signature and editing the patterns and then applying that signature under the profile.

SQL injection

All e-commerce sites use a database of some form in the backend to be able to process product orders and record them. The Web page that is at the frontend of this database should be able to detect requests that are malicious and catch them before they get to the database layer where the focus is more performance and functionality, rather than security. SQL injection attacks use knowledge of SQL commands and vulnerabilities in SQL software to be able to directly manipulate entries in the database.

Here is an example of a SQL injection attack:

1. Attacker accesses the login page of an e-commerce site.

2. The login page accepts input from valid users and displays confidential information only as it pertains to the User logged in, such as their recent orders.

3. The login works using a SQL query that is run against a credentials table. For example `SELECT username FROM User_table WHERE username='input_ username' AND password='input_password'`.

4. Attacker, with the knowledge of the SQL backend in place, instead of providing his username and password, enters `admin` as username and `random_password OR 1=1` as the password.

5. The `random_password` is incorrect and this login attempt should have failed. However, the query now contains an `OR` with a condition `1=1`, which will always evaluate to `true`, hence the login succeeds.

6. Attacker now has admin access to the system.

7. The following is a screenshot of an attempted SQL injection request, notice how the `employee_name` field contains an `OR`, which is a SQL keyword:

```
POST http://192.168.1.55/WebGoat/attack?Screen=6&menu=1100 HTTP/1.1
Host: 192.168.1.55
Connection: keep-alive
Content-Length: 41
Accept: */*
Origin: http://192.168.1.55
X-Requested-With: XMLHttpRequest
User-Agent: Mozilla/5.0 (Windows NT 6.1; WOW64) AppleWebKit/537.36 (KHTML, like Gecko)
Chrome/45.0.2454.93 Safari/537.36
Content-Type: application/x-www-form-urlencoded; charset=UTF-8
Referer: http://192.168.1.55/WebGoat/start.mvc
Accept-Encoding: gzip, deflate
Accept-Language: en-US,en;q=0.8
Cookie: JSESSIONID=8B171042280296316745AB30E9EB3E45;
citrix_ns_id=5rpTb1eoVvZtoCSBwWZe5JTLDHMA000;
citrix_ns_id_192.168.1.55_%2F_wat=SlNFU1NJT05JRF9f?NB2dUnEVUtEB0yS6v7CtO5Q1E9oA#p9WeT3U
cPBdPvu/06UwpvPs8KJYA&

employee_name=rvt&password=mypassword' OR '1' = '1&action=Login
```

To protect against SQL injection attacks

AppFirewall engine has been coded to recognize SQL commands and keywords so when enabled, it blocks all entries that look like SQL, unless learned and applied as exceptions:

```
Sep 20 19:23:25 <local0.info> 192.168.1.50 09/20/2015:17:23:25 GMT 192_50_ns 0-PPE-0 : AP
PFW APPFW_SQL 410 0 :  192.168.1.90 385-PPE0 - advanced-profile http://192.168.1.55/WebGo
at/attack?Screen=6&menu=1100 SQL Keyword check failed for field password="..OR '1' = '1('
)" <blocked>
```

As with XSS protection, SQL injection protection also relies on a set of keywords already predefined on NetScaler, which can be accessed at: **Application Firewall | Signatures | Default Signatures** and can be adjusted by making a copy of this signature with the necessary changes to the keyword list.

Forceful browsing attacks

Forceful browsing refers to the approach of manipulating URL paths in the browser directly instead of arriving at them by clicking on the links in the previous page. If the server doesn't prevent these, the Attackers can try to guess the path on the server and access content they are not entitled to.

As an example, consider a fictitious URL: www.example.com/users/aHacker/agenda.

While it might not be intended, the path is predictable for different users, if the name of the User is known. The attacker can try to guess the login name of the User, for example, `aUser` and try to access their agenda by force browsing to: `www.example.com/users/aUser/agenda`.

To protect against forceful browsing

AppFirewall supports **Start URLs**. Start URLs allow AppFirewall administrators to control what the starting URL for accessing a site should be. This when combined with the URL closure feature enforces the need for users to start on a certain landing page for the site and users will only be allowed to visit pages for which the URL was seen being provided by the server – that is they will need to click and move between pages instead of being able to manually edit the URLs.

Attacks based on Parameter tampering

Web-based applications use parameters such as cookies and hidden form fields to track the state information for an ongoing customer order. Unless these fields are being monitored, an Attacker can tamper with cookies or hidden fields to modify the price or a product prior to purchasing, thus potentially buying it for much cheaper than the displayed price. Let's look at a few examples of such attacks.

Cookie tampering

Web applications rely heavily on cookies for functionality. Cookies serve primarily to identify users, thus they are very critical to a site's security. **Cookie tampering** (also called **cookie poisoning**) refers to an Attacker being able to modify cookies that denote something important about the transaction, such as the price or the User's identity.

To protect against cookie tampering

When the Server sets a cookie, AppFirewall starts watching it by hashing and signing the cookie and then including that hash as part of each request/response. It will then compare the cookie hash on all subsequent requests from the User to the original value to confirm that the cookie hasn't been tampered with.

In my example, I tried to mess with the `PRICEID`, a cookie that tracks the price of all items in the shopping cart at the time of checkout. I tried to buy an item of $15000 (HEX 3A98) for a price of $5000 (HEX 1388). AppFirewall detects this modification and rejects the cookie.

The original request is as follows:

```
Cookie: PRICEID=3A98; citrix_ns_id=5rpTbleoVvZtoCSBwTLDHMA000; citrix_ns_
id_192.168.1.55_%2F_wat=9f?NB2dUnEVUtEB0yS6v7CtO5Q1E9oA#p9WeT3UcPBdPvu/06
UwpvPs8KJYA&
```

The tampered request is as follows:

```
Cookie: PRICEID=1388; citrix_ns_id=5rpTbleoVvZtoCSBwTLDHMA000; citrix_ns_
id_192.168.1.55_%2F_wat=9f?NB2dUnEVUtEB0yS6v7CtO5Q1E9oA#p9WeT3UcPBdPvu/06
UwpvPs8KJYA&
```

AppFirewall will block the request with cookie `PRICEID=1388` since the hash no longer matches after the modification. The log will look like this:

```
Sep 20 23:29:07 <local0.info> 192.168.1.50 09/20/2015:21:29:07 GMT 192_50_ns 0-PPE-0 : AP
PFW APPFW_COOKIE 546 0 :  192.168.1.90 702-PPE0 0p4BlpuaRyAvXKqqql14NRkQvjcA000 advanced-
profile http://192.168.1.55/esite/scart?Stage=preval Cookie validation failed for PRICEID
<blocked>
```

> Note that to track the application cookies, AppFirewall groups all the cookies together, hashes, and then signs them. It will generate one `wlf` cookie to track all persistent application cookies, and one `wat` cookie to track all application session cookies. CTX131488 discusses this behavior.

Hidden field tampering

Many interactive websites use hidden fields to keep track of User choices such as the item chosen, its price, and so on. These form fields while *hidden* from the User's view and are still available to see when looking at the source code of a web page, at which point they can also be modified. Attackers can use this property to modify, for example, the price of items before they pay, thereby buying something at a much lower price than advertised by the site.

Here's a quick illustration using WebGoat as the vulnerable site:

Shopping Cart		
Shopping Cart Items -- To Buy Now	Price	Quantity
56 inch HDTV (model KTV-551)	2999.99	1
The total charged to your credit card:	$2999.99	Purchase

The field **Price** is also present as a hidden field that the server uses to track the final price of the purchase. Fiddler has a hidden **fields** tab that allows you to see hidden fields and even modify them. In the following screenshot, I lowered the value of hidden field **Price** from **$2999.99** to just **$10.99**:

Original value for Price		Modified value for Price	
Name ▲	Value	Name ▲	Value
as_fid	tClEqVnFaTESZgxfrTdo	as_fid	tClEqVnFaTESZgxfrTdo
Price	2999.99	Price	10.99
QTY	1	QTY	1
SUBMIT	UpdateCart	SUBMIT	UpdateCart

Image: "Price" in Form fields modified to buy TV for cheaper

If this change isn't detected and blocked, Attacker can purchase the TV for a fraction of its price.

To protect against hidden field tampering

When **Form Field Consistency** check is enabled, AppFirewall keeps track of the hidden fields and what their values were at each step in the session. When the same modification is repeated with AppFirewall **Form Field Consistency** (which is the name of the protection that enables this) enabled, the change in **Hidden Field** value during one of the requests is detected and blocked. Following is a log entry of a block:

```
Sep 22 23:24:02 <local0.info> 192.168.1.50 09/22/2015:21:24:02 GMT 192_50_ns 0-PPE-0 : APP
168.1.90 695-PPE0 5M/hFzrLrd42z6is04xf52GrzUEA000 advanced-profile http://192.168.1.55/Web
consistency check failed for field "" <blocked>
```

Buffer overflow attacks via long URLs and queries

All programs use buffers, that is, memory allocations to which parts of the program can be moved to for editing/manipulating before it's executed. Buffer sizes are finite.

During a buffer overflow attack, an attacker forces the application to accept more data than its buffers are designed to handle. By pushing the buffers past their limits, the Attacker can overwrite memory areas related to other functions, and in the process change the return address of those functions.

Return addresses are how a program knows the next instructions to process. So effectively, the attacker can change the application's flow of processing through a buffer overflow attack. For example, they can cause the authentication function to be bypassed.

To protect against buffer overflow attacks

AppFirewall can be configured to limit input values for URLs, Headers, and Cookies. The following is a block seen when the URL length exceeds what has been configured as allowed on AppFirewall:

```
Sep 22 22:55:16 <local0.info> 192.168.1.50 09/22/2015:20:55:16 GMT 192 50
ns 0-PPE-0 : APPFW APPFW_BUFFEROVERFLOW_URL 446 0 :  192.168.1.90 387-PPE0
 rgKDYh1BX/YZ0Hh7Wvz7i6a/PhoA000 advanced-profile URL length(20) is greate
r than maximum allowed(10): http://192.168.1.55/ <blocked>
```

Cross Site Request Forgery

Cross Site Request Forgery (CSRF) attack, as its name suggests, relies on the Attacker forging requests, such as bank transfers via a victim who is logged in to their account when the attack happens. The `logged-in` is important here, as this is important for the attack to succeed:

1. The Attacker crafts a malicious link and gets the victim to click on it.
2. This might be done by means of social engineering.
3. The victim clicks on the malicious link.
4. If the victim happens to be logged in to their bank website, at this time.
5. The browser while executing the link, might also include the necessary cookies since the session is still open.
6. This results in an amount being illegally transferred from the victim's bank account to the Attackers.

To protect against CSRF attacks

AppFirewall uses two key mechanisms:

- CSRF Form Tagging
- Referer Header Validation

With CSRF Form Tagging enabled, all forms sent by the server (such as forms for funds transfers) are tagged with a **Form ID (fid)**, which is a randomly generated code.

Form IDs are embedded within the HTML source of the page. Here is what they look like when examining using fiddler:

```
as_sfid [#] (hidden) : AAAAAAVap-pXJLaAsTzlj_DB6pUgKwyVwvY5Da3lph42-VNGaN2z
as_fid [#] (hidden) : KBUhP1cn6shbBEjCvKiQ
```

When the User returns the completed form, NetScaler checks to see if the returned form contains the Form ID provided to the User earlier. This way even if the Attacker manages to get the victim to unknowingly generate a request with all the necessary cookies, the transfer will fail since the form to be used was never seen being served by the server. Here is an example of an attempt blocked by AppFirewall due to the Form ID being missing in the returned form:

```
Sep 27 17:04:08 <local0.info> 192.168.1.50 09/27/2015:15:04:08 GMT 192_50_ns 0-PPE-0 : APPFW
APPFW_CSRF_TAG 568 0 : 192.168.1.90 615-PPE0 7OHTLfhFRxnZkTgsXXSTTReTjxsA000 advanced-profile
http://rvbank.lab/transfer?pname=hk3r&amount=10000 CSRF Tag validation failed. <blocked>
```

> Note that the Integrated Caching feature and CSRF form tagging are not compatible.

The `referer` header is used to provide information to the server on the origin of the current request, that is, what site the User was previously on before being redirected to the current page. For example, if you visited `http://www.example1.com/` and were redirected to `http://example2.com/`, the `referer` header on the redirect, if present, will show **Referer: https://example.com**.

The `referer` header can only be generated by the browser and cannot be forced by an attacker, which makes it a formidable mechanism in protecting against CSRF attacks. It means that the AppFirewall (through appropriate configuration) can restrict which redirect-based requests are admitted and which ones are dropped, based on the domain name of the original site.

Enabling the `referer` header validation is done in the **Start URL Settings** since both protections rely on this check:

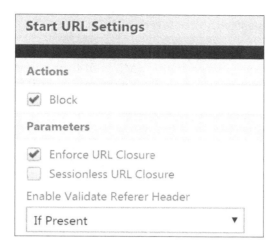

On enabling `referer` header validation, NetScaler looks to see if the value of the `referer` header matches any of the exceptions configured in the start URL whitelist. If not, the request is rejected.

The following screenshot is an example of a block due to `referer` header mismatch:

```
Sep 27 17:44:40 <local0.info> 192.168.1.50 09/27/2015:13:44:40 GMT 192_50 ns 0-PPE-0 : APPFW
APPFW_REFERER_HEADER 412 0 : 192.168.1.90 355-PPE0 gVmAXEeviopbpsRezj6InjZuhh4A000 advanced-
profile http://rvbank.lab/transfer?pname=hk3r&amount=10000 Referer header check failed: refe
rer header URL 'http://blog33rs.lab/comments.php' not in Start URL or closure list <blocked>
```

Referer mismatch

 Note that some browsers may not present `referer` headers or this might be turned off for privacy reasons, so an option to validate only if present is also available.

XML protections

In the current e-commerce landscape, web services serve a very important purpose, allowing application servers to talk to each other over the Internet. XML, using HTTP as the transport protocol, is a core component of Web Services and as such, needs to be protected.

Web services share some of the same vulnerabilities as HTML applications, which is why you see some of the protections offered to be the same, such as XML, XSS, and XML SQL injection protections. However, XML does have its uniqueness that is a result of how XML requests are structured.

Security offered by AppFirewall for XML mainly takes the form of understanding this structure and inspecting requests for XML well-formedness. XML is a lot stricter than HTML in terms of how the tags (called elements in XML) are used. If a poorly formed XML request is not caught, it can cause the XML Parser to crash and result in a denial of service.

The following is a simple example of a malformed request; here the poorly formed request has a mismatch between the opening and closing tags.

Well Formed XML Request	Poorly Formed XML Request

`GET / HTTP/1.1`
`Content-type: application/xml`
`Host: 10.72.142.85`
`Accept: */*`
`Content-Length:230`
 	
`<?xml version="1 .0" encoding="ISO-8859 -1"?>`
`<Bio>`
`    <Name>`
`        <First> Raghu</First>`
`        <Last> Varma </Last>`
`    </Name>`
`    <Status Employed=" Yes">`
`        As an Engineer`
`    </Status>`
`</Bio>`
	`GET / HTTP/1.1`
	`Content-type: application/xml`
	`Host: 10.72.142.85`
	`Accept: */*`
	`Content-Length:233`
	
	`<?xml version="1 .0" encoding="ISO-8859 -1"?>`
	`<Bio>`
	`    <Name>`
	`        <First> Raghu</First>`
	`        <Last> Varma </Last>`
	`    </Name>`
	`    <JobStatus Employed=" Yes">`
	`        As an Engineer`
	`    </Status>`
	`</Bio>`

On seeing the mismatched tag, AppFirewall throws an XML Format check failed error, as shown in the following screenshot:

```
Feb 29 20:05:03 <local0.warn> 127.0.0.2 02/29/2016:19:05:03 GMT ns 80 0-PPE-0 :
default APPFW APPFW_XML_ERR_NOT_WELLFORMED 1642 0 :  10.68.16.22 1671-PPE0 - we
b20 http://10.72.142.85/ XML Format check failed: Message is not a well-formed
XML.Error string is 'syntax error'.  Offset:16 <blocked>
```

The error is not necessarily the most intuitive to follow, as it doesn't tell you what tag to correct. But this is where the knowledge of well-formedness rules comes in handy. The main rules to consider for well formedness are:

- XML documents must have a root element
- XML elements must have a closing tag
- XML tags are case sensitive

- XML elements must be properly nested
- XML attribute values must be quoted

Source: `http://www.w3schools.com/tags/tag_doctype.asp`

 Regardless of the other protections being enabled for XML, a request is first processed for well-formedness if enabled. If this check fails, the rest of the checks won't be done, to conserve resources, the request is immediately blocked.

Signatures

Signatures use knowledge of known vulnerabilities, but also allow you to create your own rules using the current signature as a template.

To understand what each rule in the signature looks for, you can click into the signature and look at the **Rule Patterns**. The following is a random example I picked for demonstration.

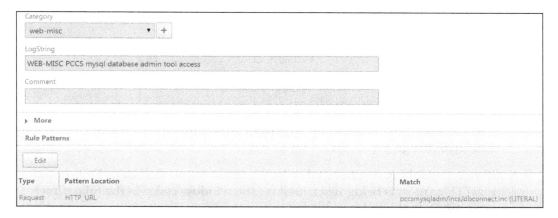

This rule protects against a vulnerability that existed in the PCCS MySql database admin tool, where, by simply browsing to the path in the **Match** column, anyone could get a hold of the `Admin` password. To use signatures correctly, you need to know what your servers are in terms of OS and applications they are running, and based on this knowledge, you choose the rules that form the signature.

You can also customize each signature, using expressions, which gives you the flexibility of the NetScaler policy engine or writes Regex for maximum flexibility. A recommendation here is to use the **fastmatch** option where possible, which greatly reduces CPU overhead when looking for patterns. This option is available when adding a new *Signature Rule*, under the **Rule Patterns** page.

Troubleshooting

AppFirewall is powerful, but not necessarily plug and play as we discussed. Issues with AppFirewall arise in the form of applications failing when the feature is turned on.

Identifying application Firewall blocks

It is important to know how to tell if the application is failing because AppFirewall is blocking it. There are several ways to identify if this is the case:

- Under the **Profile** settings, you can configure an error object that can be useful when a User calls in to the helpdesk with an application access issue caused by AppFirewall blocking the request:

  You can configure this text under **Application Firewall | Profile | Profile Settings**.

- If you are looking at a trace taken on NetScaler or on the User's PC where a HTTP request is being reset, look for the window code. In the following screenshot, that window code is 9845:

Source	Destination	Length	Info
Client IP	VIP Protected by	118	51382→80 [SYN] Seq=0 Win=8192 Len=0 MSS=1460 WS=256 SACK_PERM=1
VIP Protected by AppFw	Client IP	112	80→51382 [SYN, ACK] Seq=0 Ack=1 Win=8190 Len=0 MSS=1460
Client IP	VIP Protected by	106	51382→80 [ACK] Seq=1 Ack=1 Win=64240 Len=0
Client IP	VIP Protected by	627	POST /transferFunds.do?acctId=123456 HTTP/1.1
VIP Protected by AppFw	Client IP	112	80→51382 [ACK] Seq=1 Ack=522 Win=65535 Len=0
VIP Protected by AppFw	Client IP	112	80→51382 [RST, ACK] Seq=1 Ack=522 Win=9845 Len=0

  9845 means the reset has been sent because an AppFirewall protection policy has been triggered.

- If you have set up your profile for troubleshooting that is, with the log option enabled for the protections that have been set to block, you should see a log entry every time a request is blocked. This entry is worth gold since it gives you a lot of important detail. Look at the following screenshot for an example:

```
Sep 27 17:47:58 <local0.info> 192.168.1.50 09/27/2015:15:47:58 GMT 192_50_ns 0-PPE-0 : APPFW
APPFW_REFERER_HEADER 653 0 : 192.168.1.90 736-PPE0 B+hVVhWXOhMu7mKkxFKED2gpUmYA000 advanced
-profile http://rvbank.lab/transfer?pname=hk3r&amount=10000 Referer header check failed: ref
erer header not present <blocked>
```

AppFirewall log entry displaying a number of useful details

In the preceding screenshot, we have date and time in the local time zone, NSIP, which is useful if you are trying to parse logs based on NSIP, AppFirewall protection that is triggering the block, Client IP, AppFirewall profile hit that was triggered, URL, and keyword that triggered the block.

- You can also use `nsconmsg` and `grep` for the counter `as_err`. It will help you identify what AppFirewall violations are seen as well as the rate. The command: `nsconmsg -g as_err -d current`:

```
root@192_50_ns# nsconmsg -g as_err -d current
Displaying performance information
NetScaler V20 Performance Data
NetScaler NS10.5: Build 58.11.nc, Date: Jul 14 2015, 13:28:13


reltime:mili second between two records Sun Sep 27 19:21:41 2015
  Index   rtime totalcount-val      delta rate/sec symbol-name&device-no
      0   21001              37          1        0 as_err_missing_referer
```

- The `stat AppFirewall` command will help you get a quick overview of what violations AppFirewall is seeing when enabled. This allows you to build a threat profile for your environment.

HTML/XML Violation Statistics	Rate (/s)	Total
Start URL	0	2
Deny URL	0	0
Referer header	0	0
Buffer overflow	0	15
Cookie consistency	0	0
CSRF form tag	0	9
HTML Cross-site scripting	0	10
HTML SQL injection	0	0
Field format	0	20
Field consistency	0	0
Credit card	0	0
Safe object	0	0
Signature Violations	0	43

Users reporting XXXX patterns in web pages

AppFirewall is also capable of transforming and sometimes, removing content in the responses when it finds them unsafe, or in the case of credit card numbers, confidential:

```
Sep 27 21:02:07 <local0.info> 192.168.1.50 09/27/2015:19:02:07 GMT 192_50_ns 0-PPE-0 :
APPFW APPFW_SAFECOMMERCE_XFORM 1060 0 :  192.168.1.90 1356-PPE0 - advanced-profile
http://rvbank.lab/cc.html Transformed (xout) potential credit card numbers seen in
server response <transformed>

Sep 27 21:02:07 <local0.info> 192.168.1.50 09/27/2015:19:02:07 GMT 192_50_ns 0-PPE-0 :
APPFW APPFW_SAFECOMMERCE 1061 0 :  192.168.1.90 1356-PPE0 - advanced-profile http://rv
bank.lab/cc.html Maximum number of potential credit card numbers seen <blocked>
```

When you see unexpected xxxx where it should be, check the profile settings to see if any credit card protections have been configured. This has the potential to sometimes trigger false positives since a lot of numbers can resemble credit card numbers. You will need to configure exceptions for these.

Performance issues when enabling AppFirewall

The following are the performance issues when AppFirewall is enabled:

- A very tempting expression when configuring AppFirewall policies, is the expression `true`. This is useful during troubleshooting, since it provides a guaranteed way for AppFirewall to trigger. However, if used for actual production, depending on how much traffic and how comprehensive the protection policies, this can easily result in a significant performance hit. A better practice is to create policies that match the profile of requests, such as: `HTTP.REQ.HOSTNAME.EQ("example.com")`.

- Similarly, Regex, which is a particular favorite of administrators coming from the scripting world, is very tempting to use and is sometimes absolutely necessary to achieve a certain level of flexibility. However, Regex too when applied to too many requests has a performance impact. Where possible, use literal matches and the **fastmatch** option we talked about in the *Signatures* section.

- A final performance issue is that of scanning large files. To be able to protect effectively, AppFirewall needs to look at each file and request it in its entirety, and not as individual packets that only contain part of the information. This is not a problem for most HTTP requests and responses, which are generally in the range of kilobytes. File uploads, however, can get much larger. They have the potential to cause AppFirewall to hang. To avoid such situations, the maximum size that AppFirewall will accept is set to 20000000 bytes (~20 MB) by default. The downside of this setting is that AppFirewall will throw an error when the size exceeds this limit. You can, of course, increase this limit but will need to carefully weigh out the performance impact.

- NetScaler 11.0 now allows requests to be streamed instead of accumulating all of the request. A certain amount is still accumulated, but only as much as necessary at the time to be able to run its checks. AppFirewall streaming can be enabled on a profile using the following command:

```
> set AppFirewall profile web20 -streaming ON
```

Ruling out AppFirewall as a potential cause

There will be occasions where, having confirmed AppFirewall as the source of a problem, you want to bypass it for a subset of users or URLs.

The easiest way to do this is to bind the APPFIREWALL_BYPASS profile to an appropriately chosen policy. The following is an example that does this for traffic to OWA:

```
add AppFirewall policy bypass_AppFirewall_for_owa "http.REQ.URL.PATH.
CONTAINS(\"/owa/\")" APPFIREWALL_BYPASS
```

Summary

In this chapter, we introduced Application Firewall and discussed the deployment considerations. We then looked at how AppFirewall modifies various HTTP aspects of the packet, before exploring the most common attacks, how they work, and how AppFirewall protects against them. Finally, we concluded the chapter with a look at common issues and troubleshooting. In the next chapter, we will take a look at NetScaler gateway.

NetScaler Gateway™ 7

NetScaler Gateway (formerly known as **Access Gateway Enterprise Edition**) is the remote access feature of NetScaler. It has all the usual bells and whistles of an enterprise class hardened VPN solution, and is also the secure frontend of choice for XenApp, XenDesktop, and XenMobile.

As a frontend for XenApp and XenDesktop solutions, NetScaler Gateway understands how to work with **ICA** (**Independent Computing Architecture**) and can provide policy-based control for published applications and desktops.

 ICA is a Citrix proprietary protocol which is optimized for published applications and desktop delivery.

As a frontend for XenMobile, NetScaler provides a MicroVPN capability that is critical for enabling Worx applications to communicate securely with the backend services.

We will cover the necessary background and troubleshooting for these features in the following order:

- Basic and Smart Access modes
- NetScaler Gateway VPNs
- NetScaler integration with XenApp and XenDesktop
- NetScaler integration with XenMobile

Basic and Smart Access Modes

Before we look at the individual features, it's important to understand the different modes that the Gateway VPN Vserver can be set to. Depending on the vServer mode chosen, which in turn permits specific functionalities, you might require additional licenses called **Concurrent User (CCU)** licenses for its functioning. Here's a quick summary of what Basic and Smart Access Modes provide.

Basic mode

The following are the characteristics of Basic Mode:

- Does not consume or need any CCUs
- Provides secure (encrypted) access to published applications or desktops (ICA Proxy)
- No VPNs or **Endpoint Analysis (EPA)** capabilities are provided
- This mode is very similar in functionality to the legacy Secure Gateway product

Smart Access mode

This consumes one CCU per session. Here are the additional things you can do with a Smart Access vServer:

- SSL VPN tunnels
- Split tunneling
- EPA and quarantining
- Policy-based access to published apps and desktops (Smart Access)
- MicroVPNs for XenMobile
- RDP Proxy

Following is a show license screenshot, which shows that 105 CCUs are installed; these can be used for VPN tunnels, Smart Access or for XenMobile Micro VPNs. On the other hand, the number of ICA proxy sessions has no limit:

```
> sh license | grep VPN

SSL VPN: YES   (Maximum users = 105)   (Maximum ICA users = Unlimited)
```

CCU licenses are tied to the configured hostname of NetScaler, unlike feature licenses, which are tied to the HostID (which is a MAC address).

NetScaler Gateway comes installed with five free Smart Access licenses. The 105 licenses seen in the screenshot are because I added a 100-CCU license.

Also, XenApp and XenDesktop Platinum licenses already provide you with a certain number of CCU licenses, so you might not need to purchase them separately if you are using NetScaler Gateway with the platinum versions of these products.

NetScaler Gateway™ VPNs

To get a baseline idea of what a successful login and resource access should look like, over the next few pages we will examine the various stages of a NetScaler Gateway VPN session using a Wireshark capture. The intent is to provide you with the knowledge of a *known good trace* that you can compare against when troubleshooting issues.

We will then follow up with a discussion of the troubleshooting tools and techniques for troubleshooting NetScaler Gateway VPNs.

Examining VPN session launch using Wireshark

VPN session establishment is a multi-step process where the client and NetScaler exchange a number of control messages. To make this exchange easier to digest, let's break this into different phases:

- **Phase 1**: The EPA exchange
- **Phase 2**: The authentication exchange
- **Phase 3**: Post login exchange

 To avoid duplication, we will assume the SSL handshake was successful. SSL handshake troubleshooting would be exactly the same as covered in the SSL section of *Chapter 2, Traffic Management Features*.

Phase 1 – The EPA exchange

Pre-authentication, if configured, will be the first step of the exchange:

	Source	Destination	Protocol	Info
				http && ssl
201	VPN Client	VPN Vserver	HTTP	GET / HTTP/1.1
202	VPN Vserver	VPN Client	HTTP	HTTP/1.1 302 Object Moved (text/html)
275	VPN Client	VPN Vserver	HTTP	GET /epatype HTTP/1.1
276	VPN Vserver	VPN Client	HTTP	HTTP/1.1 200 OK (text/html)
301	VPN Client	VPN Vserver	HTTP	GET /epaq HTTP/1.1
303	VPN Vserver	VPN Client	HTTP	HTTP/1.1 200 OK
331	VPN Client	VPN Vserver	HTTP	GET /epas HTTP/1.1
333	VPN Vserver	VPN Client	HTTP	HTTP/1.1 200 OK (text/html)
347	VPN Client	VPN Vserver	HTTP	GET /vpn/index.html HTTP/1.1
363	VPN Vserver	VPN Client	HTTP	HTTP/1.1 200 OK (text/html)

1. The client tries to load the VPN login page and, since pre-authentication is configured, gets redirected to /epatype page (Packet 275).

2. The Client visits /epatype and learns what the settings for EPA and device certificate check are. In our example, EPA was enabled and device certificate check is off, which is reflected in NetScaler's response:

```
Line-based text data: text/html
Epa:on;deviceCert:off;
```

3. Now that the client knows EPA is configured, it needs to find out what those EPA checks to be carried out are. To do this, it sends a GET to /epaq.

4. In our test, we are doing a check for domain membership. Hence, the client sees the following text in the response:

```
Hypertext Transfer Protocol
HTTP/1.1 200 OK\r\n
TunnelType:nocmp\r\n
Set-Cookie: NSC_ERRM=xyz;Path=/;expires=Wednesday, 09-Nov-1999 23:12:40 GMT\r\n
CSEC: reg_0_HKEY_LOCAL_MACHINE\\SYSTEM\\CurrentControlSet\\Services\\Tcpip\\Parameters_Domain_xmx.lab;\r\n
```

5. The EPA plugin on the client runs this check and returns a CSEC value that represents the result. In our case, that check passes since the machine is a domain member. So, the GET /epas contains 0, which indicates success. In the troubleshooting section, we will talk about how to interpret this value.

```
Hypertext Transfer Protocol
GET /epas HTTP/1.1\r\n
Cookie: NSC_EPAC=ec0d6a4e008047bfea7f65bf7e8bec6b\r\n
CSEC: 0\r\n
```

6. The client then receives the **Login** page from NetScaler.

Phase 2 – The authentication exchange

The User provides their credentials. As a result, authentication and group extraction happen.

 By default, it is the NSIP that gets used for communication with the authentication server. However, using a Netprofile, you can force this to be a specific SNIP to suit your firewall rules.

1. The User authentication happens as a `POST` request with the credentials.

```
398  Client PC        Gateway VIP      HTTP   POST /cgi/login HTTP/1.1  (application/x-www-form-urlencoded)
409  NSIP             Active Directory LDAP   bindRequest(1) "administrator@xmx.lab" simple
412  Active Directory NSIP             LDAP   bindResponse(1) success
414  NSIP             Active Directory LDAP   searchRequest(2) "dc=xmx,dc=lab" wholeSubtree
416  Active Directory NSIP             LDAP   searchResEntry(2) "CN=bob leroy,CN=Users,DC=xmx,DC=lab"  | se
418  NSIP             Active Directory LDAP   bindRequest(3) "CN=bob leroy,CN=Users,DC=xmx,DC=lab" simple
420  Active Directory NSIP             LDAP   bindResponse(3) success
423  NSIP             Active Directory LDAP   unbindRequest(4)
429  Gateway VIP      Client PC        HTTP   HTTP/1.1 302 Object Moved
455  Client PC        Gateway VIP      HTTP   GET /vpns/choices.html HTTP/1.1
465  Gateway VIP      Client PC        HTTP   HTTP/1.1 200 OK  (text/html)
509  Client PC        Gateway VIP      HTTP   GET /cgi/setclient?agnt HTTP/1.1
511  Gateway VIP      Client PC        HTTP   HTTP/1.1 302 Object Moved  (text/html)
```

2. The NetScaler first uses its credentials to authenticate itself, in order to be able to talk to the LDAP server (packet 409).

3. NetScaler then sends the User provided credentials to the server (packets 414 and 418) for authentication and group extraction.

 Notice how packet 509 shows the path as `/cgi/setclient?agnt`. The `/cgi/setclient` path is what helps NetScaler identify the client device so it can handle the VPN request appropriately. `agnt` indicates a VPN plugin. For a clientless VPN, this would be `/cgi/setclient?cvpn`.

Phase 3 – Post-login exchange

The following successful authentication, depending on whether client choices are configured in the session profile, the NetScaler Gateway presents the User with a list of options. The possibilities here are:

*   **FULL VPN:** Layer 3 Intranet connectivity
*   **Clientless VPN**: Web Access (HTTP and HTTPS) and ICA access
*   **ICA PROXY**: ICA only access

If ICA Proxy is set to **ON**, the client choices will not be displayed and the User will go directly to the **Storefront** page. Sometimes users might report seeing **Error: Logins Exceeded** on successful authentication. This might happen for one of three reasons:

- There are not enough licenses
- The global AAA User limit hasn't been raised from the default of 5
- The MaxUsers setting on the VPN vServer is being hit

Let's now look at a trace from a scenario in which the User chooses FULL VPN:

1. The client is sent to a plugin **Detection** and **Download** page.

2. Clicking on the **Download** link starts the plugin download and installation.

3. Once the installation is complete, there will be a number of HTTPs exchanges between the client and the VPN vServer to get the connection established.

	Source	Destination	Protocol	Info
12178	VPN Client	VPN Vserver	HTTP	GET /cfg HTTP/1.1
12179	VPN Vserver	VPN Client	HTTP	HTTP/1.1 200 OK (text/html)
12196	VPN Client	VPN Vserver	HTTP	GET /cs HTTP/1.1
12197	VPN Vserver	VPN Client	HTTP	HTTP/1.1 200 OK
12214	VPN Client	VPN Vserver	HTTP	GET /vpns/services.html HTTP/1.1
12215	VPN Vserver	VPN Client	HTTP	HTTP/1.1 302 Object Moved (text/html)
12252	VPN Client	VPN Vserver	HTTP	GET /cs HTTP/1.1
12256	VPN Client	VPN Vserver	HTTP	GET /cs HTTP/1.1
12262	VPN Vserver	VPN Client	HTTP	HTTP/1.1 200 OK
12263	VPN Vserver	VPN Client	HTTP	HTTP/1.1 200 OK
12264	VPN Client	VPN Vserver	HTTP	GET /dns HTTP/1.1
12266	VPN Vserver	VPN Client	HTTP	HTTP/1.1 200 OK
12267	VPN Client	VPN Vserver	HTTP	GET /dns HTTP/1.1
12268	VPN Vserver	VPN Client	HTTP	HTTP/1.1 200 OK

(http && ssl) || ldap

4. Following is description of the requests:

   ° /cfg requests are configuration download requests from the VPN client.

   ° /cs requests are connection setup messages.

   ° /dns requests are DNS requests. By default, they are exchanged as HTTP and get converted to a regular DNS protocol in NetScaler, before being sent to the DNS server.

5. At the end of this connection setup, the User has full layer 3 connectivity for the company network and can start accessing resources.

6. At the end of the session, once the User clicks on **Logout**, a request is sent to /cgi/logout, redirecting the User to the post-logout page. If configured, a clean-up script will be triggered at this point.

7. If the User chooses **CLIENTLESS ACCESS** instead, the /cgi/setclient path will be set to cvpn. In that case, you will not see any control messages (/cfg, /dns).

```
351   Client PC     Gateway VIP    HTTP   GET /cgi/setclient?cvpn HTTP/1.1
353   Gateway VIP   Client PC      HTTP   HTTP/1.1 302 Object Moved  (text/html)
402   Client PC     Gateway VIP    HTTP   GET /cvpn/http/127.0.0.1/vpns/services.html HTTP/1.1
403   Gateway VIP   Client PC      HTTP   HTTP/1.1 302 Object Moved  (text/html)
408   Client PC     Gateway VIP    HTTP   GET /cvpn/aHR0cDovL2ludHJhbmV0LnhteC5sYWI HTTP/1.1
411   Gateway VIP   Client PC      HTTP   HTTP/1.1 302 Object Moved  (text/html)
```

Instead a /cvpn/ path will be added to the path the original request will be either shown as is, base64 encoded or encrypted based on the Clientless Access URL Encoding setting.

Troubleshooting NetScaler Gateway™ VPNs

There are a number of tools and techniques available to troubleshoot the VPN feature. We will explore these in the following order:

- Debug logs from the client's PC
- The aaad.debug log file for authentication issues
- The ns.log on NetScaler for session information
- The pol_hits nsconmsg counter to verify which policies are getting hit
- The active User sessions GUI tool
- Capturing traces

Collecting debug logs from the client's PC

These logs contain a wealth of information across several files on the client's PC. In order to capture the maximum detail, you need to enable debug. This can be enabled in two ways:

1. Push this setting from the NetScaler Gateway to the VPN plugin on the client machine, using the **Client Debug** option under **Session Profile | Client Experience | Advanced Settings**. The User will need to log out and log back in so that the change takes effect.

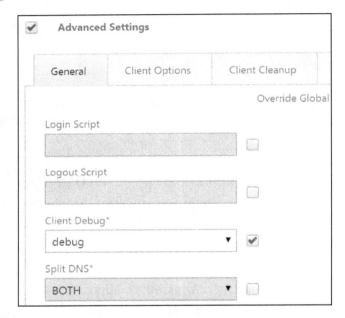

2. Have the User select the **Record detailed debugging messages** option. This is found by right-clicking on the VPN plugin in the system tray and going to the **Trace** tab in the options:

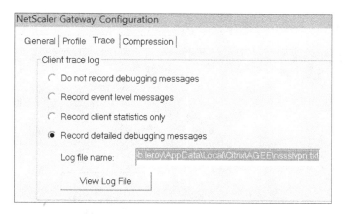

Once the issue has been reproduced, you can ask the User to run the `nsClientCollect.exe` script, which will create a ZIP file containing all the necessary logs so they can be easily shared with you. Here is a sample run of the command:

```
C:\Users\bob.leroy>"C:\Program Files\Citrix\Secure Access Client\nsClientColl
.exe" bob_clientlogs.zip
agClientCollect version 1.0.0.10
Running as user 'bob.leroy'
Logon as user 'bob.leroy' domain 'XMX'

Collecting System info ...
  OS Info
  IP Config
  Route Table
  ARP Table
  Registry Info
  NDIS Driver Info
  C:\Users\BOB~1.LER\AppData\Local\Temp\agClientCollect_sysinfo.txt
Collecting AGEE AllUser logs ...
  C:/ProgramData/Citrix/AGEE/nscltapi.txt
  C:/ProgramData/Citrix/AGEE/nsinst.txt
  C:/ProgramData/Citrix/AGEE/nsinst2.txt
  C:/ProgramData/Citrix/AGEE/nsverctl.txt
Collecting AGEE User logs ...
  C:/Users/bob.leroy/AppData/Local/Citrix/AGEE/npagee.txt
  C:/Users/bob.leroy/AppData/Local/Citrix/AGEE/nsepa.txt
  C:/Users/bob.leroy/AppData/Local/Citrix/AGEE/nssslvpn.txt
  C:/Users/bob.leroy/AppData/Local/Citrix/AGEE/nswcclog.txt
  C:/Users/bob.leroy/AppData/Local/Citrix/AGEE/stopCA.txt
  C:/Users/bob.leroy/AppData/Local/Citrix/AGEE/~nssslvpn.txt
  C:/Users/bob.leroy/AppData/Local/Citrix/AGEE/ns1profile.ini
```

Diagnosing EPA failures

Let's troubleshoot an example EPA failure.

The issue that the User reports that he cannot log in and sees an error that the client machine doesn't meet the security requirements:

From the details in the error it's clear that it's EPA and not authentication that is failing. To see the reason for this failure, the file nsepa.txt picked up by the nsclientcollect utility would be the best resource for identifying the problem. Open this file and look for a header called CSEC. This field contains values – usually 0 or 3 – for each of the checks:

- 0 indicates a success

- 3 indicates a failure

Now let's consider the following screenshot:

```
22:19:18.778 ns_HTTPrequest: https://vpn.xmx.lab:443epas
22:19:18.778
<GET epas HTTP/1.1

Cookie: NSC_EPAC=*********************************

CSEC: 03
```

Here, the value 03 means that there are two checks (since there are two digits) and that the first check succeeded (0) but the second failed (3). So you need to look at the EPA policy to identify what the second expression is, and then match it to the User's situation to see if it's the User's machine or the expression that needs to be addressed. As well as `nsepa.txt`, a decrypted trace would also show this information.

The check for domain joined is a popular one; you can set it up in this way:

```
add aaa preauthenticationaction allow_xmx.lab_machines
add aaa preauthenticationpolicy is_domain_xmx.
lab q/CLIENT.REG('HKEY_LOCAL_MACHINE\\\\SYSTEM\\\\
CurrentControlSet\\\\Services\\\\Tcpip\\\\Parameters_
Domain').VALUE == xmx.lab/ allow_xmx.lab_machines
```

Using aaad.debug for authentication issues

The file `aaad.debug`, which we briefly visited in the AAA chapter, is the one you would look at for authentication issues with VPN as well. `aaad.debug` is especially valuable when using multiple authentication policies, as it allows you to see which of the several authentication policies is failing before you engage in more specific troubleshooting.

Another indispensable `aaad.debug` feature is the ability to display User group memberships. This is really helpful for identifying situations where incorrect group association is the reason why a User doesn't see the expected resources.

The following screenshot is an example of running cat `/tmp/aaad.debug`, showing which groups the User is part of:

```
/usr/home/build/rs_105_58_5/usr.src/netscaler/aaad/ldap_drv.c[377]: receive_ldap_user_searc
Sun Oct 25 10:43:42 2015
 /usr/home/build/rs_105_58_5/usr.src/netscaler/aaad/ldap_drv.c[474]: receive_ldap_user_sear
CN=Outlook Users Group,CN=Users,DC=xmx,DC=lab
CN=IT Users Group,CN=Users,DC=xmx,DC=lab
CN=vpnusers,CN=Users,DC=xmx,DC=lab
CN=Remote Desktop Users,CN=Builtin,DC=xmx,DC=lab
```

One aspect of group extraction that has been a challenge for a long time is ensuring the right group is picked up when the User is part of more than one group. NetScaler by default picks up whichever group is returned first, which might not necessarily be the one you are looking for. In other words, a priority is missing.

A solution has been included, starting with version 10.1, in the form of the parameter `defaultauthenticationgroup`. When this parameter is set, upon successful authentication, NetScaler assumes the User to be part of this group and applies the policies bound to this group.

Using ns.log to see authorization and session information

The file `/var/log/ns.log` should be a familiar one to you by now as we have relied on it for troubleshooting several other feature issues. It is especially useful in a NetScaler Gateway context, since the logs for this feature are captured in a very detailed fashion. Let's explore its usefulness by trying to troubleshoot another example issue.

The issue is that a User passes EPA and authentication successfully, but instead of seeing a homepage, experiences a browser hang followed by a timeout:

Upon running a tail -f on the `ns.log` file (tail -f /var/log/ns.log) and having the User access the page at the same time, it becomes evident that it's the session policy `192.168.1.55_443_pol` that is denying access:

```
- User bob.leroy - Client_ip 192.168.1.101 - Nat_ip "Mapped Ip" - Vserver 192
- Source 192.168.1.101:51706 - Destination 192.168.1.30:80 - Total_bytes_send
ytes_recv 0 - Denied_by_policy "192.168.1.55_443_POL" - Group(s) "vpnusers"
```

At this point, you will need to look at the settings in the **Security** tab of the session policy to ensure that either the default authorization setting is adjusted, or that an appropriate authorization policy is used.

`ns.log` also captures a ton of other information for VPN issues:

- Timestamps in GMT and local time zones
- The username
- The session ID
- The client IP and port
- Session start and end time
- Whether it was mapped IP/SNIP or an **Intranet IP (IIP)** that was used
- The VPN vServer IP
- Destination IP and port (server)
- Any error messages
- The policy that kicked in
- The group that the User was being considered as part for policy evaluation
- Total TCP connections, UDP flows

Using the pol_hits counter to examine policy hits

When users log in to NetScaler Gateway VPN, who gets access to what resources and on satisfying what conditions is governed by a combination of policies and profiles. Issues such as users seeing resources or options they aren't meant to see can happen due to the inheritance behavior of NetScaler Gateway policies.

Therefore, it is important to understand how inheritance works. NetScaler Gateway policies, be they pre-auth, session, or traffic policies, follow this processing order:

```
User level > Group level > VSERVER level > Global
```

In addition, certain policies, such as pre-auth, can only be bound at the global or vServer level since the User has not yet presented their username and cannot be identified as a result.

The `pol_hits nsconmsg` counter is a very useful means of identifying what the resultant set of policies is. Taking an example, in the following screenshot we can see that for the User who just logged in, the LDAP authentication policy (`ldap_LDAP_pol`), the global session policy (`SETVPNPARAMS_POL`), and a more specific session policy (`192.168.1.55_443_POL`) are being hit:

```
root@192_50_ns# nsconmsg -g pol_hits -d current
Displaying performance information
NetScaler V20 Performance Data
NetScaler NS10.5: Build 58.11.nc, Date: Jul 14 2015, 13:28:13

reltime:mili second between two records Sat Oct 24 17:57:27 2015
  Index    rtime totalcount-val       delta rate/sec symbol-name&device-no

      1    14000           34           4       0 pol_hits Policy(ldap_LDAP_pol)
      2   133002           35           1       0 pol_hits Policy(ldap_LDAP_pol)
      3     7000            2           1       0 pol_hits Policy(SETVPNPARAMS_POL)
      4        0            1           1       0 pol_hits Policy(192.168.1.55_443_POL)
```

 In a busy environment, this command can present a lot of information in a short time. Furthermore, you might also have a challenge in being able to tell which User the output is for, when several users are logging in. For this reason, it would be best to use the command during a window when you are able to limit the users logging in, such as after hours.

Seeing and managing the users who are logged in

When troubleshooting you will often times need to make a configuration change to vServer or policies. This introduces a need to be able to:

- Find out if and how many users are logged in
- Get users to re-process policies by having them log out and log back in

The **Active User sessions** tool in the NetScaler **Gateway** tab is great for this purpose:

Sessions					
Terminate					
Username	Client IP	Client Port	Server IP	Server Port	Intranet IP
bob.leroy	192.168.1.101	52136	192.168.1.55	443	0.0.0.0
bob.leroy	192.168.1.101	52154	192.168.1.55	443	0.0.0.0

Capturing traces for troubleshooting

Considering that NetScaler Gateway exchanges are basically SSL conversations, it's easy to see why Wireshark is a critical tool for troubleshooting. All troubleshooting that we looked at in the SSL Chapter automatically applies here, including:

- SSL Handshake failures due to certificates not being trusted
- TLS versions not matching
- No matching Ciphers between receiver and NetScaler
- Ports being blocked

The following points are important to remember while taking traces:

1. Where possible always identify a test User and note down the username so logs and traces can be correlated.

2. Disable SSL reuse on the VPN vServer so that the trace can be decrypted.

   ```
   > set ssl vserver vpn.xmx.lab -sessReuse DISABLED Done
   ```

 Notice that in the preceding example, I used `set ssl vserver` and not `set vpn Vserver`. This is how you set any SSL-related settings, even if the vServer is a VPN vServer.

3. Set the trace size to 0. If you leave it at the default 164-byte truncated size, the complete certificate will not be captured, so the decryption will fail.

4. Have the test User close their session and only log in after you have started the trace.

5. Always take simultaneous traces between client and NetScaler and the backend server for backend access issues.

NetScaler Gateway™ Integration with XenApp® and XenDesktop®

NetScaler Gateway's ability to act as a secure and intelligent proxy for XenApp and XenDesktop is a major reason for its success in the field.

To be able to deliver published apps and desktops securely, NetScaler works closely with the following components:

- **Storefront Server**: This is a web-based service that hosts a number of named stores. Each store is a collection of applications with a specific path on the server, hosted by specific servers, and with specific Gateway settings. It has been, for several years now, used as the replacement for Citrix Web Interface, which is a similar solution but on its way out. If you are deploying a new XenApp/XenDesktop environment, you should consider Storefront, as web interface is being phased out.

- **Secure Ticketing Authority (STA)**: This is an XML service that provides short-lived tickets (32 characters long) to help validate User requests and launch published apps or desktops.

- **Delivery Controller**: This is a brokering service that enables communication between the different XenApp/XenDesktop components, and is the component responsible for providing the list of applications and desktops for Storefront to share with receiver.

Given the integrated nature of these deployments, an understanding of the sequence from a User getting to a logon page (or a dialog box if using receiver) to seeing their list of applications or desktops and launching them, is critical in order to identify where the underlying communication is breaking. Let's move on to examining what an application or desktop launch looks like under the hood if you were to take a trace.

Published application/desktop launch process

The launch processes for XenApp and XenDesktop are practically the same, especially with the current version of these products since they use the same components. We will use XenDesktop for our demonstration.

The process can seem lengthy as it involves many steps. So, to make it simpler to digest, let's break it into two phases:

- **Phase 1**: Desktop enumeration, that is displaying the list of desktops
- **Phase 2**: Desktop launch

Phase 1 – steps involved in desktop enumeration

These are the steps involved in desktop enumeration:

1. Similar to our VPN example, the User logs in with their credentials. As with the previous cases, this results in an LDAP exchange between NetScaler and the authentication server. On successful authentication, a request is made to /cgi/setclient?wica (packet 1896):

```
1844      Client          Gateway VIP      HTTP   POST /cgi/login HTTP/1.1  (application/x-www-form-urlencoded)
1858      NSIP            Active Directory LDAP   bindRequest(1) "administrator@xmx.lab" simple
1861  Active Directory       NSIP          LDAP   bindResponse(1) success
1863      NSIP            Active Directory LDAP   searchRequest(2) "dc=xmx,dc=lab" wholeSubtree
1865  Active Directory       NSIP          LDAP   searchResEntry(2) "CN=bob leroy,CN=Users,DC=xmx,DC=lab"   | se
1867      NSIP            Active Directory LDAP   bindRequest(3) "CN=bob leroy,CN=Users,DC=xmx,DC=lab" simple
1869  Active Directory       NSIP          LDAP   bindResponse(3) success
1872      NSIP            Active Directory LDAP   unbindRequest(4)
1877   Gateway VIP         Client          HTTP   HTTP/1.1 302 Object Moved
1896      Client          Gateway VIP      HTTP   GET /cgi/setclient?wica HTTP/1.1
1898   Gateway VIP         Client          HTTP   HTTP/1.1 200 OK  (text/html)
```

2. Recall from the earlier cases that the query part of this string indicates the type of access. Here wica means the User wants to launch a published app or desktop. Though this request could also come from a browser, it is most commonly issued by the receiver client. By expanding this packet (1896) you can also see the version of receiver that this request is coming from, which is very handy during troubleshooting:

```
Hypertext Transfer Protocol
 GET /cgi/setclient?wica HTTP/1.1\r\n
 Cache-Control: no-cache\r\n
 Connection: Keep-Alive\r\n
 Pragma: no-cache\r\n
 Accept-Language: en-US\r\n
 Cookie: NSC_AAAC=f76847107af6a2bc45989263e50a01bc0af181f2645525d5f4f58455e445a4a42\r\n
 User-Agent: CitrixReceiver Windows/6.1 AuthManager/7.0.0.8243 (Release) X1Class\r\n
 X-Citrix-Gateway: vpn.xmx.lab\r\n
 Host: vpn.xmx.lab\r\n
```

3. At this point, the client side (receiver) kicks off the discovery process with a GET to /AGServices/discover. Recall that when you log in with receiver, you are free to put in anything – an email address or an FQDN. Receiver doesn't have any idea yet which of these it will be, and making that determination is the purpose of this discovery request.

For this discovery to work flawlessly, TCP Service (SRV) records need to be added. Take a look at this blog for details: `https://goo.gl/uZzuZU`.

4. At this point at a number of headers also come into play:

    ○ **X-Citrix-Gateway**: This contains the VPN VIP FQDN.

    ○ **X-Citrix-Via**: This also contains the VPN VIP FQDN. This is used by Storefront to make the optional callback.

    ○ **X-Citrix-Via-VIP**: This header serves a similar purpose as X-Citrix-Via, but instead contains an IP. This is necessary since in a GSLB-based environment with multiple NetScaler Gateways, the FQDN will always be the same, so an IP is used to lead to a specific VPN VIP.

    ○ **X-Forwarded-For**: This will contain the Client IP.

5. Receiver now tries to obtain details concerning what stores are available on the Storefront server, by making a call to `/Citrix/Roaming/Accounts`. This step involves a number of authentication calls using a process called CitrixAGBasic and hence the 401s in the following screenshot:

Source	Destination	Length	Info
SNIP	Storefront	447	GET /Citrix/Roaming/Accounts HTTP/1.1
Storefront	SNIP	383	HTTP/1.1 401 Unauthorized (text/html)
SNIP	Storefront	543	POST /Citrix/Authentication/auth/v1/token HTTP/1.1 (application/vnd.citrix.requesttoken+xml)
Storefront	SNIP	447	HTTP/1.1 401 Unauthorized (text/html)
SNIP	Storefront	543	POST /Citrix/Authentication/auth/v1/protocols HTTP/1.1 (application/vnd.citrix.requesttoken+xml)
Storefront	SNIP	975	HTTP/1.1 300 Multiple Choices (application/vnd.citrix.requesttokenchoices+xml)
SNIP	Storefront	543	POST /Citrix/Authentication/CitrixAGBasic/Authenticate HTTP/1.1 (application/vnd.citrix.requesttoken+xml)
Storefront	SNIP	271	HTTP/1.1 401 Unauthorized (text/html)
SNIP	Storefront	543	POST /Citrix/Authentication/CitrixAGBasic/Authenticate HTTP/1.1 (application/vnd.citrix.requesttoken+xml)
Storefront	SNIP	1263	HTTP/1.1 200 OK (application/vnd.citrix.requesttokenresponse+xml)
SNIP	Storefront	543	POST /Citrix/Authentication/auth/v1/token HTTP/1.1 (application/vnd.citrix.requesttokenresponse+xml)
Storefront	SNIP	975	HTTP/1.1 200 OK (application/vnd.citrix.requesttokenresponse+xml)
SNIP	Storefront	735	GET /Citrix/Roaming/Accounts HTTP/1.1
Storefront	SNIP	479	HTTP/1.1 200 OK (application/vnd.citrix.roamingaccounts+xml)

6. Storefront then makes a callback to the address it sees in the `X-Citrix-Via-VIP` header. This is what the callback looks like:

```
POST /CitrixAuthService/AuthService.asmx HTTP/1.1
User-Agent: Mozilla/4.0 (compatible; MSIE 6.0; MS Web Services Client Protocol 4.0.30319.18408)
Content-Type: text/xml; charset=utf-8
SOAPAction: "http://citrix.com/SecureAccessManager/AuthenticationService/V3.0/GetAccessInformation"
Host: vpn.xmx.lab
Content-Length: 473
Expect: 100-continue
Connection: Keep-Alive

HTTP/1.1 100 Continue

<?xml version="1.0" encoding="utf-8"?><soap:Envelope xmlns:soap="http://schemas.xmlsoap.org/soap/
envelope/" xmlns:xsi="http://www.w3.org/2001/XMLSchema-instance" xmlns:xsd="http://www.w3.org/2001/
XMLSchema"><soap:Body><GetAccessInformation xmlns="http://citrix.com/SecureAccessManager/
AuthenticationService/V3.0"><sessionId>53776b91cee486e8430b65777dec2ba0</sessionId><username>bob.leroy</
username><domain>xmx.lab</domain></GetAccessInformation></soap:Body></soap:Envelope>HTTP/1.1 200 OK
Cache-Control: no-store
Content-Type: text/xml; charset=utf-8
Connection: close

<?xml version="1.0" encoding="utf-8"?><soap:Envelope xmlns:soap="http://schemas.xmlsoap.org/soap/
envelope/" xmlns:xsi="http://www.w3.org/2001/XMLSchema-instance" xmlns:xsd="http://www.w3.org/2001/
XMLSchema"><soap:Body><GetAccessInformationResponse xmlns="http://citrix.com/SecureAccessManager/
AuthenticationService/V3.0"><GetAccessInformationResult><StatusCode>0</StatusCode><StatusString>Success</
StatusString><ClientAddress>172.16.1.101</ClientAddress><FarmName>_XD_vpn.xmx.lab</
FarmName><FarmId>172.16.1.55</FarmId><MpsAccessMode>Direct</
MpsAccessMode><SmartAccessConditions><string>PL_OS_172.16.1.55</string><string>SETVPNPARAMS_POL</
string></SmartAccessConditions></GetAccessInformationResult></GetAccessInformationResponse></soap:Body></
soap:Envelope>
```

7. In its response, NetScaler includes the tag `<smartAccessConditions>` to indicate what session policy has been evaluated for the request. The name of this session policy matches a filter configured on the XenApp server, thereby providing preconfigured policy-based access from XenApp, based on the session policy evaluation on NetScaler. This integration is what is called **Smart Access**.

 Any failures in the callback will result in a `Cannot complete your request` error.

8. The Storefront server does its own authentication in addition, using Kerberos. Ensure that the necessary ports – Port 88, 445 and Global Catalog 3268 – are open between Storefront Server and Active Directory:

Source	Destination	Length	Info
StoreFront	AD	66	49473→3268 [SYN] Seq=0 Win=8192 Len=0 MSS=1456 WS=256
AD	StoreFront	66	3268→49473 [SYN, ACK] Seq=0 Ack=1 Win=8192 Len=0 MSS=1
StoreFront	AD	54	49473→3268 [ACK] Seq=1 Ack=1 Win=66816 Len=0
StoreFront	AD	404	searchRequest(34) "<ROOT>" baseObject
AD	StoreFront	58	3268→49473 [ACK] Seq=1 Ack=351 Win=66816 Len=4[Malform
AD	StoreFront	2239	3268→49473 [PSH, ACK] Seq=5 Ack=351 Win=66816 Len=2185
StoreFront	AD	54	49473→3268 [ACK] Seq=351 Ack=2190 Win=66816 Len=0
StoreFront	AD	1607	bindRequest(36) "<ROOT>" sasl
AD	StoreFront	60	3268→49473 [ACK] Seq=2190 Ack=1904 Win=66816 Len=0
AD	StoreFront	264	bindResponse(36) success
StoreFront	AD	320	SASL GSS-API Integrity:
AD	StoreFront	252	SASL GSS-API Integrity:
StoreFront	AD	97	SASL GSS-API Integrity: [Malformed Packet]

9. At the end of this exchange, Storefront provides a token that equals the store ID which the client uses in subsequent requests. During this process, the client also receives the beacons, as configured on Storefront:

```
point><Services version="1.0"><Service type="store"><SRID>3178163479</
SRID><Name>xmxstore</Name><Address>https://sf.xmx.lab/Citrix/xmxstore/discovery</
Address><Gateways><Gateway Name="vpn.xmx.lab" Default="true" Edition="Enterprise"
Auth="Domain" RewriteMode="NONE"><Location>https://vpn.xmx.lab</Location></Gateway></
Gateways><Beacons><Internal><Beacon>https://sf.xmx.lab/</Beacon></
Internal><External><Beacon>https://vpn.xmx.lab</Beacon><Beacon>http://www.citrix.com</
Beacon></External></Beacons></Service></Services></Discovery>
```

> Beacons serve to help receiver understand if the User is on the same local network as Storefront, or if it is connecting through the Internet. This is done by providing at least two beacons, one of which is accessible only when the client is on the LAN. In this way, receiver knows when it has to go through the NetScaler Gateway VIP (and the associated authentication process) and when it can be bypassed.

10. Storefront then obtains the list of Applications by talking to the delivery controller (one of the XenApp/XenDesktop servers designated for this purpose) and passes the list of applications/desktops that it receives to the client via the Gateway VIP. Here is a fiddler trace taken on the client machine that shows what this list looks like:

```
clienttypes
  ica30
  rdp
description=desktops and apps for xmx group users
desktopassignmenttype=assigned
desktophostname=windesk01
iconurl=Resources/Icon/L0NpdHJpeC94bXhzdG9yZS9yZXNvdXJjZXMvdjIvTTNkT01VZE5Sa1YwVDBkMGEwTnJZV
id=xaxdcontroller.desktopsandapps $P2
isdesktop=True
launchstatusurl=Resources/GetLaunchStatus/eGF4ZGNvbnRyb2xsZXIuZGVza3RvcHNhbmRhcHBzICRQMg--
launchurl=Resources/LaunchIca/eGF4ZGNvbnRyb2xsZXIuZGVza3RvcHNhbmRhcHBzICRQMg--.ica
name=desktopsandapps
path=\
position=1
poweroffurl=Resources/PowerOff/eGF4ZGNvbnRyb2xsZXIuZGVza3RvcHNhbmRhcHBzICRQMg--
shortcutvalidationurl=Resources/ValidateAppShortcutLaunch/eGF4ZGNvbnRyb2xsZXIuZGVza3RvcHNhbmRhcHB
subscriptionstatus=subscribed
subscriptionurl=Resources/Subscription/eGF4ZGNvbnRyb2xsZXIuZGVza3RvcHNhbmRhcHBzICRQMg--
```

11. Receiver processes this list and displays the list of apps and desktops to the User.

Phase 2 – Steps leading to the launch of the published desktop

Once the User sees the list of desktops and clicks on one of them, the following steps happen, leading to the desktop being presented to the User:

1. The User clicking on the desktop in receiver results in a request to Storefront via the NetScaler Gateway and Storefront needs to present an ICA file. The steps involved in this process are:

    1. Storefront queries the delivery controller to find out which XenApp virtual desktop the client should be directed to. As part of this query, storefront provides the details of who it is obtaining the information for by including their credentials.

    2. Storefront also presents the SmartAccess information it received from NetScaler. Recall that this policy, named PL_OS_172.16.1.55, is what was provided as the value for SmartAccessConditions during the callback.

```
<Credentials>
    <UserName>bob.leroy</UserName>
    <Password encoding="ctx1">ODDEPEDEPDCFOEHAOH</Password>
    <Domain type="NT">xmx.lab</Domain>
</Credentials>
<ClientName>RVT-WIN7</ClientName>
<ClientAddress addresstype="dot">172.16.1.101</ClientAddress>
<SessionContext>
    <SessionContextEntry name="Citrix.SessionProductType">MSAM</SessionContextEntry>
    <SessionContextEntry name="Citrix.SessionProductVersion">1</SessionContextEntry>
    <SessionContextEntry name="Citrix.FarmName">_XD_vpn.xmx.lab</SessionContextEntry>
    <SessionContextEntry name="Citrix.FarmID">172.16.1.55</SessionContextEntry>
    <SessionContextEntry name="Citrix.SessionID">53776b91cee486e8430b65777dec2ba0</SessionContextEntry>
    <SessionContextEntry name="Citrix.Condition">PL_OS_172.16.1.55</SessionContextEntry>
    <SessionContextEntry name="Citrix.Condition">SETVPNPARAMS_POL</SessionContextEntry>
```

2. The delivery controller will do another round of authentication using these credentials and also consider the SmartAccess details it receives from Storefront. After processing, it provides the details of the target virtual machine to Storefront. This is what that response will look like:

```
<LeasingStatus>working</LeasingStatus>
<RetryDelayHint>0</RetryDelayHint>
<ServerAddress addresstype="dot-port">192.168.1.32:1494</ServerAddress>
<ServerType>win32</ServerType>
<ConnectionType>tcp</ConnectionType>
<ClientType>ica30</ClientType>
<TicketTag>00bc527d-ecca-411b-83ec-e924ec9f3d93</TicketTag>
<CGPAddress addresstype="port">2598</CGPAddress>
<Ticket>7998882D9BFA904B05A8915ECECA78</Ticket>
<LaunchRef>7F419CA2CC285E098EE2110C401352</LaunchRef>
```

3. Storefront then needs to obtain an STA ticket that the User can use when launching the ICA connection for desktop 192.168.1.32 (shown in the preceding screenshot). It does so with a POST to /scripts/ ctxsta.dll on the STA server.

 You will see this POST a lot of times in the trace, because this is also how NetScaler verifies that the STA is up.

4. The response to this POST will contain the STA ticket that gets passed on to the client as part of the ICA file and is provided each time by the client to confirm it has been authenticated and has access to this resource.

```
<?xml version="1.0" encoding="UTF-8"?>
<!DOCTYPE CtxSTAProtocol SYSTEM "CtxSta.dtd">
<CtxSTAProtocol version="4.0">
    <ResponseTicket>
        <AuthorityID authorityType="STA-v1">STA304540071</AuthorityID>
        <Ticket ticketType="STA-v4">B2D0FB2E5B16A4F44FF595AAB5EBA9</Ticket>
        <TicketVersion>40</TicketVersion>
        <TicketLifetime>100</TicketLifetime>
    </ResponseTicket>
</CtxSTAProtocol>
```

5. Storefront packages the various details into an ICA file that then gets forwarded to the client via the Gateway VIP. This file is human readable and contains all the necessary information, such as the application name, its connection properties, and the ticket. The IP of the desktop will not be presented as is; instead it points to the access Gateway, which stays in the path of access:

```
[WFClient]
ProxyFavorIEConnectionSetting=Yes
ProxyTimeout=30000
ProxyType=Auto
ProxyUseFQDN=Off
RemoveICAFile=yes
TransportReconnectEnabled=Off
Version=2
VirtualCOMPortEmulation=On

[ApplicationServers]
desktopsandapps $P2=

[desktopsandapps $P2]
Address=;40;STA304540071;D065A8E6DDA3DD9C58B3A8225A907F
AutologonAllowed=ON
BrowserProtocol=HTTPonTCP
CGPSecurityTicket=On
ClearPassword=50255D66DBBB8E
ClientAudio=On
ConnectionBar=1
DesiredColor=8
DesiredHRES=4294967295
DesiredVRES=4294967295
DesktopRestartAllowed=1
Domain=\5CD78225FAED7EE5
DoNotUseDefaultCSL=On
FontSmoothingType=0
HTTPBrowserAddress=!
InitialProgram=#desktopsandapps $P2
LaunchReference=BF2C34619FD683429F2AFEEDCF6D95
LocHttpBrowserAddress=!
LogonTicket=50255D66DBBB8E5CD78225FAED7EE5
LogonTicketType=CTXS1
LongCommandLine=
LPWD=4882
NRWD=884
ProxyTimeout=30000
ProxyType=Auto
SecureChannelProtocol=Detect
```

3. On receiving the ICA file, receiver submits a connection request to the NetScaler Gateway, including the ticket.

4. NetScaler Gateway talks to the STA to verify that the ticket is valid and exchanges it for the IP address of the actual resource, the desktop. It then establishes a connection to the desktop on either port TCP 2598 or 1494, depending on whether the **Session Reliability** feature is enabled or disabled.

What is Session Reliability?

It is a feature of XenApp and XenDesktop which allows ICA sessions to continue to run in the background on the server during a network disconnection while the session is in progress. This is nice from a User experience perspective, as it means that the User doesn't need to go through the entire process of launching an application again when they encounter network disruption. Also, any working data, such as text typed into a document, is preserved during this disconnection period.

Troubleshooting XenApp® and XenDesktop® launch issues

We've just gone through a marathon discussion of the flow that is involved in an application or desktop launch. Let's now discuss some troubleshooting steps to consider in case of issues in this area:

1. Verify that NetScaler is able to resolve DNS, especially if you have added the various components by their hostname/FQDN.

2. Try to qualify the issue as either an enumeration or a launch issue. As we've seen in our trace examination, the steps for each phase are different.

3. If application enumeration is failing:

    1. Check your group memberships, especially if only a subset of users are seeing the problem.

    2. Check what session profile is getting hit and if the Storefront address in the Profile is correct.

    3. Check Storefront status and reachability. If you are seeing **Http/1.1 Internal Server Error**, Storefront reachability is likely the problem.

    4. Check that the XML service is running and that the configured port is correct. It can run on its own port or share the port with IIS. CTX104063 discusses how to change it, if there is a conflict.

4. Verify the callback URL configured. It is optional, but if configured, needs to be successful. Otherwise users will see a **Cannot complete your Request** error. Common reasons why your call back might fail are as follows:

    ◦ SSL certificate is not trusted

    ◦ Incorrect configuration of Callback URL

    ◦ DNS resolution on Storefront failing

    ◦ Firewalls blocking the communication

If you cannot have the Storefront talking to the public Gateway vServer IP due to firewall rules, a common trick that is employed is to configure a second VPN vServer on the same NetScaler Gateway. In some cases, values need to be added to the hosts file on the Storefront servers to enable proper name resolution.

5. If you are load balancing the Storefront servers, incorrect persistence can also be a problem. The recommendation is to use Source IP. To rule out problems in this area as a root cause, try this with a single Storefront server first.

6. Also when using load balancing, not having the Client IP header on the services can be an issue. This needs to be enabled using the `X-Fowarded-For` header in the service settings, so that the Storefront server can see the real client IP.

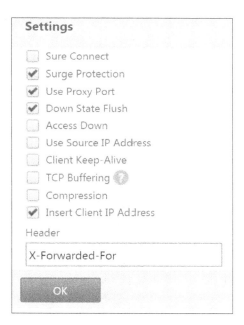

7. Enable logging on receiver to get some hints to look at in the form of error messages. You can do this for Windows receiver by following the instructions in the article CTX134101 (`http://goo.gl/V70uw7`). It is even simpler for mobile devices; the options are available in **Settings | Support | Log Options**. Note down the time, set the log level to debug just for the period of the troubleshooting, reproduce the issue and click on request help from support to send the logs to yourself.

8. Once you have the logs (which are usually in the form of CSV files), look for the keywords **Error** or **Failed** around the timestamp in question.

9. A commonly reported error is **There are no Apps or Desktops Assigned to you at this time** when rolling out a new deployment. This is a Storefront communication failure and one way this failure commonly happens is when the Administrator configures Storefront for one method of access (say HTTPS) but configures the Storefront URL on NetScaler as HTTP. Verify that this matches in both places. HTTPS is recommended.

If applications/desktops enumerate but fail to launch:

1. Check that the STA servers are all UP. One way to do this is to run `show vpn Vserver <Vserver name>`. This will show you the status of all STAs bound to the Gateway VIP.

2. Remember that when adding by hostname, DNS plays a role and that can be a point of failure. Re-add by IP to rule out DNS issues.

3. Verify that the STAs added on NetScaler and Storefront match. The ticket provided by an STA can only be validated by the same STA, so a mismatch here will mean launch failures due to ticket validation failures.

 CTX120589 is a very useful article in this context, it shows you how to modify `CtxSta.config` to enable and look at STA debug level logs.

4. Also try to spot patterns in failures; sometimes the issue is intermittent, which tells us that one of the components where there is redundancy, such as multiple STAs, Storefront servers, or XenApp/Desktop servers, is failing. Try to further isolate the issue by having only one of each component for a start.

5. Try changing the Storefront settings to bypass the Gateway and access the store. This will help you validate if the XenApp/XenDesktop infrastructure is working properly without the NetScaler Gateway in the picture.

6. Verify that the NetScaler Gateway can talk to the XenApp Server on 1494 or 2598 and that there are no firewalls blocking this.

7. If you are seeing the problems with iOS receiver but Android works, check to see if Port 1494 is getting blocked somewhere. Receiver for iOS doesn't support Session Reliability. This makes it possible for situations to arise where Android works because Firewall ports only allow Session Reliability Port 2598, but iOS cannot fallback and work because 1494 is blocked.

8. Finally, try turning off SSL Session Reliability for troubleshooting. While Session Reliability being enabled is not a problem on its own, turning it off will provide you with a more detailed error message, along with an error code. These error codes are a great first hint as to what is going wrong. Here are some common examples:

   ° **SSL Error 61**: Receiver does not trust the SSL certificate

   ° **SSL Error 4**: This is usually STA related; enable logging and look for ticket validation failures

   ° **SSL Error 38, SSL Error 29, SSL Error 43**: Proxy Denied Access NetScaler is unable to reach STA, NetScaler is unable to reach XenApp or XenDesktop servers and Gateway max users getting hit; for example, the default limit (5) has not been raised

NetScaler Gateway™ integration with XenMobile®

XenMobile is Citrix's Enterprise Mobile Management suite. It allows enterprises to maintain better control over how their IT users interact with company data, when connected through either company-provided or employee-owned mobile devices. The importance of such a solution is easy to see when you consider how ubiquitous mobile devices have become and also how they offer better on the run access to information, something hugely important to the mobile workforce of today.

Before we dive into troubleshooting XenMobile integration, let's look at some fundamentals.

XenMobile components

From an integration perspective, the key components are as follows:

1. The XenMobile Server, a Linux virtual machine which is an amalgamation of the following:

   ° The AppController service, which provides mobile application management, but also acts as an STA for ticketing

   ° The MDM service, which provides mobile device management

2. The WorxHome component, which is the application on the mobile device that takes care of User enrolment, as well as handling application enumeration and subscription.

3. The Worx applications, such as WorxMail, WorxWeb, or even custom applications.

4. A SAAS-based sharing platform which allows users to store and share files. It works both as a standalone application and as a connector built into other WorxApps, such as WorxMail, allowing users to attach files directly from the cloud.

The Ports used for NetScaler integration are as follows:

- **LDAP and Global Catalogue**: TCP ports 389/636 and TCP ports 3268/3269
- **DNS**: UDP port 53
- **User Enrolment and WorxStore access**: TCP port 8443 between NetScaler and XenMobile server

 The complete XenMobile solution uses a lot more ports. Please see the XenMobile eDocs page for the exhaustive list.

XenMobile launch process with NetScaler Gateway

Let's take a look at a communication flow that demonstrates NetScaler's integration with XenMobile server using the most popular use case for this integration, WorxMail. We will once again break this into phases to make it easy to digest:

- **Phase1**: Authentication and discovery
- **Phase2**: Mobile application enumeration and launch

Phase 1 – Authentication and discovery

When User Bob launches WorxHome on his mobile device, it sends a GET to the path `/zdm/cxf/public/getserverinfo` on XenMobile server. This for the purpose of discovery and results in a redirect to the NetScaler Gateway VIP:

```
GET /zdm/cxf/public/getserverinfo HTTP/1.1
Accept: application/xml
Host: mvpn.xmx.lab:443
Connection: Keep-Alive

HTTP/1.1 302 Object Moved
Location: /vpn/index.html
Connection: close
```

Bob logs in and his credentials are verified with the LDAP server.

```
Bob's Android   VPN VIP        GET /vpn/index.html HTTP/1.1
VPN VIP         Bob's Android  HTTP/1.1 200 OK  (text/html)
Bob's Android   VPN VIP        POST /cgi/login HTTP/1.1  (application/x-www-form-urlencoded)
192.168.1.70    192.168.1.30   bindRequest(1) "administrator@xmx.lab" simple
192.168.1.30    192.168.1.70   bindResponse(1) success
192.168.1.70    192.168.1.30   searchRequest(2) "dc=xmx,dc=lab" wholeSubtree
192.168.1.30    192.168.1.70   searchResEntry(2) "CN=bob leroy,CN=Users,DC=xmx,DC=lab"  | se
192.168.1.70    192.168.1.30   bindRequest(3) "CN=bob leroy,CN=Users,DC=xmx,DC=lab" simple
192.168.1.30    192.168.1.70   bindResponse(3) success
192.168.1.70    192.168.1.30   unbindRequest(4)
VPN VIP         Bob's Android  HTTP/1.1 302 Object Moved
Bob's Android   VPN VIP        GET /cgi/setclient?andr HTTP/1.1
VPN VIP         Bob's Android  HTTP/1.1 302 Object Moved  (text/html)
Bob's Android   VPN VIP        GET /cfg HTTP/1.1
VPN VIP         Bob's Android  HTTP/1.1 200 OK  (text/html)
```

Use `aaad.debug`, as in the VPN scenario, for any issues with authentication. Along with the credentials, WorxHome also tells NetScaler Gateway what kind of device Bob is connecting from, by using the `User-Agent` header:

User-Agent: CitrixReceiver/com.zenprise build/10.2.2 Android/4.4.2 KOT49H.N5110XXDNF1 VpnCapable

 The VpnCapable part of the string is used to say that the client component can handle `microvpns`.

This results in a redirect to the path `/cgi/setclient?andr`. The `andr` here stands for Android. The redirect also contains the NSC_AAAC cookie, which identifies all further requests from this User:

```
Hypertext Transfer Protocol
⊕ HTTP/1.1 302 Object Moved\r\n
  Location: /cgi/setclient?andr\r\n
  Set-Cookie: NSC_AAAC=459ef221cc3d71ca275
```

The discovery finishes with the VPN client receiving the XenMobile server's details:

```
GET /AGServices/discover HTTP/1.1
Accept: */*
Accept-Language: en-US, en
X-Citrix-Gateway: mvpn.xmx.lab
Host: mvpn.xmx.lab
Connection: Keep-Alive
User-Agent: CitrixReceiver/com.ze
Accept-Encoding: gzip
Cookie: NSC_AAAC=459ef221cc3d71ca
Cookie2: $Version=1

HTTP/1.1 200 OK
Content-Length: 27
Cache-control: no-cache, no-store
Pragma: no-cache
Content-Type: text/plain
https://xmsvip.xmx.lab:8443
```

Phase 2 – App enumeration and Launch

Once discovery is complete, WorxHome on the User's mobile device needs to be able to show the list of Worx Applications available to them. This is called application enumeration.

 The callback URL in XenMobile is optional, just as with Storefront. The recommendation is to leave it blank by default.

WorxHome requests a list of available applications through a series of POST, the last of which is to /StoreWeb/ws/Resources/List. So if it's enumeration that's failing, this is the request you'd be looking for. The response will be a list of apps and info about these apps, such as where to pull the icons from, their app ID, and their SSO details:

Source	Destination	Info
Bob's Android	VPN VIP	POST /cvpn/https/xms:8443/StoreWeb/ws/Home/Configuration HTTP
Bob's Android	VPN VIP	POST /cvpn/cp HTTP/1.1 (text/plain)
VPN VIP	Bob's Android	HTTP/1.1 200 OK (text/html)
VPN VIP	Bob's Android	HTTP/1.1 200 OK (application/json)
Bob's Android	VPN VIP	POST /cvpn/https/xms:8443/StoreWeb/ws/Resources/List HTTP/1.1
VPN VIP	Bob's Android	HTTP/1.1 200 OK (application/json)
VPN VIP	Bob's Android	HTTP/1.1 200 OK (application/json)

```
f 70 65 72 74 69 65    s":[],"p ropertie
4 65 73 63 72 69 70    s":null, "descrip
2 78 4d 61 69 6c 22    tion":"W orxMail"
```

The app ID here is very useful because if you have app launch failures you can search using this value, and identify all pertinent requests. In the following screenshot the app ID is `MobileApp2`:

```
3f6-99fc-603f1f1f5a01%7E2629651449/image","linkurl":"https://xms:8443/Citrix/
("id":"Citrix.MPS.Doc.Farm 1.MobileApp2"), "name":"WorxMail","path":"\\Default\
```

At this point Bob clicks on the WorxMail icon and this results in the application being fetched for installation. We can follow the exchange using a filter such as `http contains MobileApp2`. This should show something similar to the following:

```
Bob's Android   VPN VIP          1015 POST /cvpn/https/xms:8443/StoreWeb/ws/Resources/MobileInsta
SNIP            XenMobileServer   144 POST /StoreWeb/ws/Resources/MobileInstall/Citrix.MPS.Doc.Fa
XenMobileServer SNIP              400 HTTP/1.1 200 OK  (application/json)
VPN VIP         Bob's Android     250 HTTP/1.1 200 OK  (application/json)
XenMobileServer SNIP               32 HTTP/1.1 200 OK  (application/vnd.citrix.resources+xml)
VPN VIP         Bob's Android    4736 HTTP/1.1 200 OK  (application/vnd.citrix.resources+xml)
Bob's Android   VPN VIP           648 GET /cvpn/https/xms:8443/Citrix/v1/download/app/MobileApp2
SNIP            XenMobileServer   768 GET /Citrix/v1/download/app/MobileApp2 HTTP/1.1
XenMobileServer SNIP            10384 HTTP/1.1 200 OK  (application/vnd.android.package-archive)
VPN VIP         Bob's Android    3640 HTTP/1.1 200 OK  (application/vnd.android.package-archive)
```

The really large 200 OK is the WorxMail package. At this point, communication starts between the mobile end point and the end server, which is exchange in the case of WorxMail, and the User should see their mail:

```
Bob's Android   VPN VIP          656 GET /cvpn/https/xms:8443/Citrix/Store/Policy/V1/Citrix.MPS.Doc.Farm%201.MobileApp2 HTTP/1.1
VPN VIP         Bob's Android   6040 HTTP/1.1 200 OK  (application/vnd.citrix.policies+xml)
Bob's Android   VPN VIP          688 POST /cvpn/https/xms:8443/STA/get_ticket_v1 HTTP/1.1
VPN VIP         Bob's Android    280 HTTP/1.1 200 OK  (text/plain)
SNIP            Exchange Server  304 OPTIONS /Microsoft-Server-ActiveSync?Cmd=OPTIONS&User=null&DeviceId=workmailc1402373954&DeviceType=SAMSUNGGTN5110 HTTP/1.1
Exchange Server SNIP            1536 HTTP/1.1 401 Unauthorized  (text/html)
SNIP            Exchange Server  400 OPTIONS /Microsoft-Server-ActiveSync?Cmd=OPTIONS&User=xmx.lab%5Cbob.leroy%40xmx.lab&DeviceId=workmailc1402373954&DeviceType=SAMSUNGGTN5110
Exchange Server SNIP             640 HTTP/1.1 200 OK
SNIP            Exchange Server  496 POST /Microsoft-Server-ActiveSync?Cmd=FolderSync&User=xmx.lab%5Cbob.leroy%40xmx.lab&DeviceId=workmailc1402373954&DeviceType=SAMSUNGGTN5110
```

For WorxMail, this will appear as a series of ActiveSync requests.

Troubleshooting XenMobile® and NetScaler integration

Now that we know what the flow looks like for a XenMobile application when connecting via NetScaler, let's look at some troubleshooting suggestions. Both XenMobile and NetScaler provide some excellent tools to support this integration.

Using the wizard for configuration

XenMobile can be complex to configure manually. There are many components and operating systems (IOS, Android, Windows) each with their own characteristics, which means a lot of policies. Citrix has made this job a lot simpler by providing a wizard in NetScaler Gateway to help create these policies with just a few clicks. If you see issues during your deployment, I would highly recommend redoing the configuration using the wizard. This is available in the **Integrate with Citrix Products** section of the GUI:

Using the connectivity checks

Between the client devices, NetScaler, the XenMobile server, and the backend infrastructure, there are a lot of connectivity points that need verifying. Citrix provides three excellent tools to help verify that the necessary connectivity and configurations are in place:

- **On the NetScaler Gateway**: Go to the **Integrate with Citrix Products** section where the wizards are. Click on **XenMobile** and you will find a **Test Connectivity** button in the top right-hand corner. This button runs through a number of important checks for you and verifies the following:
  - DNS Suffix is configured (this is very important for Android devices when split tunneling is configured)
  - DNS server is configured and reachable
  - LDAP binding works correctly
  - XenMobile servers are set up and respond correctly

○ The XenMobile VIP is up and running:

Connectivity Checks

Connectivity Checks

DNS Suffix

⬤ **xmx.lab**

'xmx.lab' is resolved by configured DNS servers.

DNS

⬤ **192.168.1.30**

Server '192.168.1.30' is reachable.

Port '53/udp' is open.

'192.168.1.30' is a valid DNS server.

Domain records are properly configured.

LDAP Authentication Server for Netscaler Gateway

⬤ **192.168.1.30**

Server '192.168.1.30' is reachable.

port '389/tcp' is open.

'192.168.1.30' is a valid LDAP server.

LDAP Policy is configured with proper credentials.

XenMobile AppController Server

⬤ **xmsvip.xmx.lab:8443**

Server 'xmsvip.xmx.lab' is reachable.

port '8443/tcp' is open.

'xmsvip.xmx.lab' is not a valid AppController server.

STA Server

⬤ **xmsvip.xmx.lab:8443**

Server 'xmsvip.xmx.lab' is reachable.

port '8443/tcp' is open.

'xmsvip.xmx.lab' is a valid STA server.

- **On the XenMobile server**: Go to the page at `https://<XenMobile_Server_IP>:4443/support.html` (or click on the wrench on the configuration screen) and you will have the means to test connectivity to NetScaler and see whether the necessary settings are in place:

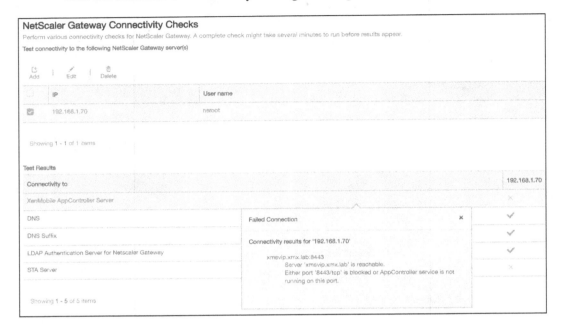

- **Using the XenMobile Cerebro Utility**: Cerebro is a small diagnostic utility (it needs Excel on your PC) that can either run checks against NetScaler if your PC has direct access to it, or alternatively accept an `ns.conf`, analyze it and tell you whether the necessary configuration pieces are all in place. This tool is available at KB Article CTX141060 (`http://goo.gl/jZSH6V`).

Knowing where the logs are

Just as with other NetScaler Gateway scenarios the authentication exchange and any issues are captured in `aaad.debug`. The connection attempts and the start and end of sessions are captured in `ns.log`.

WorxHome and XenMobile server have their own logs as well. These can sometimes seem unintuitive, especially when captured with the level set to debug (as this may sometimes contain references to internal functions). Nonetheless, coupled with the timestamp of the issue, they can provide you with a good starting point by looking for the keywords `Error` or `Failed`.

The procedures to collect these logs are covered in the *XenMobile Logs Collection Guide*. You can use the shortened URL `https://goo.gl/tBtjtV` which points to this document. This article covers the following topics:

- How to capture logs for WorxHome and its applications for different Operating Systems – iOS, Android, and Windows

- How to capture debug level logs on the XenServer

- Exchange ActiveSync logs, which are useful for troubleshooting WorxMail issues

> Remember to reset the log levels from debug to default. While the debug level of logging is useful for troubleshooting, it is resource intensive and can impact performance if left enabled indefinitely.

Common integration issue areas

Here are some of the integration issues that commonly get reported in the XenMobile-NetScaler field.

Licenses

MicroVPNs tunnels each use up a VPN license, one per device. So ensure that sufficient licenses are in place.

Network settings for the application

For any issues involving WorxApps being unable to connect, verify the following:

- The DNS suffix configured is correct – this is very important for Android, since an incorrect setting means the VPN tunnel does not start and any resources that are only accessible via the gateway VIP will be unreachable.

- Network access is set to the right value. This is a setting on the XenMobile server, which is independently set for each application. There is a very popular blog that shows sample settings for WorxMail; you can access it here: `https://goo.gl/fXiB3v`.

- Whether the application traffic uses the tunnel or not depends on this setting. Here is a screenshot of the options and what they mean in NetScaler VPN parlance:

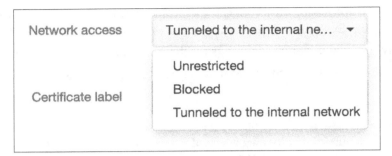

- Following is the explanation of the preceding options
  - ○ **Unrestricted**: Split tunnel ON
  - ○ **Blocked**: No network access at all
  - ○ **Tunneled to the Internal Network**: Split tunnel OFF

If you choose the **Tunneled to the internal network** setting, you need to be sure that NetScaler SNIP can reach the backend server without any firewall issues.

The following XenMobile Apps are most commonly impacted by an incorrect setting here:
- WorxMail, which needs access to the Exchange Server
- ShareFile, which needs access to the ShareFile cloud-based service and the Storage Zone Controller
- WorxWeb, which if tunneled to the internal network needs access to the website the User is trying to access

Account services address

Verify that this field is configured on the session profiles. If this is missing, WorxHome autodiscovery will fail. Here is an example taken from my lab. The URL should point to the XenMobile server or an LB VIP representing it:

Persistence issues when Load Balancing XenMobile servers

If you are load balancing multiple XenMobile servers, verify that persistence is set to ACNODEID, and that this ACNODEID is being received in the requests, by looking at a trace. Try disabling all but one XenMobile server to rule out load balancing issues as a cause of the problem:

```
POST /cvpn/https/xms:8443/Citrix/StoreWeb/Tiffany/store/launch HTTP/1.1
Accept: application/json
Accept-Language: en-US, en
X-Citrix-Device-ID: NYJcLRM0iPMi8H8CoPKPShW6wiD00n+Xu12fjdVA9Vk=
X-Citrix-Gateway: mvpn.xmx.lab
Content-Length: 0
Host: mvpn.xmx.lab
Connection: Keep-Alive
User-Agent: CitrixReceiver/com.zenprise build/10.2.2 Android/4.4.2 KOT49H.N5110XXDNF1 VpnCapable
Accept-Encoding: gzip
Cookie: NSC_AAAC=85bd309c1a6c3d3ec03f2622ecd87aec0c3a01f5a45525d5f4f58455e445a4a42; ACNODEID=3232235816
Cookie2: $Version=1
```

ShareFile SSO issues

SAML-based SSO for ShareFile is a very popular use case. Consider the following three steps if you see any issues here:

1. Verify that the ShareFile account works by logging into the ShareFile site without SAML.

2. Ensure that the times are set correctly on NetScaler and the XenMobile server. As we discussed in our AAA chapter, time skews will cause SAML authentication to fail, as the assertions will be deemed invalid.

3. To validate that the configuration is set correctly, open a web browser (this can even be on your PC) and access the following URL: `https://<subdomain>.sharefile.com/saml/login`. For example `https://bobleroy.sharefile.com/saml/login`.

This should present you with the NetScaler login page without any errors. You should be able to log in and see all your ShareFile files and folders. If this doesn't work, the SSO URL configured on the XenMobile server might be incorrect or there might have been a certificate failure.

Summary

In this chapter, we covered a lot of information, so let's take a few minutes to summarize it. We discussed Basic and Smart Access modes, how they different in functionality, and that Smart Access mode uses Concurrent User licenses. We broke the rest of the chapter down into three sections.

In the *NetScaler Gateway as a VPN* section, we looked at the exchange that happens when a User launches a full VPN connection using a VPN client. We contrasted this with a Clientless VPN, before proceeding to discuss some troubleshooting tools and techniques for VPN connections, and how to capture debug information.

In the *NetScaler Gateway integration with XenApp and XenDesktop* section, we began by discussing the components involved. Before examining a XenDesktop session, we discussed the steps for enumeration and for published desktop launch. We then discussed the troubleshooting steps for each of these two phases.

In the *NetScaler Gateway integration with XenMobile* section, we discussed the components involved before examining the steps involved in the discovery, enumeration, and launch of Worx applications, using WorxMail as an example. We then discussed the excellent tools Citrix provides for troubleshooting this integration – namely the connectivity checks in XenMobile Server and NetScaler, and the Cerebro utility. We then wrapped up the section with a discussion of some common XenMobile integration issues.

I hope you found this chapter useful. Please join me for the next chapter, where we will look at system issues that can impact NetScaler at a system level.

8
System-Level Issues

Up until this point, our focus has been on troubleshooting individual features. While working with NetScaler, one can also run into issues impacting the NetScaler system as a whole. These can range from licensing issues, to the unit itself becoming inaccessible. Troubleshooting such system-wide issues are the focus of this chapter.

We will focus on the following key areas:

- Licensing issues
- NTP issues
- SNMP issues
- CPU and memory issues
- Disk issues
- Crash and hang issues

Licensing issues

You can check the status of licensing on your NetScaler by running the `show license` command. This should show which features are licensed:

```
> show license
        License status:
                               Web Logging: YES
                          Surge Protection: YES
                           Load Balancing: YES
                         Content Switching: YES
                        Cache Redirection: YES
                             Sure Connect: YES
                      Compression Control: YES
```

The NetScaler editions page available at https://goo.gl/sE8Pth is an excellent resource for understanding what features each of the license types includes.

These feature licenses are tied to a value called the hostID, an ID which is based on the MAC address of one of the interfaces that you provide when allocating your licenses on the Citrix portal:

```
root@rvtns# lmutil lmhostid -ether
lmutil - Copyright (c) 1989-2013 Flexera Software LLC. All Rights Reserved
The FlexNet host ID of this machine is "1a2b3c4d5e6f"
```

If there is a mismatch between what is provided during allocation versus the ID of the device, the license will fail to apply. Consequently, this ID is an important focus area when troubleshooting licensing.

To troubleshoot licensing issues, use the following method:

1. Go to shell.
2. Change the directory to /var/log.
3. Run a cat license.log | grep hostid and look for any errors.

The following Wrong hostid error is an indication that this needs to be resolved by reallocating the license with the correct hostID:

```
root@rvtns# cat /var/log/license.log | grep hostid
16:58:36 (CITRIX) Wrong hostid on SERVER line for license file:
16:58:36 (CITRIX) SERVER line says ce89cf62cffb, hostid is 1a2b3c4d5e6f
16:58:36 (CITRIX) Invalid hostid on SERVER line
16:58:36 (CITRIX) No valid hostids, exiting
```

 A licensing aspect that is commonly confused is feature/platform licenses versus VPN Concurrent User Licenses (CCUs). The former use the hostID, while CCUs rely on the hostname configured on the NetScaler.

NTP issues

NTP (**Network Time Protocol**) allows machines to synchronize their time and date with a master server that is always considered to be accurate. There are several reasons why accurate time and date on the NetScaler are important:

- Authentication protocols such as Kerberos and SAML rely on timestamps to check that the tokens issued are still valid. Authentication will fail if the time on the NetScaler is incorrect.

- Caching relies on the time set on the NetScaler to determine if `http` objects are still valid.

- When performing log analysis and trace analysis, it is important that the date and time correspond across different devices, to be able to match the times across various logs.

 Citrix article CTX120952 provides the necessary steps to configure NTP on NetScaler.

Before discussing troubleshooting, here's a quick summary of the steps that happen when a NetScaler is configured to synchronize its time with an NTP server:

1. The NetScaler contacts the NTP Server and sets the original timestamp field to a time in the past, to indicate that it needs to synchronize:

```
Network Time Protocol (NTP Version 4, client)
⊞ Flags: 0xe3
   Peer Clock Stratum: unspecified or invalid (0)
   Peer Polling Interval: 6 (64 sec)
   Peer Clock Precision: 0.000002 sec
   Root Delay:    0.0000 sec
   Root Dispersion:    0.0088 sec
   Reference ID: (Initialization)
   Reference Timestamp: Jan  1, 1970 00:00:00.000000000 UTC
   Origin Timestamp: Oct 18, 2015 13:09:26.765140000 UTC
   Receive Timestamp: Oct 18, 2015 13:08:07.675643000 UTC
   Transmit Timestamp: Oct 18, 2015 13:09:13.619097000 UTC
```

2. The server responds with its value of time, always considered accurate, using the receive timestamp.

3. Several exchanges of timestamps occur, each involving similar requests and responses as Steps 1 and 2. This process generally takes several minutes.

4. Eventually, the NetScaler updates itself to the Server indicated time. At this point, the origin and receive timestamps will both have the same value:

```
Network Time Protocol (NTP Version 4, client)
⊞ Flags: 0x23
   Peer Clock Stratum: secondary reference (4)
   Peer Polling Interval: 6 (64 sec)
   Peer Clock Precision: 0.000002 sec
   Root Delay:     0.1012 sec
   Root Dispersion:    0.0804 sec
   Reference ID: mail.my-inbox.co.uk
   Reference Timestamp: Oct 18, 2015 13:30:40.857382000 UTC
   Origin Timestamp: Oct 18, 2015 13:30:40.837825000 UTC
   Receive Timestamp: Oct 18, 2015 13:30:40.857382000 UTC
   Transmit Timestamp: Oct 18, 2015 13:31:44.799994000 UTC
```

 NTP needs UDP port 123 to be open between NSIP and the NTP Server.

Troubleshooting NTP synchronization

If your NetScaler is configured for NTP but shows the date and time incorrectly, start by checking the status of NTP on the NetScaler. To do this, use the following command:

`'> show ntp status'`

```
> show ntp status
     remote          refid       st t when poll reach   delay   offset  jitter
===============================================================================
*81.168.77.149  82.219.4.30     3 u   37   64  377   57.885  127414.  0.538
Done
```

This output will provide a number of useful bits of information. The preceding output is taken from a working NTP setup. The important fields are as follows:

- `remote`: The IP address/DNS name of the server
- `refid`: The IP address of the source of the time for the NTP server itself—a higher stratum server
- `st`: The stratum level of the server
- `when`: How much time has passed since the last response
- `poll`: How often, in seconds, the NetScaler will poll this server
- `reach`: How many attempts by the NetScaler to reach the server were successful

- `delay`: Round trip time to the NTP Server
- `Offset`: This value indicates the time difference between the NetScaler and the server

Following on from the previous screenshot, the time skew of 127,414 milliseconds (127.414 seconds) will result in a `clock_step` update. This will be visible in `/var/log/ntpd.log`, which is the NTP log file:

```
20 Mar 17:32:22 ntpd[94942]: 0.0.0.0 c615 05 clock_sync
20 Mar 17:32:23 ntpd[94942]: 0.0.0.0 c618 08 no_sys_peer
20 Mar 17:40:27 ntpd[94942]: 0.0.0.0 c613 03 spike_detect +127.414157 s
20 Mar 17:43:47 ntpd[94942]: 0.0.0.0 c61c 0c clock_step +127.414157 s
```

Jitter in NTP verifies several samples of time, which is why the convergence takes time. Jitter is a value indicative of the differences in time between those samples.

 Once the time is corrected using a `clock_step` action, all ntp statistics are reset.

Let's now look at a failing NTP setup. In this case, the status will be stuck in INIT and the delay, offset, and Jitter will all show zeroes:

```
> show ntp status
     remote          refid      st t when poll reach   delay   offset  jitter
================================================================================
mail.my-inbox.c .INIT.         16 u    -   64    0    0.000    0.000   0.000
```

As part of troubleshooting, you can also query the NTP server using the `ntpdate -q` command, which will help you identify any communication issues. If the command returns errors because the NetScaler cannot reach the NTP server, you will need to investigate this as a network issue.

You can also use the `ntpdate -u <ntp_server_ip>` shell command to update the time instantaneously and let NTP maintain the time from then on:

```
root@ns_80# date
Sat Nov 28 11:15:14 CET 2015
root@ns_80# ntpdate -q 81.168.77.149
server 81.168.77.149, stratum 3, offset 110519.099892, delay 0.08241
28 Nov 11:15:26 ntpdate[71315]: step time server 81.168.77.149 offset 110519.099892 sec
```

SNMP issues

SNMP is the most commonly used method to monitor the health of NetScaler and the services configured on it. It involves polling specific strings, called **OIDs (Object Identifiers)**, that represent various NetScaler properties such as interface stats, or NetScaler entities such as vServers and services, using external tools to monitor health and performance characteristics.

The NetScaler eDocs cover how to set SNMP using the various versions (SNMP v1, v2, v3), but at a basic level, you need the following configuration:

- An external SNMP manager, or your own PC if you use an SNMP browser.

- The SNMP **MIB (Management Information Base)**, which contains, in a tree-like structure, all the properties of NetScaler and its objects that you can poll, and what their OIDs are. These are located in the /netscaler/snmp/ folder. You can also download the MIB files from the GUI:

```
root@ns_80# cd /netscaler/snmp
root@ns_80# ls
NS-MIB-smiv1.mib          mib.txt
NS-MIB-smiv2.mib          traps.txt
```

- SNMP community configuration, which needs to match what is configured on the server side.

- Adding the SNMP Manager on the NetScaler

Troubleshooting SNMP on a NetScaler

Most issues in this area come down to one of three areas, as follows:

- **Reachability issues**: Take a trace to verify that the SNMP requests are getting through to the NetScaler. For example, are ports UDP 161 and 162 open? Also, ensure that access to and from the NSIP is allowed through the firewall, or use an appropriate netprofile.

- **Configuration issues**: If you are seeing no response at all, check if the community string and versions match on both sides. Verify permissions such as GET, SET, and BULK. This is part of the community configuration. For example, add snmp community london_snmp_goup ALL. If you're using SNMP V3, also ensure that authentication is set up correctly. Ensure you are polling the correct OID. You can browse through the MIBs for this purpose, or alternatively use the file mib.txt, which handily lists in all system-level OIDs.

To browse through the MIB, you could also use a tool (my favorite is MIB browser, by `iReasoning`) to click around and discover all the available OIDs. Another excellent alternative for quick testing is `snmpwalk`.

- **SNMP Manager missing in the list**: If there are SNMP Managers configured on NetScaler, ensure that your SNMP Manager is in that list, otherwise the requests may fail. You can use the command `show snmp manager` for this purpose. This a common configuration issue when working with Command Center discovery of NetScaler.

CPU and memory issues

Most high CPU and memory issues will require working with tech support to conclude the root cause through adequate code-level analysis. There are, however, actions you can take, including collecting useful information, both to speed up the investigation, but also to avoid having to wait for the issue to recur for that information to be captured.

Types of NetScaler CPU

NetScaler has two CPUs that do very different things:

- The Management CPU handles mainly bookkeeping tasks and parts of the NetScaler code that run in FreeBSD, such as the various protocol daemons (for example, `snmpd`). A high management CPU usage, unless prolonged, does not impact packet handling, and a momentary spike should be expected when logs are compressed as part of a rollover.

- The Packet Engine CPU is entirely dedicated to handling packets, therefore, a saturation of this CPU can impact your production traffic and needs to be dealt with immediately.

SNMP is the best way to detect high CPU events as it is not practical to constantly monitor the dashboard. NetScaler has specific traps that get sent out when a CPU goes high. You can configure these values by navigating to **System | SNMP | Alarms**. The following is a typical example:

CPU-USAGE	Enabled	80%	40%	-N/A-	Critical	ENABLED
MGMT-CPU-USAGE	Enabled	100%	30%	-N/A-	Major	ENABLED

Consider the following steps when you see CPU staying pegged at 100%:

1. Use `stat cpu` on the NetScaler CLI to see what the actual packet engine CPU consumption is. If it shows near 100%, try the following steps to lower potential impact to traffic:

   1. Stop any running traces.
   2. Disable USIP if not absolutely needed.
   3. Where possible, turn off rewrite policies that use regex.
   4. Ensure SSL reuse is enabled on all SSL vServers. It is by default, but as you recall from the *Chapter 2, Traffic Management Features*, it will need to be turned off momentarily to obtain a decryptable trace. If, however, left for long in production, a CPU increase can be expected along with SSL card utilization.

   If this is a VPX or SDX, also consider adding additional packet engines. Citrix article CTX139485 shows how to do this for a VPX.

2. If it's the Management CPU that is shooting to 100%, run the shell command `top` and look for processes other than NSPPE that are taking up high CPU percentage – this can be because of any of the daemons that run in `userland` `nsaaad` and `httpd`. Save this output to a file (for example, `top > /var/top.txt`) to include with the case information when engaging Citrix Tech Support.

 When you check the `top` output, you will see the **NSPPE** (**NetScaler Packet Processing Engine**) processes taking up 100%. This is normal, since FreeBSD on the NetScaler offloads all of the CPUs except one (the Management CPU) to the NetScaler OS.

3. Generate a `show techsupport` file and share it with Citrix Tech Support to assist with the root cause analysis. The easiest way to do this is from the GUI, under the diagnostics tab.

Exploring high memory issues

Memory build ups happen more gradually than CPU build ups. As a result, apart from SNMP monitoring, periodically looking at the dashboard or running `stat` commands on the NetScaler is a good way to catch them.

Memory build ups can result from:

- High traffic
- Memory leaks
- The use of certain features

Troubleshooting high memory issues

To troubleshoot memory issues, start by plotting the memory usage versus traffic being handled. The easiest way to do this is to use the *CPU versus Memory versus HTTP Requests Rate* graph. You will find this graph in the dashboard:

- If the graph instead only shows memory increasing and never dropping, even after peak hours, this could be due to a memory leak resulting from a function not releasing memory it no longer needs. Memory leaks are bugs that need engaging with technical support with the help of a `techsupport` file. It will be useful to note any details of features recently enabled or new services being created on the NetScaler for faster identification.

- If the memory usage is high but it increases and decreases with traffic, it means you have an insufficiently sized NetScaler. You might, in the short term, handle the situation by reducing the amount of memory assigned to caching and TCP buffering, or by turning off certain protections in AppFirewall. Another option that you have with AppFirewall is to use the `sessionless` forms of protection (for example, `sessionless` form field consistency).

- The shell command `nsconmsg -s ConMEM=2 -d oldconmsg | more` produces a snapshot of the current memory consumption, giving you an insight into the amount of memory that each of the features is consuming. This will help you understand if your NetScaler is undersized for the traffic it needs to handle, or if particular application is receiving more traffic than you planned for:

MEMPOOL	MaxAllowd	CurAlloc Bytes (Own%)(Overall%)	ErrLmtFailed	ErrAllocFailed	ErrFreeF
TotalMEM: (5481921792/5674893312)	Allocated: 4202086336(74.05%)	ActualInUse: 3115640569(54.90%)			
MEM_PE	62914560	3663168(5.82% 0.06%)	0	0	0
MEM_LB_SERVER	12884901885	10339776(0.08% 0.18%)	0	0	0
MEM_LB_SESSION	408944640	1642112(0.40% 0.03%)	0	0	0
MEM_LB_SERVICE	12884901885	394752(0.00% 0.01%)	0	0	0
MEM_CSWMEM	75497472	94272(0.12% 0.00%)	0	0	0
MEM_IOH	15728640	0(0.00% 0.00%)	0	0	0
MEM_LOGGING	12884901885	16785408(0.13% 0.30%)	0	0	0
MEM_CONN	12884901885	2791464960(21.66% 49.19%)	0	0	0
MEM_SNMP	12884901885	664576(0.01% 0.01%)	0	0	0
MEM_DEBUG	786432	4992(0.63% 0.00%)	0	0	0
MEM_MISC	12884901885	12460672(0.10% 0.22%)	0	0	0
MEM_SERVMON	12884901885	2194752(0.02% 0.04%)	0	0	0
MEM_IPFRAG	12884901885	0(0.00% 0.00%)	0	0	0
MEM_URLMON	47185920	0(0.00% 0.00%)	0	0	0
MEM_TCPBUFFP	254454442	6291456(2.47% 0.11%)	0	0	0
MEM_DCC	31457280	0(0.00% 0.00%)	0	0	0
MEM_DNS	12884901885	25232832(0.20% 0.44%)	0	0	0
MEM_GSLB	12884901885	1728(0.00% 0.00%)	0	0	0
MEM_POLENG	402653184	5056128(1.26% 0.09%)	0	0	0
MEM_AUDITLOG	150994944	1332672(0.88% 0.02%)	0	0	0
MEM_PI_CONFIG	12884901885	47819264(0.37% 0.84%)	0	0	0
MEM_APPSECURE	4768557456	595027904(12.48% 10.49%)	0	31	0

> Memory issues can also manifest due to failed memory hardware. Since memory is detected at boot time, `dmesg` is a great place to find this info. Use the shell command `dmesg | grep memory`. If the real memory is less than what is advertised when you purchased the unit, you could be looking at an RMA. A quick way to verify what it should be is by looking at the HA peer, since the units are generally both the same model.

Disk issues

There are two kinds of disk issues that NetScaler administrators may come across:

- **Disk hardware issues**: There are three ways to identify disk hardware issues:
    - SNMP Alerts is one way to identify it. You can configure the alarm `HARD-DISK-DRIVE-ERRORS`

    ○   Look for entries in the `/var/log/messages` file – the keyword is `TIMEOUT`

```
May 15 16:42:01  LILLE-NETSCALER kernel: ad4:
TIMEOUT - WRITE_DMA retrying (1 retry left) LBA=233764177
```

    ○   Run the hardware analysis file `/netscaler/ns_hw_err.bash`, which will run through all the log files and capture the TIMEOUT entries for you.

> Note that a very occasional `TIMEOUT` can occur with a perfectly healthy NetScaler. There is, however, a problem if you see a few of them in succession and that is the symptom you are looking for. RMAs can involve either simply replacing the SSD, which is less disruptive, or sometimes replacing the unit, if it's the controller which is failing (which is a lot rarer).

- **Disk space issues:** NetScaler relies on the hard disk not just for storing logs and traces, but also as swap space to improve performance. Consequently, when the hard disk fills up, you might run into a number of issues. The most commonly reported of these issues is logins failing. For this reason, it is always good to periodically check the free disk space using the `df -h` shell command and clear up space by deleting older traces or installation files under `/var/nsinstall` that are no longer in use.

Crash and hang issues

Crashes and hangs can happen with any device running software, and the NetScaler is no different in this regard. While a large percentage of them get picked up during testing, the complexity involved in catching all use cases and packet combinations means that some will make their way to the Customers. The good news is that most are usually fixed by the next revision of the software. This is one of the biggest reasons to stay current in terms of NetScaler builds.

Let's first start by differentiating these crashes and hangs. While their impact on your application's availability can be the same, the underlying issues are very different, and how you have to approach them as an Administrator are different as well.

Understanding crashes

A NetScaler crash can happen due to several reasons:

- The NetScaler encounters a coding error by which it arrives at an invalid condition such as an invalid pointer reference, due to which it gives up on processing and proceeds to dump a core.

- One of the packet engines becomes too slow to respond and fails to send out its heartbeats to a system process that monitors all packet engines. This can happen because the packet engine is doing something very CPU-intensive, such as processing a huge regex policy.

- While rare, a crash of the FreeBSD software itself will eventually crash the system and result in a core file under /var/crash.

Working with crashes

Most administrators will notice a crash in the form of an unexpected reboot or a failover. One way to verify whether the issue was due to a crash is to look for newly created files in /var/core or /var/crash.

You will need to engage Citrix Technical Support to help identify the root cause for the crash and get advice on corrective steps, which will often involve upgrading to a build that contains the fix. To facilitate the investigation, capture the following information to share with the engineer:

- The core file under /var/core or /var/crash that matches the time of the issue

- The show techsupport file

- Note down and provide details of any recent changes in configuration, such as introducing new services or enabling new features before the crash

While waiting for the engagement to complete, consider reverting to an earlier build if the crash is seen immediately after an upgrade. If you are using a very out of date build, consider upgrading to the latest by looking up the release notes for similar potential issues that are fixed, or alternatively consider one of the Citrix-certified **Safe Harbor builds** (see the upcoming section about the various build types).

Working with hang issues

A hang is a situation where the NetScaler is stuck in a race condition because two functions mutually waiting on each other, or because a process is running in a never-ending loop. One sign of a hang is when the device appears to power up but doesn't respond to any input. There are also cases where the device continues to handle traffic while being unreachable via GUI/SSH/Console.

In the case of a hang you will not see any core dumps. A reboot will almost certainly restore access to the unit, but it should not be the first line of troubleshooting as this will result in important diagnostic information being lost. You should instead attempt to dump a core.

Dumping a core on a VPX/MPX when console is available

You can dump a core by aborting one of the packet engines from console. Here are a quick set of steps taken from the knowledge base article CTX207598 on how to do this:

1. Go to shell.
2. Run the command `pb_policy -o abort`. This tells the NetScaler to dump cores if packet engines are interrupted.
3. Do a `ps -aux` and note down the PID of all the packet engines.
4. Use the `kill -6` command and list the PIDs of all packet engines in the command. For example, `kill -6 325 326 327 328`.
5. This will dump a core and restart the packet engines.
6. Once the core dumps are complete, reset the `pb_policy` back to its default by running the shell command `pb_policy -d`. This is important, as the `abort` mode of running the system is performance-intensive.

Dumping a core when NetScaler is completely unresponsive

On MPX units, if NetScaler is unresponsive via console, you can dump a core using the **NMI** button. This is a recessed button at the back of NetScaler. Once the cores are available, you will need to engage tech support using the core and a collector file for the root cause analysis to be carried out.

Understanding NetScaler Build names

GA (General Availability) builds are available for all Citrix customers to use. This is a good thing. It means that there is a very large install base for such builds and any issues present will have a greater chance of being reported and fixed in the next iteration. GA builds are of two types:

- **Maintenance builds (.M builds)** are what nearly all customers run. The difference between one MR and the next is mainly bug fixes and security fixes. Unless there is a clear reason, this is the build you are most encouraged to use.

- **Enhancement builds (.e builds)** are a superset of a GA builds and contain features that are not yet available in the GA version. Usually, the features that are included in the current `.e builds` make it into the maintenance builds of the next release of code. For example, features introduced in `10.5.e` became available in the regular 11.0 version.

11.0 releases introduced naming changes in the form of **.M builds** (Maintenance – containing bugs and security fixes) and **.F builds** (which introduce new features). Then, there are the special builds:

- A **Private build** (the opposite of a GA Build) is limited to a small set of customers. These are provided under very specific conditions such as a customer needing the fix even before the complete range of tests are finished on the build, primarily because the bug has a very high impact. Consequently, the tradeoff needs to be very carefully considered.

- A **Debug build** is one that Citrix Engineering produces in a targeted manner to capture a problem which is not reproducible in the Citrix Lab environment and for which the conditions of the failure are not well understood. The build will not fix the issue, but it does contain additional instrumentation to help diagnose the issue when it happens next.

A **Safe Harbor** build is a GA build that has been available publicly for at least six months and on which customers have reported very few issues. Citrix clearly calls out these builds on the download page so they are easy to notice. At the time of writing, the latest safe harbor build available is 10.5 56.22. There are no 11.0 safe harbor builds yet, but this is subject to change.

An **NDPP build** is a build for certain sectors, such as government agencies. Such organizations are governed by regulations that require that the security status of networking devices (such as NetScaler) are independently verified as conforming to a specific standard, namely the NDPP standard. This particular build has passed that standard.

Summary

In this chapter we have looked at various issues that impact the NetScaler system as a whole. We've learned how to identify issues with system level functions such as licensing, NTP, and SNMP. We've looked at what to do when certain processes unexpectedly drain system resources such as memory and CPU, and also how to deal with the system becoming unresponsive during crash and hang situations. Finally, we have reviewed the different build types available to you as a NetScaler owner.

In our final chapter we will take a detailed look at the various tools that NetScaler provides to help us during troubleshooting.

Troubleshooting Tools

9

NetScaler has extensive logging and tracing capabilities and includes some GUI-based tools that help you with issue analysis. To complement these, Citrix also provides external tools to support you with your NetScaler deployments and associated troubleshooting. A discussion of these various tools is the focus of this chapter. We will touch on these utilities in the following order:

- The nsconmsg utility
- NetScaler packet tracing (nstrace)
- The showtechsupport utility
- NetScaler dashboard and reporting
- Citrix insight (TAAS)
- Command Center and Insight Center

The nsconmsg utility

Nsconmsg is a logging process that runs nonstop on the NetScaler. It contains a snapshot of all the available counters taken once every 7 seconds. There are an excess of 10,000 counters each with specific conditions for specific features, which makes this such a formidable troubleshooting tool in identifying if a problem condition has been hit.

The logs produced by this utility are available in /var/nslog. By default, they roll over once every two days or on reaching a size of 300 MB whichever is first. The file newlog will always be latest (current log file). They can go up to 99 files after which they restart from 0.

nsconmsg syntax and options

`nsconmsg` is used from the shell prompt with the following syntax:

```
nsconmsg -K <path> -g <counter_name> -d <display_option>
```

The commonly used options are as follows:

- `-K`: This is used to specify the name of the log file; if not used, current values of counters are shown.

- `-g`: This is used to grep for the values of specific counters, making `nsconmsg` more usable. For example, use `-g ssl` to see all available SSL counters before narrowing down to specific ones.

- `-d`: This is used to specify the type of operation. The common ones are:
    - `setime`: This displays the start and end time of the `newslog` file.
    - `current`: This displays the current value of each counter, on a 7-second basis.
    - `event`: This displays all events during that log period. It is useful for looking for any service or monitor failures and HA-related events.
    - `oldconmsg`: This is used for load balancing and content switching; it allows you to see a variety of information such as the number of requests received by each service, number of active transaction, and how the surge queue looks at each 7-second interval.
    - `stats`: This displays the current statistics. It is useful to see whether a particular counter (and thus a specific error condition) has ever been incremented.
    - `statswt0`: This displays only counters that incremented during the current log.
    - `memstats`: This displays memory-related statistics.
    - `consmsg`: This displays console messages.

Here are some useful examples:

- Use `setime` to display the time covered by the logs. If you know the time of the issue, this command will help zero in on the `newslog` file you need for analysis:

```
nsconmsg -K /var/nslog/newnslog.x.tar.gz -d setime
```

```
root@ns# nsconmsg -K /var/nslog/newnslog.17.tar.gz -d setime
x newnslog.17/
x newnslog.17/newnslog.ppe.0
Displaying start and end time information
NetScaler V20 Performance Data
NetScaler NS11.0: Build 62.10.nc, Date: Aug  8 2015, 22:30:34

start time Sun Dec 20 07:16:41 2015
end    time Mon Dec 21 06:06:03 2015
total duration      00.22:49:22
data size 35,277,352 bytes
```

- Use current to find out the rate at which a counter is incrementing:

```
nsconmsg -K /var/nslog/newnslog -g <counter name> -d current
```

In the following example, I am trying to identify whether a rate limit is being hit and at which point packets will be dropped. The pattern I would grep for this would -g _rl_.

```
root@ns_80# nsconmsg -K newnslog -g allnic_err_rl_rate_pkt_drops -d current
Displaying performance information
NetScaler V20 Performance Data
NetScaler NS11.0: Build 62.10.nc, Date: Aug  8 2015, 22:30:34

reltime:mili second between two records Wed Dec 12 12:31:50 2015
   Index    rtime totalcount-val      delta rate/sec symbol-name&device-no
       1     7002          1289        379      54 allnic_err_rl_rate_pkt_drops
       2     7004          1588        299      42 allnic_err_rl_rate_pkt_drops
       3     7002          1790        202      28 allnic_err_rl_rate_pkt_drops
       4     7005          1968        178      25 allnic_err_rl_rate_pkt_drops
       5     7002          2190        222      31 allnic_err_rl_rate_pkt_drops
       6    28014          2321        131      18 allnic_err_rl_rate_pkt_drops
```

The easiest way to arrive at the counters you need is to Google search for various NetScaler counters. For example, to find the rate limiting counter I used in the screenshot, I looked for all NetScaler NIC-related counters and found the article CTX132772. Similar articles exist for all features. You can then use the –g option to see whether the counter is being hit.

Some of the common patterns I use are -g ssl_err, -g http_err, -g tcp_err, -g nic_err, and –g csw_err.

- Use event to look at event-related data:

```
nsconmsg -K /var/nslog/newnslog -d event
```

This command is very useful to see if and when a particular failure event such as a HA failover (by grepping for the word node) has occurred.

```
root@ns_80# nsconmsg -K newnslog -d event | grep node
1342      0 PPE-0 remote node 192.168.1.81: DOWN       Wed Feb 10 22:21:26 2016
1343      0 PPE-0 self node 192.168.1.82: Claiming     Wed Feb 10 22:21:26 2016
1344      0 PPE-0 self node 192.168.1.82: Primary      Wed Feb 10 22:21:26 2016
1348      0 PPE-0 remote node 192.168.1.81: UP         Wed Feb 10 22:21:29 2016
1349      0 PPE-0 self node 192.168.1.82: Secondary (peer: Primary, UP) Wed Feb 10
1350      0 PPE-0 remote node 192.168.1.81: Primary    Wed Feb 10 22:21:29 2016
1351      7 PPE-0 remote node 192.168.1.81: INIT       Wed Feb 10 22:21:29 2016
1352      0 PPE-0 self node 192.168.1.82: Claiming     Wed Feb 10 22:21:29 2016
1353      0 PPE-0 self node 192.168.1.82: Primary (peer: Secondary, INIT) Wed Feb
1358      0 PPE-0 remote node 192.168.1.81: UP         Wed Feb 10 22:21:32 2016
```

Another important use case for event data is checking for services and vServer flaps.

- Use oldconmsg to obtain traffic management data. Load balancing as well as other feature level info such as for content switching, SSL, or monitors can be extracted using the -d oldconmsg switch by specifying the -s feature-specific switch. For example:

```
nsconmsg -K /var/nslog/newnslog -s ConLB=1 -d oldconmsg
```

```
nsconmsg -K /var/nslog/newnslog -s ConCSW=1 -d oldconmsg
```

The output of these commands were discussed in detail in *Chapter 2, Traffic Management Features*.

Using nstrace to capture a packet trace

While the logs on the NetScaler help build a picture of what happened, it is oftentimes necessary to delve deeper and identify what device is responsible for the issue (for example, is it the Server, NetScaler, or the Network?). Examining a network trace taken on the NetScaler helps identify the next steps by narrowing down the focus area.

Steps to run a trace

You can take a trace using the GUI, the CLI, or the shell. The recommended way is to do this over the GUI, which provides easy dropdown-based filtering choices as well as an option to download the trace once it's captured.

To take a trace from the GUI, use the **start new trace** option in the *Diagnostics* section.

Let's take a look at some general recommendations for running a trace.

- Always attempt to capture simultaneous traces to start with—on the client machine, NetScaler and server.

- Run the trace with a packet size of 0 unless the packets you are looking for are really small, especially SSL traces. The certificate that needs to be captured will be larger than the 164 bytes and that would mean the trace is not decryptable.

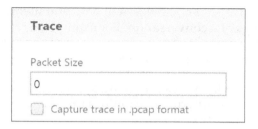

 Versions 11.0 and later offer the ability to directly capture decrypted SSL Packets. To do this select the `Decrypted SSL packets` `(SSLPLAIN)` option

- Leave the capture trace in the `.pcap` format unchecked. This will capture the trace in the proprietary NetScaler format—a format that captures a wealth of NetScaler-specific info that you can see by opening up the `NetScaler Packet Trace` header:

```
Frame 3939: 150 bytes on wire (1200 bits), 150 bytes
NetScaler Packet Trace
  Operation: TXB (0xad)
  Nic No: 0
  Activity Flags: 0x00000000
  Capture Flags: 0x00000000
  Errorcode: No Error (0x00)
  App: TEST (0x17)
  Core Id: 0
  Vlan: 1
  PcbDevNo: 0x000696d5
  Linked PcbDevNo: 0x000696d9
  TCP Debug Info
    TcpCwnd: 112880
    TcpAck: 170
    TcpTsrecent: 0
    HTTPabrtReason: connection is trackable (0)
```

Here are some of the most helpful NetScaler packet trace fields:

- The `Operation` field that shows whether the packet is transmitted or received.
- The `Nic No` field shows you the interface on which the packet was received. For example, the trace shows `0` and show interface shows `Interface 1/1 (NetScaler Virtual Interface) #0`, hence we know this packet was transmitted on `1/1`.
- The `VLAN ID` field.
- `PcbDevNo` and `Linked PcbDevNos` will help you identify the frontend and backend legs of a conversation. For example, `nstrace.pdevno == 0x000696d5 || nstrace.l_pdevno == 0x000696d9` based on the preceding screenshot will give you both legs of the conversation.

If you exactly know the packet you are looking for and are running a huge amount of traffic, you can rely on the filtering capabilities provided in the GUI. This is a great way to capture smaller traces. However, where possible, my recommendation when you first start troubleshooting a problem is to take unfiltered traces so you can see the full picture, for example, you are looking for why HTTP is failing but the problem is originating due to ARP or DNS failures.

So, start by capturing a short trace of all packets and work your way up to more specific traces.

The Showtechsupport utility

The show techsupport utility runs a perl script to collect a number of log files and command outputs. The utility's primary purpose is for Citrix Techsupport Engineers to collect all necessary logs and debug info via a single command. But it is also useful to you as an Administrator as it provides you a means to export all the useful logs to your local machine, which might have your preferred tools, such as Textpad, to examine them.

Running the utility

The easiest means is to use the GUI. It is available under **System | Diagnostics | Generate Support File**. You can also run the command `showtechsupport` from CLI or shell and then export the file that gets created in the folder `/var/tmp/support/`.

What does it contain?

The file itself is named with the convention—`collector_<primary or secondary (denoted as P/S)>_NSIP_Date_Time`. Here's a summary of the useful info it contains.

The shell directory

This is a collection of files each with the output of CLI or shell commands. The key ones are as follows:

- `showcmds.txt`, which contains:
    - Version and hardware info
    - Features and modes configured
    - Interfaces and their states and VLAN bindings
    - All vServers, Services, and ServiceGroups along with their states
    - Policies and their hits
    - Routes and bridge table entries
    - A copy of the running configuration—very useful as it helps look at the config at the time as opposed to what you find in the `ns.conf` file, which might have changed since
- `statcmds.txt`, which contains statistics both for the system as well as for all features
- `/var` folder output, which helps check whether a crash has happened recently
- `top`, which is the shell command output showing which FreeBSD processes are consuming the most CPU
- The ZebOS routing configuration in the way of `vtysh` commands (`vtyshcmds.txt`)

The var directory

This contains all the logs. The `/var/log` folder is especially useful for spotting anomalies quickly since the contents here are all ASCII. The important ones here are the `ns.log`, `messages`, `license.log`, and `auth.log` files. The `/var/nslog` contains the newnslogs, which we discussed earlier.

The nsconfig directory

This contains the configuration files. The SSL certificates and especially the private keys are not picked up for obvious security reasons.

Dashboard and Reporting tabs

NetScaler provides a couple of very useful GUI utilities in the **Dashboard** and the **Reporting** tabs. The **Dashboard** tab allows you to get a quick glance of the vital parameters of the NetScaler, such as what the current CPU and memory levels are.

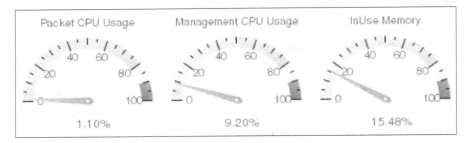

Dashboard also provides you with a number of built-in graphs that allow you to plot traffic and connection characteristics. A popular example is the client versus server connections. The following screenshot shows equal numbers, a sign that there is not a lot of connection multiplexing happening:

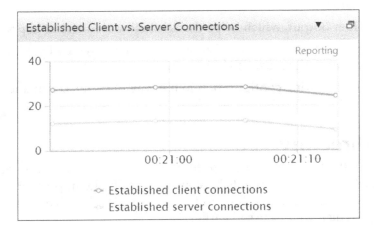

Another useful purpose that the **Dashboard** serves is as an event viewer. The **Event** logs available here help you catch ongoing issues more easily due to the red color coding. You can in addition search for specific text patterns, for example, DOWN to zero in on problematic entries.

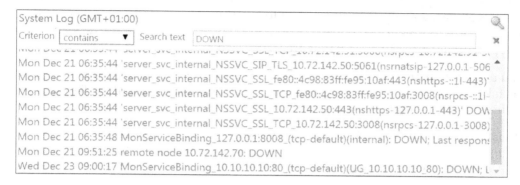

The **Reporting** tab provides historical reporting by extracting data from newnslogs. A very handy functionality here is the ability to create custom reports, which allows endless flexibility around the counters that can be used as part of the report.

Once a report is created and displayed, you can zoom in and out to control the level of granularity (for example hourly, daily).

A problem that some customers report here is the NO DATA error when displaying results. This is often because the duration selected falls outside what is covered by the log file.

Web-based analysis with Citrix Insight® Services

TAAS (Techsupport As A Service) or Citrix Insight Services, as it is now called, is a Citrix web-based analysis utility geared towards providing customers more visibility into their environment. All it takes is signing up for a MyCitrix account, something you potentially already have if you are the person managing your NetScaler.

You can then go on to `https://cis.citrix.com/` and upload a `showtechsupport` file taken from your NetScaler by clicking on the **Upload Data** button. The strength of this tool lies in automation based on years of NetScaler knowledge.

Statistics that you would otherwise have to use newnslogs commands for can be readily obtained using the site. The benefit is that you can plot CPU, Memory, SSL, TCP, and HTTP statistics and identify any trends coinciding with the time of the issue.

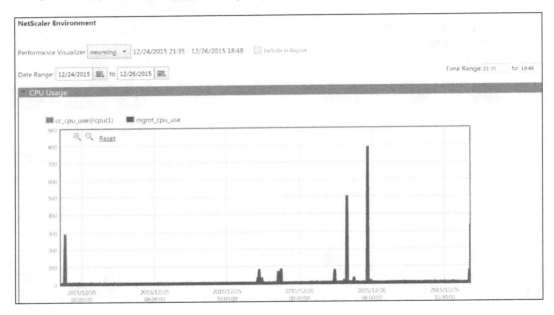

The tool will also highlight any deviation from NetScaler's best practices. The following is a sample best practice that recommends dropping invalid HTTP requests.

Invalid requests, that is, requests that are not HTTP RFC-compliant, can form the basis for certain HTTP-based attacks and should be dropped.

Citrix Command Center

Command Center is Citrix's own management solution and is highly customized to manage NetScalers. It allows you to get a quick bird's eye view of your NetScaler infrastructure from where you can dig deeper into individual issues.

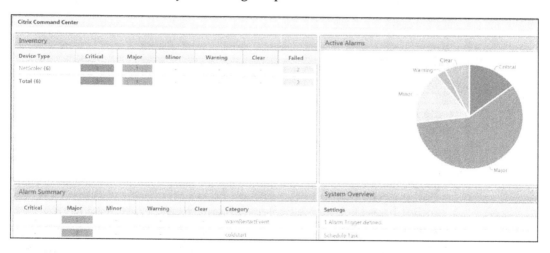

Command Center also includes extensive backup capabilities. Once a NetScaler is discovered, that is to say added to the inventory of managed devices, **Command Center** periodically backs up configuration and certificates for these devices. This allows you to quickly restore to an earlier good configuration when necessary.

What makes **Command Center** a very effective troubleshooting tool is its ability to make sense of NetScaler-generated alerts. The **Events** and **Alarms** sections of **Command Center** display very clear messages based on the alerts received.

To take this usefulness one step further, **Command Center** allows you to create automated actions when a problem is detected. Examples of such actions can be to send an e-mail to an Administrator or to failover to a different service as part of a contingency plan.

Troubleshooting tips

Consider the following steps if you run into issues with **Command Center**:

1. Ensure the following ports are open between **Command Center** and the NetScaler:
   - UDP port 161 for SNMP polling
   - UDP port 162 for SNMP traps
   - TCP ports 80 (HTTP) 443 (SSL) for NITRO (API) communication and utilities such as NetScaler CLI, which can be invoked from **Command Center**
   - TCP port 22 for SFTP and SSH for running commands (for example, Tasks)

2. If you have SNMP managers already configured, ensure **Command Center** is already present in that list or discovery will fail.

3. Verify that discovery is set to use the following:
   - Correct SNMP community
   - Correct security credentials
   - Correct SSL/TLS settings

4. **Command Center** software needs to be installed on top of Windows or Linux. This can sometimes mean interference from other software on the machine or a missing prerequisite due to which **Command Center** fails to start. To identify the reason for such issues, take a look at `wrapper.log` located in the `Logs` directory. The `Logs` directory will be present in the folder for **Command Center** you chose during installation.

Insight center

Insight center can be best described as an application visibility tool. It allows application and network owners to see how the applications hosted via the NetScaler are performing and the point of origin of delays, which helps narrow down areas for troubleshooting. It also helps identify the top users for applications and the applications that are most used. These applications can be standard web applications hosted by the NetScaler (web insight) or XenApp and XenDesktop Applications (HDX insight). The following screenshot is a sample HDX Insight showing the various delays adding up to slow application launches:

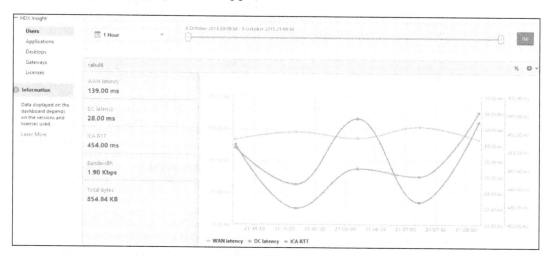

Source: Image from Citrix eDocs

There are a couple of technologies at the heart of Insight Center: IPFIX and AppFlow.

IPFIX is an IETF standard that allows TCP/UDP flow level information, that is, the 5-tuple info that contains Source IP, Destination IP, Source Port, Destination Port, and Protocol.

AppFlow is an extension to IPFIX that then adds application info to this mix by using a provision in the standard to include details such as URLs, request methods, and status codes. An excellent use of this provision is to include ICA information, such as the published app that is accessed (used by an Insight Center feature called HDX insight).

When NetScaler is set up for insight center, it knows to send IPFIX records with the AppFlow information added information to it. The application level info present in these records then allows insight center to provide in-depth visibility into how the applications are performing in the form of a wide range of performance reports.

Troubleshooting insight center

Consider the following steps if you run into issues with Insight Center:

1. Ensure the following ports are open between Insight Center and NetScaler:
   ° UDP port 4739 used by IPFIX and AppFlow
   ° TCP ports 80 (HTTP) 443 (SSL) for NITRO (API) communication. SSL can also be enforced though configuration. NITRO to query NetScalers for details such as the vServers that are configured.
   ° TCP port 22 for SSH between Insight Center and the NetScaler
   ° ICMP which Insight Center uses to verify reachability

2. Verify that the feature is enabled and configured on the VIP.

3. Ensure that the times are in sync; any inaccuracies here will mean there will be a skew in the reports.

4. There is a dependency between the Insight Center version and the NetScaler version. Ensure that the Insight Center version is the same as the NetScaler version or higher.

5. HDX Insight (ICA) reporting also has a dependency on the NetScaler license so ensure that NetScaler is adequately licensed. HDX Insight is not available for NetScaler Standard and is only available with certain granularities for the Enterprise Edition.

Summary

In this chapter, we discussed the tools available to you as an Administrator to help troubleshoot NetScaler issues. We began by looking at the `nsconmsg` binary logging utility, its syntax, and some useful examples. This was followed by the tracing utility nstrace and what proprietary information it can capture. We then looked at the different pieces of information that get picked up by the `TechSupport` file, before covering the **Reporting** and **Dashboard** pages.

In the second half of the chapter, we looked at Citrix Insight Services, which takes as input the `TechSupport` file and produces recommendations based on NetScaler best practices and highlights any deviations.

We concluded the chapter by briefly discussing **Command Center** and Insight Center, two tools that help to manage and gain better visibility into your Application environment. We also touched some quick troubleshooting tips for these tools.

Index

ns.log file
  reference link 197
  used, for viewing authorization
      information 174, 175
  used, for viewing session
      information 174, 175
  using 196
nstrace
  trace, running 220-222
  using, for capturing packet trace 220
NTLM (NT LAN Manager) 93
NTLM SSO (401 Based Authentication)
  about 93
  authentication flow 93, 94
  troubleshooting 94, 95
NTP (Network Time Protocol)
  about 203
  issues 203
  synchronization, troubleshooting 204, 205

O

OIDs (Object Identifiers)
  core, dumping 206

P

Path MTU Discovery 14
Payment Card Industry Data Security
      Standard (PCI-DSS) 141
pol_hits counter
  used, for examining policy hits 175, 176
Ports, for NetScaler integration
  DNS 190
  Global Catalogue 190
  LDAP 190
  User Enrolment 190
  WorxStore access 190
Prefer Direct Route option 21, 22
promiscuous mode 131
Protocol Transition (S4USELF) 100
proximity
  based methods, troubleshooting 60, 61
  dynamic 60
  static 60

published application/desktop
      launch process
  about 178
  desktop enumeration 179-182
  launching 183-185

R

RADIUS protocol
  about 86
  authentication flow 86
  ports 86
  troubleshooting 86-88
Remote Integrated Services
      Engine (RISE) 14
Reporting tab 224, 225
Request Switching 8, 9
Response time (RspTime) 33
RISE modes
  RISE_APBR (RISE Auto PBR) 15
  RISE_RHI (RISE Route Health Injection) 15
RPC
  considerations 57
  related issues 59

S

SAML SSO
  troubleshooting 116
Secure Ticketing Authority (STA) 178
Security Assertion Markup
      Language (SAML)
  about 110
  canonicalization 111
  certificates 111
  Identity Provider (IDP) 111
  IDP initiated SSO 114, 115
  Service Provider (SP) 110
  SP Initiated SSO 112-114
  User 110
Sessionization 143
Session Reliability 186
session-reused handshake 41, 42
SFTP 11
ShareFile
  about 198
  URL 199

shell 10
Showtechsupport utility
    about 222
    nsconfig directory 224
    running 222
    shell directory 223
    var directory 223
signatures 157
Smart Access 181
Smart Access mode
    about 164
    features 164, 165
SNMP issues
    about 206
    configuration issues 206
    reachability issues 206
    SNMP Manager missing in list 207
    troubleshooting 206
SNMP MIB (Management
        Information Base) 206
SQL injection attack
    about 148
    example 148
    protecting against 149
SSL
    about 35
    card failures 49
    certificates 36-38
    deployment, considerations 35, 36
    handshake 38-41
    issues, troubleshooting 45
    key, sharing with Citrix tech support 44
    security concerns 50
    session-reuse, and troubleshooting 42
    session-reused handshake 41, 42
    Wireshark troubleshooting, for
        SSL failures 45-49
    Wireshark, used for decrypting trace 42, 43
    Wireshark, used for examining
        handshake 38
SSL handshake 38-41
Standard Network Firewalls 141
Storefront Server 178
Subnet IP (SNIP)
    about 6
    using 13

successful authentication
    verifying, counters used 116
system level issues
    about 201
    CPU and memory issues 207
    crash and hang issues 211
    disk issues 210
    licensing issues 201, 202
    NTP issues 203
    SNMP issues 206

T

TAAS (Techsupport As A Service) 226
TCP Buffering 16
TCP Service (SRV)
    reference link 180
troubleshooting
    HA Failovers 123
troubleshooting, Application Firewall
    AppFirewall, ruling out as
        potential cause 161
    application Firewall blocks,
        identifying 158, 159
    users reporting XXXX patterns,
        in web pages 160, 161

U

User interface, options
    CLI 10
    console 10
    GUI 10
    Nitro 11
    SFTP 11
    shell 10
Use Source IP (USIP) 15, 20

V

Virtual IP (VIP) 6
VMACs (Virtual MACs) 129
VPN session launch
    authentication exchange 167
    EPA exchange 166
    examining, with Wireshark 165
    post-login exchange 167-169

W

web application firewalls 141
web-based analysis
  with Citrix Insight Services 226, 227
Wireshark
  used, for examining handshake 38
  used, for examining VPN session
      launch 165
wizard
  used, for XenMobile configuration 194
WorxMail
  about 198
  reference link 197
WorxWeb 198

X

XenApp
  launch issues, troubleshooting 186-189
  NetScaler Gateway, integrating with 178
XenDesktop
  launch issues, troubleshooting 186-189
  NetScaler Gateway, integrating with 178

XenMobile
  app enumeration 192, 193
  authentication 190, 191
  discovery 190, 191
  integrating, w ith NetScaler Gateway 189
  key components 189
  LAU 192, 193
  launch process 190
  Ports, using 190
XenMobile and NetScaler integration
  connectivity checks, using 194-196
  ns.log file, using 196, 197
  troubleshooting 193
  wizard, used for configuration 194
XenMobile and NetScaler integration issues
  account services address 198
  licenses 197
  load balancing issues 199
  network settings 197, 198
  ShareFile SSO issues 199, 200
XenMobile Cerebro Utility
  URL 196
  using 196
XML protections 155, 156